NOTABLE
SOUTHERN
FAMILIES

VOLUME IV

The Sevier Family

COMPILED BY

ZELLA ARMSTRONG

JANAWAY PUBLISHING, INC.
Santa Maria, California

Notice

In many older books, foxing (or discoloration) occurs and, in some instances, print lightens with wear and age. Furthermore, this reprint's original printing was, by today's standards, of mediocre quality and included uneven type with numerous unintended ink markings throughout the text. Reprinted books, such as this, often duplicate these flaws, notwithstanding efforts to reduce or eliminate them. The pages of this reprint have been digitally enhanced and, where possible, the flaws eliminated in order to provide clarity of content and a pleasant reading experience.

Notable Southern Families. Volume IV

The Sevier Family

Copyright © 1926, by Zella Armstrong

Originally published
Chattanooga, Tennessee
1926

Reprinted by:

Janaway Publishing, Inc.
732 Kelsey Ct.
Santa Maria, California 93454
(805) 925-1038
www.janawaygenealogy.com

2018

ISBN: 978-1-59641-397-9

Made in the United States of America

To my uncle
Robert A. J. Armstrong
This book is affectionately dedicated

The Sevier Family

IN SIX PARTS

FOREWORD

THE history of John Sevier and his family is interlocked with the history of thousands upon thousands of citizens of Tennessee and every other Southern State. A speaker said not long ago that no where else in the United States than in the mountains of Tennessee can a man address a crowd of two or three thousand people with not a foreign born hearer, or a hearer whose parents are foreign born. No where else are traditions so deeply ingrained of the pioneers who won the land. The ancestors of every man and woman in the section participated with Sevier in the Winning of the West and were on more or less intimate terms with the Great Commander.

Many of the things that are here set down will therefore be twice told tales, as around every fireside in the mountains stories are still told of the prowess and courage of the Good Governor, Nollichucky Jack, of the beauty of Bonny Kate or the sweetness and bravery of Sarah Hawkins, who was the first Madame Sevier; of the charm of the Sevier girls and the bravery of the sons; of the heroic fortitude of Valentine Sevier III, and his sorrow of six sons and daughters killed by Indians; of the almost king-like reign of John Sevier in Tennessee and of the fact that, had he so desired, perhaps he might have truly reigned, a king, for the Spanish proposals were many and various. Yet, lest the knowledge of these things should pass as the generations go and lest the dates and names should become confused, these facts are gathered from many sources.

Before closing the chapters of this History of the Sevier Family I take this opportunity to thank Charles Lyman Sevier, Robert A. J. Armstrong, Mrs. Eugene Coile, Miss Kellogg, of the Wisconsin Historical Society, Custodian of the Draver papers, Mrs. Sessler Hoss, Elston Luttrell, Miss Augusta Bradford, of the Chattanooga Library, A. N. Turner, A. V. Goodpasture, William Drane, Miss Lucy M. Ball, Mrs. Sophia Hoss French, Charles Sevier, Mrs. Florence Underwood Eastman, John Trotwood Moore, Tennessee State Librarian, A. P. Foster, Assistant Tennessee State Librarian, Miss Cora Sevier, Mrs. Theodore Francis Sevier, Mrs. Louise Sevier Giddings, Mrs. Gray Gentry (Evelyn Sevier), the late Charles Bascom Sevier, Mrs. John Trotwood Moore, Daniel Vertner Sevier, Jr., Benjamin F. Wyley, W. H. Waddell, Mrs. Ruth Catherine Hoyt, Mrs. N. B. Pearman, Samuel Sevier Kirkpatrick, Fain Anderson, Miss Kate White, J. J. Brown, Mrs. G. L. Wing, Mrs. Ida Barclay Tucker, Mrs. William P. Bowdry, Mrs. M. W. Barney, Seldon Nelson, Mrs. Sabine, Miss Lucy M. Ball, and many other members of the family whose information and interest contributed so largely to the value of the record.

ZELLA ARMSTRONG

BIBLIOGRAPHY.

Not all of the hundreds of books studied during the preparation of the Sevier Family History can be listed here but some of the important volumes whose contents contributed valuable information should be mentioned. Among them are:

Ramsey's Annals of Tennessee

Ramsey's History of Lebanon Church

Wheeler's History of North Carolina

Wheeler's Reminiscences of North Carolina

Goodspeed's History of East Tennessee

Waddell's Annals of Augusta County

Chalkley's Abstracts of Augusta County

White's King's Mountain

Draper's Heroes of the Revolution

Haywood's History of Tennessee

Ellett's Pioneer Women of the West

North Carolina Colonial Records

North Carolina State Records

Roosevelt's Winning of the West

Putnam's History of Middle Tennessee

Taylor's Historic Sullivan

Sumner's History of Southwest Virginia

Turner's Life of General John Sevier

Heiskall's Andrew Jackson and His Times

Lenoir's History of Sweetwater Vally

Lineage Books D. A. R.

Lineage Books S. A. R.

Gilmore's John Sevier

Thompson's Life of Loyola

Allison's Dropped Stitches

PART ONE
Antecedents and Emigration

The Sevier Family

ANTECEDENTS AND EMIGRATION

THE Sevier family name, originally Xavier, had its earliest history in the Kingdom of Navarre, an independent monarchy until its sovreign, Henry III, succeeded to the throne of France as Henry IV. He ruled Navarre and France in a romantic period and as Henry of Navarre is one of the best known characters in history. The "White Plume of Navarre" was a rallying cry and is one of the famous phrases of history and literature.

Navarre lay on two sides of the Western Pyrenees. The territory is now in Spain and France; it is now the Spanish province of Navarra and a part of the French Department of Basses-Pyrenees. Pamplona is the capitol of Navarre.

Henry IV, (Henry III, of Navarre) was born in Castle Pau, Bearne, in 1553. He was the third son of Antoinne de Bourbon and Jeanne d'Albret, daughter of Henry II of Navarre and Margaret, sister of Francis I, of France, and succeeded to the throne of France through Margaret, after Francis' grandsons had died without heirs. Henry III had married his cousin Margaret of France, grand-daughter of Francis.

This brief understanding of Navarre and its rulers is necessary to the story of the Xaviers, as they were prominent in the history of the country and intimate friends and kinsmen of the royal family.

The first mention I have seen of the Xaviers is in the time of King Jean III, known as Jean d'Albret, King of Navarre. One of his counselors was Don Juan de Jassu. Don Juan married, doubtless with the King's full approval and assistance, the King's ward, the orphan Marie de Xavier and Azpileuta. This young girl was sole heiress to the houses of both her father and her mother, Xavier and Azpileuta. The Xavier castle and estate lay in what is now Spain. At that time both estates were of course in Navarre.

It is frequently said in family traditions and records that the Xaviers were close kin to the reigning family and that they were of Bourbon descent through Charles of Orleans. That is indication

1

of very close kinship and the loyalty of the family through a long and stormy period of time is proof that a close tie of some sort certainly existed.

In later years a King of France had among his several names Xavier. Louis Stanilaus Xavier, Count of Provence, became King of France as Louis XVIII, but I think it is possible that he was given a complimentary name of Saint Francis de Xavier, perhaps however, partly because Saint Francis was a kinsman.

Marie de Xavier, heiress of that name and title, who was also heiress of the Spanish name Azpileuta, was a matrimonial prize in the court of Navarre in the latter part of the fifteenth century. Don Juan de Jassu, upon his marriage to her, assumed her titles. The marriage took place about 1485. When a large family was born to them, one half the children took the name Xavier and one half Azpileuta. It is said that the eldest children assumed Azpileuta and the youngest children Xavier, from which I conclude the Spanish name was more important and that probably the fortune was larger, since the eldest born children took it.

Among the children born to Marie and Don Juan Xavier and Azpileuta whose names we know are:

Phillip de Xavier.
Miguel de Xavier.
Juan de Xavier.
Valentine de Xavier.
Francis de Xavier.
Magdalen de Xavier, a nun in the convent of St. Clare and Gandia.

These all took the name de Xavier and were therefore according to history and tradition among the younger children.

Among the youngest, and said by many to be the youngest child, was Francis de Xavier. He was born April 7, 1506, and it is by his birth that I predicate the probable marriage of his parents, since he was the youngest or nearly the youngest of a large family. It is shown on the above list that at least five sons were born in the "younger half" of the family since these five took the name of Xavier. Francis Thompson's Life of Loyola mentions Esteban and Diego d'Equia as first cousins of Francis Xavier.

Francis was born, as were his brothers and sisters, in the Castle de Xavier, eight leagues from Pamplona, the capitol of Navarre.

Francis studied for the priesthood and became one of the greatest missionaries of the world. He was subsequently pronounced a saint by the Catholic Church. As Saint Francis de Xavier he is the best known member of his family with the exception of his many times great nephew John Sevier, First Governor of Tennessee.

Francis de Xavier was born April 7, 1506, in the Castle de

Xavier, eight leagues from Pamlona, close to the little village of Sanguesa. His full name was Francois de Jassu de Xavier, which shows that for a generation the children used their father's name with their mother's. His mother was sole heiress of the Spanish House of Azpileuta and her father was heir to the house of Xavier, or Xavarro. She herself was an only child and much sought at the Court of Navarre. The King of Navarre was her guardian and over-lord and doubtless by his wish she was betrothed to his chief Counselor of State, Don Juan de Jassu.

Upon his marriage Don Juan dropped his name which does not appear again in the family annals except in the first name, Juan which in the Anglicized form of John is many times repeated.

Francis de Xavier is said by many to be the youngest child of the couple, while all historians concur in saying he was one of the youngest. I conclude that all the children who took the Azpileuta name were born in the latter part of the fifteenth century 14——, and that some of the Xaviers were also born in that century. The history of St.Francis de Xavier is interesting and dramatic and is given in full in the Catholllic Enclycopedias. Many biographies have been written also, and from his life, details of his family history can be gathered.

"From his infancy he was of a complying, winning humor, and discovered a good genius and great propensity to learning to which of his own notion he turned himself, whilst all his brothers embraced the profession of arms," is a quaint quotation from one Life of Saint Francis.

His studious inclination determined his parents to send him to Paris in the eighteenth year of his age where he entered the College of Saint Barbara. He took his degree as Master of Arts in 1530, and taught philosophy as Beauvais College, although he still lived at Saint Barbara. Saint Barbara was headquarters for Spanish and Portuguese students.

St. Ignatius came to Paris in 1528 intending to finish his studies. Francis de Xavier was then twenty-two years old. Ignatius had conceived a plan to organize a society which we know now as the Society of Jesuits. At St. Barbara he formed an intimate friendship with Francis de Xavier and Peter Faber, a Savoyard, who was a school mate and friend of Fancis. Peter Faber yielded almost immediately to the influence of Ignatius and fell in with his plans. But to quote the old books. "Francis de Xavier, whose head was full of ambitious thoughts, made a long and vigorous resistance."

However in time, through the influence of St. Ignatius he became a devoted convert to religion and his life thereafter was given to apostolic work. In 1534 he was of the seven persons who first took the oath of the Society of Jesuits. He became one of the great missionaries of the world and traveled far and wide teaching the

gospel. Much space could be filled with his life and works, but as
he is not a direct ancestor of the Sevier family the information will
be condensed.

After many years of evangelical work in India and Japan, Francis de Xavier turned to Sancian, an island off the south Chinese
coast, to wait for a favorable moment to enter China to pursue his
missionary work. He died there December 2, 1552, before he had
made his entry into China. A shrine has been erected to his memory
on this island where he died. It is an interesting fact that recently
(March, 1924) American Catholics have been given charge of the
Island of Sancian and the little shrine, devoted to the memory of
Francis de Xavier.

Announcement was made in March, 1924, from Rome that the
French priests of the Paris-Foreign Missions had relinquished the
island to the care of the Catholic Foreign Missionary Society of
America. The island was made a "prefecture apostolic" at the same
time. The chief point of interest on the island is the shrine of St.
Francis.

Francis was beatified two years after his death, canonized ten
years after his death, and now, nearly four hundred years after his
death, the scene of his last days comes into the possession of American Catholics.

St. Francis' life was written in Latin by Turselin in six books
and was first published in Rome in 1594. The same author translated into Latin and published in 1596 his Letters in four books. His
Life was also written by Orlandino and was written in Italian by
Bartoli, in Portuguese by Luzena and in Spanish by Garcia. See
Nierenberg's Illustrious Men, Histories of India, Histories of Japan,
etc. His History was published in French and in English by Dryden
in 1688.

Interesting details of the Sevier family are revealed in Henry
Dwight Sedgwick's Life of Ignatius Loyola. Francis Xavier was one
of the early converts to Loyola's Society of Jusus, and all histories
of Loyola mention Xavier. Dr. Sedgwick says:

"Loyola's second disciple, Francois de Jassu et de Xavier, was
of the same age as Lefevre, (the first disciple)_ but from a different
social class. An official document declares him to be a hijodalgo, a
gentleman according to feudal standards. His people dwelt in the
kingdom of Navarre, which at that time lay on both sides of the Pyrenees. His father's family had lived to the north of the mountains,
his mother's to the south, at Xavier, the family castle and estate
where Francois was born some twenty-five miles southeast of Pamplona. The parents resided at Xavier and had been prosperous until
King Ferdinand invaded and annexed Southern Navarre in 1512, when
they, as partisans of the French claimants, were dispossessed of a
part of their estates, at least, and left camparatively poor.   Four
years later on Ferdinand's death, there was a rising on behalf the

old royal house, but this was quickly put down, and Cardinal Ximenes, at that time regent for young King Charles, ordered all the strongholds throughout Spanish Navarre to be destroyed. The castle of Xavier shared the common fate, its towers and fortifications were torn down, leaving it defenseless, almost a ruin. As the duke of Najera, viceroy of Navarre, executed these orders, it may be that Loyola had a hand in the demolition. Besides the injury to the castle the family were stripped legally and illegally of various rights; their former tenants, finding them outside the pale of royal favor, denied rents and feudal dues; drivers taking cattle across their land refused to pay toll howerer long established; and later on at the time of the French invasion, neighboring farmers occupied their fields and lawless peasant cut down their timber. For these latter doings there was some excuse, since Xavier's two elder brothers, Miguel and Juan, were among the inhabitants favorable to the old royal house who took arms and declared for their former allegiance. So it came to pass that while Loyola, in the Spanish army, was fighting to defend the citadel at Pamplona, Xavier's brothers were serving with the French troops.

"The insurrection, if it may be called, came to an end in 1524; the two fighting brothers made their peace with the Spanish government and returned home to find the family affairs in a pitiable condition. Francis, in the meantime, had stayed with his mother. He was only six years of age in 1512 and ten years of age in 1516, and had acquired enough schooling to prepare himself for the course in Philosophy at Saint-Barbe, and to Paris he went in time for the October term in 1525, where he had the good fortune to fall in with Pierre Lefevre. While studying philosophy of the schools under Juan Pena, so his biographers say, he was applying himself with great fervor to a better philosophy of a different kind, the knowledge of self and the service of God. This better philosophy he owed at first to Pierre Lefevre and only afterward to Loyola; for it seems that Xavier, in the beginning at least, was less impressionable than Pierre to Loyola's persuasion. Perhaps the yong nobleman entertained more pleasureable visions of the worldly life than the young peasant, and was less disposed to renounce them; possibly the fact that Loyola had served under the Spanish colors in Navarre, against what Xavier regarded as the patriotic party, may have put some barrier between them, And besides, it seems certain that the new ideas of religious and ecclesiastical matters, that were spreading in Paris, at first possessed some attraction for Xavier; but all obstacles and causes of separation, whatever they may have been, were swept away by Loyola's passionate purpose, and Xavier became his second disciple. Xavier is the prototype of modern Christian missionaries, sans peur et sans reproche. Like Bayard on Sir Phillip Sidney, he is renowned for his modesty as for his dauntless courage."

PHILLIP DE XAVIER
AND VALENTINE DE XAVIER

Phillip de Xavier, said to be the eldest of the second half of the children of Don Juan and Marie de Xavier de Azpileuta, was born in the last year of the fifteenth century, say about 1493. It is said that Phillip was a close friend and devoted follower of the young King of Navarre, Henry, who succeeded to the throne of France as Henry IV and it is further said that Phillip married a close kinswoman of the young King, thus tightening the cord of intimacy; but I think the marriage must have been of a son or a grandson of Phillip, as Phillip, son of Marie and Don Juan was born about 1495 and King Henry of Navarre was born in 1553 The King's intimate friend and contemporary therefore, must have been a grandson of the original Phillip. The repetition of the name of Henry in the royal line and of Phillip, Valentine and Juan, in the Xavier family, is of course confusing and, when tradition is the basis of anecdote, even hopelessly confusing. Tradition tells of this marriage of a Phillip to a kinswoman of the king and it is doubtless to be relied upon. As will be seen the generations are confused also in family annals when Valentine becomes the subject of relation.

Valentine is said in some records to be the youngest son of Don Juan and Marie and this is the first time I have seen the name Valentine de Xavier, although it may have been a frequent name in the family of the heiress de Xavier and Azpileuta. The name is in frequent use to this day. John is, of course, a popular name in the family and it is interesting to observe the continued use of these names through four centuries.

Valentine and Phillip de Xavier, probably grandsons of Don Juan and Marie, espoused the Protestant cause with their friend the King of Navarre, and it is said that upon the very morning of the Massacre of St. Bartholomew, August 24, 1572, Valentine Xavier, being apprised by some friends of danger,fled from France. Other family traditions give 1685, more than a century later as the year in which Valentine Xavier escaped from France to London and the occasion, the Revocation of the Edict of Nantes. It is true that in that year also many Huguenots fled to London for safety, so, to which ever tradition you are inclined, there is much interesting evidence.

Whatever the date it was evidently a Valentine Xavier who fled from France to London, and there took up his residence. Valentine Xavier married Mary Smith in London about the year 1700, but this is obviously not the Valentine who was born to Don Juan de Jassu and Marie de Xavier de Azpileuta about the year 1503, although it may conceivably be the Valentine who fled from France in 1685 because of the Revocation of the Edict of Nantes.

Valentine Xavier, the Refugee from France, we will call Valentine Sevier I because he is really the first of the English and American

Family as we know it and because he was first to assume the English form of the name Sevier, although he was perhaps the fourth or fifth Valentine in direct line.

Having arrived in England and having assumed the name Sevier, Valentine married Mary Smith about the year 1700.

They had among other children:

Valentine Sevier, II.

William Sevier.

Some family records say that Valentine, II, was born in London in 1699, others give 1702 as the date and still others 1704 and some 1722. I think the 1699 date is several years too early and the 1722 much too late. His birth probably took place in 1702. He died in America when he was a very old man in 1803 and he was then by all accounts about one hundred and one or two years of age.

Whatever the actual date of his birth, the sons, of Valentine Sevier I, and Mary Smith Sevier were Valentine II, and William Sevier. The name was already Anglicized and from this time is always Sevier.

There is a family tradition, and it has been repeated by learned historians again and again, that the two sons, William and Valentine II, ran away from home and "took ship to America about 1740." This is repeated sometimes in the very paragraph which gives the approximate date of their birth as 1702 or even 1699. Now, either they were born later than the date 1702, as is most often given, or they did not run away from home, as we cannot imagine men of forty or thereabouts running away! Perhaps they ran away when they were quite young men and spent the years that followed before they sailed to America in some place in England, or perhaps they "took ship" much earlier than 1740. Ramsey says they emigrated to America before 1740. It is pretty certain that they "took ship" as there was no other way to arrive in America at that date, so we can be sure that a part of the family tradition is correct: "They ran away from while still young men and took ship to America."

Bishop E. E. Hoss, a descendant of Valentine II, says the emigration took place sometime in the decade between 1730 and 1740. George Washington Sevier, a grandson of Valentine II, in writing to Dr. Lyman C. Draper, says the emigration took place in 1730.

One family record referred to above, says they were born in London in 1720 and 1722. the marriage of their father, Valentine having taken place in 1715. This is completely disproved , however, by the record of Valentine Sevier II which has been carefully preserved. He died in America, December 1803, and he was then one hundred and one years old. This establishes his birth about the year 1702.

Shortly after landing in Baltimore, where the ship upon which they took passage come to port, Valentine and William each married. William Sevier married a Catholic lady, Miss————O'Neil and her name has been preserved in the family nomenclature to this day.

William Sevier and his descendants will be found in Part Two of this book. His family remained in Maryland for sometime, though later many of his descendants migrated to Tennessee, where the family of his brother Valentine II, had become established and famous.

.Valentine Sevier II married Joanna Goode, and his descendants exclusive of the descendants of his eldest son, Governor John Sevier, will appear in Part Three of this book.

PART TWO
William Sevier and His Descendants

WILLIAM SEVIER AND
HIS DESCENDANTS

WILLIAM Sevier, son of Valentine Sevier I and Mary Smith Sevier was born in London in 1702 or shortly thereafter, and sailed for America in company with his brother Valentine Sevier II. It is of them the story is told that they ran away from home and took ship for America in 1740. However the dates of birth or of running away must be wrong for it is not probable that young men of thirty eight and forty "ran away." Bishop Hoss notes the date of emigration to America as somewhere in the decade between 1730 and 1740, while George Washington Sevier, in a letter to Dr. Lyman Draper says they emigrated in 1730. This matter is fully discussed in Part One.

William Sevier shortly after his arrival in Baltimore married———— O'Neil, said to be of a prominent Catholic family of Maryland.

They had at least one son————Sevier ,who married ———— and had at least four children, namely:

(1) Theodore Francis Sevier who died at sea unmarried.

(2) Ann Sevier, who married Frederick Seyler and had no children.

(3) Sarah Sevier, who died unmarried.

(4) William Pierre Sevier, born January '9, 1793.

WILLIAM PIERRE SEVIER

William Pierre Sevier, born January 19, 1793, died December 10. 1846, ran away from home when he was still quite young and fought in the war of 1812. He was captured and taken to Dartmoor prison in England and was there at the time of the Massacre.

A family tradition is that in the massacre that his best friend Granville Sharpe Townsend was shot and that William Pierre Sevier caught his wounded friend in his arms. His devotion to this friend is proven by the fact that he named a son for him and it is interesting to note that the name is still used in the family, Colonel Granville Sharpe Townsend Sevier, United States Army, bearing it in full. William Pierre Sevier married in 1820, Lucretia Williams Weller, born———— died 1776. They lived in Russellville, Kentucky.

William Pierre Sevier and Lucretia Williams Weller Sevier had twelve children:

(1) Granville Sharpe Townsend Sevier, born February 1, 1822.

(2) Benjamin Miller Sevier, died young, born March 21, 1824.

(3) Frederick Seyler Sevier, born 1828.

11

(4)   William Pierre Sevier, born 1830.
(4)   Theodore Francis Sevier, born 1830.
(6)   John Williams Sevier, born May 14, 1834.
(7)   Elizabeth Ann Sevier, born October 6, 1836.
(8)   Sara Louisa Sevier, died young, born 1838.
(9)   —————————Sevier, died young.
(12) Kate Sevier } twins, born 1844.
(10) Jane Sevier }

Granville Sharpe Townsend Sevier, born February 1, 1822, died in California in 1852 of cholera. He went west as a physician and established a hospital.   He died in the service of others.

Benjamin Sevier died young.

Frederick Seyler Sevier, born August 16, 1851, was executed during the Lopez Expedition in Cuba.

Theodore Francis Sevier, born February 22, 1832, died in Sabucal, Texas, in 1915, leaving a widow who now resides (1924)_ with her daughter, Mrs. Frederick Giddings, in St. Elmo, Tennessee. Theodore Francis Sevier will be the subject of the last paragraph.

John Williams Sevier, born—————, died of pneumonia during the War Between the States.

Sarah Sevier died young.

Louise Sevier died young.

Ann Elizabeth Sevier, born—————————,died in Chattanooga in 1913.

THEODORE FRANCIS SEVIER

Theodore Francis Sevier, son of William Pierre Sevier and Lucretia Williams Weller Sevier, was born February 22, 1832. He died in Sabucal, Texas, 1915. He married Mary Benton Douglas November 2, 1855. Colonel Sevier is best known as Colonel Frank Sevier. He served with distinction in the Confederate Army as a Colonel of Ordnance. He as on the staff of General Albert Sidney Johnston. Mary Benton Douglass was the daughter of Kelcey Harris Douglass. She was born in the Republic of Texas in 1839.

The children of Theodore Francis Sevier and Mary Benton Douglas Sevier were:

(1)   Henry Douglass Sevier, died in infancy.
(2)   Theodore Francis Sevier, Jr., died in New York City, unmarried, in 1904.
(3)   Louise Sevier.
(4)   Granville Sharpe Townsend Sevier.
(5   Mary Douglas Sevier, died young.
(6)   Frederick William Sevier, died young.
(7)   John O'Neil Sevier, living in Baltimore.
(8)   Jessie Benton Sevier.
(9)Hal (Henry Hulme) Sevier.
(10) Lucretia Weller Sevier.

Of the foregoing:

Frank Sevier, Jr., died in New York City in 1904.

Granville Sharpe Townsend Sevier is a Colonel in the United States Army. He is unmarried.

John O'Neil Sevier, married Frances——————.They have no children.

Jessie Benton Sevier married Joseph Edward de Belle, and lives in Jacksonville, Florida. They had two children; Joseph Edward de Belle, Jr., and Jessie de Belle. Edward de Belle, Jr., died young. Jessie de Belle married Eugene Hodson Drew and had two children, Eugene Hodson Drew, Jr., who died in infancy and Edward de Belle Drew.

Louise Sevier married Frederick Giddings and had six children, namely, Elizabeth Marshall Giddings, Mary Douglas Giddings, (who died unmarried in 1923) Helen Marshall Giddings, (who died young), Louise Sevier Giddings, Rose Haines Giddings, and Frederick Giddings, Jr.

Hal (Henry Hulme) Sevier married Clara Driscoll and lives in Austin Texas.

Lucretia Weller Sevier married Kingston Pickford and died in Texas, June, 1904, a few weeks after her marriage.

PART THREE
Valentine Sevier, II
The Emigrant
AND HIS DESCENDANTS
EXCLUSIVE OF GOVERNOR JOHN SEVIER
AND HIS DESCENDANTS

VALENTINE SEVIER, II, 7HE EMIGRANT

VALENTINE SEVIER the Emigrant is known throughout this book as Valentine Sevier II, to distinguish him among the many Valentines. His father is Valentine Sevier I, of definite record, although he may have been the fifth or sixth Valentine in direct succession. Valentine Sevier I married Mary Smith in London, as noted in Part One of this volume.

Valentine Sevier II, son of Valentine Sevier I and Mary Smith Sevier, was born in London in 1702. Historians and members of the family conflict in regard to the date, varying from 1699 to 1722, but he died in 1803 at the age of one hundred and one years. With his brother William Sevier, (see Part Two of this volume), he emigrated to America about 1730 or later, landing in Baltimore. He died at his home twenty-five miles from the home of his son, Governor John Sevier, December, 1803, at the age of one hundred and one years. This establishes his birth in 1702. His death is recorded in Governor Sevier's Journal, December 14, 1803.

The family tradition that is frequently quoted by historians claims that Valentine and William Sevier "ran away from home and took ship for America in 1740." Many grave historians give the statement in the same paragraph, which gives the birth of William and Valentine as taking place in 1700 and 1702, not conscious, apparently, of the unusualness of men of thirty-eight and forty running away from home at that mature age. It is quite possible of course that they ran away from home at an earlier period spending the intervening years elsewhere in England before they "took ship" to America in 1740, if that is the year in which they sailed.

It is fairly certain that they "took ship" in 1730 or 1740, or between those dates, and that they landed in Baltimore. Bishop Hoss says that they emigrated some time in the decade between 1730 and 1740, giving no definite year, and George Washington Sevier, son of Governor John Sevier, says that they emigrated in 1730. Ramsey's Annals says they emigrated in 1730.

Valentine Sevier II married shortly after he landed in Baltimore, by the family tradition, but he evidently did not marry Joanna Good until about 1744. The tradition is that he married a "Baltimore Lady" which is a bit indefinite for genealogical records. Other statements indicate that he moved on from Maryland to Virginia before his marriage. However he married Jonna Goode or Goade (the

17

name is frequently spelled Goade). She was the grand daughter of John Goode or Goade who had emigrated to America by way of the Barbadoes in 1650. Bishop Hoss says that Valentine II met his future wife in Augusta or Culpepper County, Virginia. The marriage took place, I think, about the year 1744.

Sometimes a tradition is more nearly right that we understand. Perhaps Valentine Sevier did marry a "Baltimore Lady" shortly after landing. Perhaps his marriage to Joanna Goode in 1744 (about), when he was at least forty-two years of age, was a second marriage.

Valentine Sevier II and Joanna Goode Sevier settled shortly after their marriage in Culpepper County, Virginia, moving later to Rockingham County, (Augusta) Virginia, where John Sevier, their eldest child and the most famous member of their family, was born September 23, 1745.

Valentine Sevier was a member of Schol'- Military Company in 1742, (Waddell's Annals of Augusta County, pages 45 and 47). This clearly proves that he was already in Augusta in the year 1742. Also it is an indication that he met Joanna Goode in Virginia as claimed by Bishop Hoss, because, although he was in Virginia in 1742, the marriage probably did not take place until 1744.

The home of Valentine Sevier II, in Rockingham County, was directly on the line of travel and so great became the burden of entertainment that he presently applied to the County Court for permission to keep an Inn, declaring that he was so "infested with travellers" that it was necessary. Permission was granted and the amount to be charged for man and beast was fixed.

Valentine Sevier was a very large man, almost a giant, if we may believe tradition. His grandson, George Washington Sevier, writes to Dr. Lyman Draper that his "grandfather was a very large man and that his mind and memory at the age of one hundred years were bright and active."

In the year 1773, it is supposed after Joanna Goode Sevier's death, since no further mention of her occurs, Valentine Sevier moved from Virginia to "the mountains," arriving on the Watauga Settlement, December 25, 1773. He was accompanied "by five sons and three daughters" to join one son already there (Valentine III) leaving one daughter in Virginia. This wholesale moving from Virginia without mention of Joanna clearly indicates that she was not living. Also the fact is clear that he had six sons and four daughters living at that date.

After he reached the Watauga Settlement, although I have no means of knowing the date, Valentine Sevier II married a second time and by this marriage to Jemima, who survived him, it is presumed that he had at least two children. Descendants of his second wife may be able to furnish the name of the second wife and the names of other children. He established a home twenty five miles from the site of Governor John Sevier's home on the south side of the Holston River, probably two or three miles below the present site of Kingsport near the old Fort Patrick Henry.

He evidently reared a family in Tennessee, though the name of no child of the second marriage is positively known to me. Governor Sevier in his Journal mentions "my brother G. Sevier," whom he visited in Nashville. I have never seen any other reference to G. Sevier. It is possible, of course, in transcribing the Journal a mistake may have been made and G. is in reality C. and an abbreviation for Charles Sevier, who was probably the sixth son by the first marriage.

Valentine Sevier II after arriving in Tennessee took no active part in public affairs. He was indeed already advanced in life, although he lived thirty years after his migration to "the mountains." He arrived in Tennessee Christmas day 1773. He died in December, 1803 in, Carter County, Tennessee. In the brief mention made in Governor Sevier's Journal of his father's passing, no wife is mentioned as surviving.

There are many earlier notes in the Journal, however, which show that Valentine Sevier II maintained a separate household for many years and that it was about twenty-five miles from the Governor's home, "Plum Grove."

There is probably no way at this date to secure a complete statement of the names of the children of Valentine Sevier II. I shall therefore give the name of every child as I have heard it and the authority therefor. There were six sons by the first wife and the names of five of these sons are positively known. Also there were four or more daughters by the first marriage. Of the six sons, John, Robert, Valentine, Joseph and Abraham are known, all having participated in the Battle of King's Mountain. The name of the sixth son is uncertain but in a copy of Abraham Sevier's Bible record the name of a brother Charles appears. He may be the sixth son and I will so list him.

As for the daughters of the first marriage, many discrepancies appear in mention of them. George Washington Sevier, for instance, in writing to Dr. Draper, says that his father, John Sevier, had only two sisters. This letter is now in the Draper collection in Madison, Wisconsin. He says that Polly and Catherine are his father's only sisters. This statement can be accounted for in several ways, for instance he may have meant only surviving sisters at the date of his letter; or some of the sisters may have been half sisters and not considered sisters by the rest of the family. Bishop Hoss, says that in 1773 Valentine Sevier II migrated from Virginia to Tennessee accompanied by five sons (to join one son already in Tennessee) and three daughters, leaving one daughter in Virginia. This clearly mentions ten children, four of them daughters. I think there was another daughter by the first wife, so I conclude that George Washington Sevier meant two surviving sisters at the date he wrote to Dr. Draper.

CHILDREN OF VALENTINE SEVIER II AND JOANNA GOODE SEVIER

(The sons in this list are given first. There is no conflicting data concerning them, and no uncertainty regarding the names of the first five. I have no information as to the exact order of birth. The daughters of the first marriage I will list and I will give all the information possible concerning each, even where the data is conflicting.)

I   John Sevier
II   Robert Sevier
III   Valentine Sevier III
IV   Joseph Sevier
V   Abraham Sevier
VI   Charles Sevier
VII   Catherine Sevier
VIII Polly Sevier
IX   Bethenia Sevier
X   Elizabeth Sevier
XI   Sophia Sevier

BY SECOND WIFE JEMIMA

XII "G" Sevier

I do not try to follow the order of birth, although John, Robert and Valentine were the first, second and third sons. Abraham was thirteen years of age in 1773, which establishes the date of his birth, and Charles, if he were the sixth son, was probably much younger The daughter who was left in Virginia may have been grown and married in 1773 or she may have been very young and therefore left with kinspeople or friends.

Abraham Sevier, the fifth son, left a Bible record in his family Bible and in it is mention of Charles Sevier, a brother. This is the only mention by that name I have ever seen of this son, although it is quite clear there were six sons at the time of the migration in 1773. The record of Abraham Sevier's Bible has been preserved by Mrs. Dulcinia Gragg Swift, of Jacksonville, Illinois.

She has what she believes to be an exact copy of Abraham's Bible record, but this record includes the children of the first wife only, as neither Rebecca nor "G" Sevier, is mentioned. Mrs. Dulcinia Gragg Swift, is a descendant of Abraham Sevier.

Mrs. Sophia Hoss French, of Morristown, Tennessee, as sister of Bishop Hoss, and a descendant of Governor Sevier, through his son

John Sevier, Jr., has furnished me with a list of the children of Valentine Sevier as follows:

I   John Sevier
II   Valentine Sevier
III   Robert Sevier
IV   Joseph Sevier
V   Abraham Sevier
VI   Bethenia Sevier
VII   Elizabeth Sevier
VIII   Sophia Sevier
IX   Polly Sevier

As will be seen, all lists agree as to the names of five of the sons, discrepancies only occurring in the names of the other sons and in the names of the daughters. I will however, take up the history of each name and give all the information possible, even conflicting statements.

John Sevier, eldest child of Valentine Sevier II and Joanna Goode Sevier, will appear in Part Five of this book and his descendants in Part Six.

WILL OF VALENTINE SEVIER. THE EMIGRANT

The will of Valentine Sevier II is on record in the court house at Elizabethton, Carter County, Tennessee. In it he mentions his loving wife Jemima and three children, Catherine Abraham and Joseph. Whether Jemima Young, to whom he gives a "sadle and fether bed," is a married daughter, we have no means of knowing.

In the name of God Amen. I. Valentine Sevier of Carter County, and State of Tennessee, being low in body tho of sound mind and memory do make ordain and constitute this my last Will and Testament, and first, I give and bequeath my Soul to God who gave it and my body to be buried at the discretion of my executors. Secondly, after the discharge of all my just debts, I leave my dear and loving wife Jemima Sevier a Sufficient Maintainance to be paid her yearly by my Executor, and to Jemima Young I give and bequeath one women's sadle and one Fether Bed to be paid to the said Jemima Young after my decease, and all the Residue of my goods, lands Tenements to be equally divided between my two sons Abraham and Joseph Sevier, Abraham Sevier paying Catherine Matlock wife of William Matlock fifty pounds unyon Currency and Joseph Sevier paying said Catherine forty pounds like money. I also appoint Pharoah Cobb and John Hendricks my sole executors to this my last Will and Testament Revoke and Disannulling all Wills by me here_ tofore made declaring this to be my last Will and Testament in witness whereof I have set my hand and Seal this the 12th day of March, 1799.   VALENTINE SEVIER

     John Dunlap (Jurat)
     John Hendricks (Jurat)

I hereby certify that the foregoing is a true, full and correct copy of the Will of Valentine Sevier now on file in this office This August 29, 1924.   GEO. F. YOUNG
         Deputy County Clerk of Carter County, Tenn.

Valentine Sevier, III

VALENTINE SEVIER, III

VALENTINE SEVIER III, second child and second son of Valentine Sevier II, the Emigrant, and his wife, Joanna Goode Sevier, was born in Rockingham County, Virginia, in 1747. Entering the service of the colonies at a very early age, he was engaged in many Indian skirmishes and campaigns before the Revolution. In accounts of Dunmore's War there is mention of Valentine Sevier and his service. He was a sergeant at Point Pleasant, 1774, and in company with James Robertson discovered the attack about to be made on that Point. At Cedar Springs he commanded a company and he also commanded a company at Musgrove's Mill. He was one of the earliest settlers in Tennessee (the territory which is now Tennessee) making his settlement in 1772, the year preceeding the date that his father's entire family removed from Virginia to "the Mountains." This family arrived December 25, 1773. He was Colonel of Militia and First Sheriff of Washington County. He was Justice of Peace of Washington County. He was one of the five Sevier brothers who fought in the Battle of King's Mountain and one of the seven Seviers in the battle as two of Governor Sevier's sons also participated.

Colonel Valentine Sevier shared with his brothers, John Sevier, Robert Sevier, Abraham Sevier and Joseph Sevier, the hardships of pioneer life, as well as the glory of King's Mountain and dozens of other battles, but unlike them he lost dearly beloved children, four sons in the prime of young manhood and two daughters, in the awful struggle with the Indians, and he saw another daughter scalped before his eyes. His infant grandchildren who were murdered are literally unacounted as the names of only two are known, though we know that others fell victim to the tomahawk or were destroyed in the flames. In the Winning of the West, as President Roosevelt called the great campaign in which the Seviers, the Shelbys, the Wears and hundreds of other heroes participated, no man gave so much, not even those who gave their own heart's blood. Indeed, I know of no other record equal to this, six children killed, a seventh scalped and more than two grandchildren destroyed!

George Washington Sevier said to Dr. Draper that his uncle Valentine Sevier III, was a very large man, "larger than Valentine Sevier II,and he was very bold and gallant." A. W. Putman, in his history of Middle Tennessee, describes Colonel Sevier in this way:

"He had been a hunter in his youth, with figure erect as an Indian's, spare of flesh with a clear skin and a bright blue eye."

A. V. Goodpasture says of Colonel Sevier: "His father was a Virginian of French extraction, from whom he inherited something of the Cavalier spirit so prominent in the character of his brother, Governor John Sevier. Spare of flesh, with an errect commanding, soldierly presence, a bright blue eye and quick ear, he was at once ardent, brave, generous and affectionate.

"He had served his country faithfully, both in the Indian wars and the War of Independence. He was sergeant in Captain Evan Shelby's company at the battle of Point Pleasant, and was distinguished for vigilance, activity and bravery. He entered the Revolutionary War as captain, and commanded a company at Thicketty Fort, Cedar Springs, Musgrove's Mill and Kings Mountain.

"He was the first sheriff of Washington County, a justice of the peace, and Colonel of the County Militia. He took an active interest in the establishment of the State of Franklin, and soon after its fall in 1788, he emigrated to Cumberland, and erected a station near the mouth of the Red River, opposite the town of Clarkesville, where the extinct town of Cumberland was afterwards established, between Clarksville, and New Providence."

It was in 1789 that Colonel Sevier decided to move to the Cumberland country. He sold his land in the Watauga and in the fall of 1789, he established himself on the Red River near the present site of Clarkesville, Tennessee. He was doubtless influenced in this removal by his early friendship with James Robertson who had moved to the Cumberland Country. General Robertson settled in Nashville and became the founder of that city. Valentine Sevier established his station on the beautiful eminence overlooking the present site of Clarkesville. His location is known as Fort Sevier. It commands a magnificent view of the River and of the entire settlement. During the War Between the States its location attracted the immediate attention of military authorities and it became a fort. It was first used by the Confederate Army and later by the Federal troops. The fortifications are plainly to be seen and the property is known as Fort Sevier. This shows that though the location had long been in other hands the fact of its having been the Valentine Sevier station was familiar. Probably when the fort was built remains of the block house and palisades covered the hill, though now there is no trace of these. They were doubtless destroyed when the fort was built. An old negro man, claiming to be ninety-four and looking it, is now living nearby. His name is Sam Washington. He told me that he moved to the section about the beginning of the War, that he helped build the fortifications for the Confederates, that he was a young man at that time and that he helped later when the Federals took it for a fort. He took me to an old graveyard which he said was very old when he helped build the fort and which he said had not been used since as a graveyard. The stones are old and not in regular shape, being merely rocks brought from the river bluff a few yards away. No marking of any sort is indicated, these graves atedating by many years the formal stones with marking (in that section.) One stone is carefully cut and shaped and is marked 1844, but a difference of at least fifty years is apparent.

Undoubtedly the victims of the massacre were buried in this plot, probably in one large grave or perhaps in two or three openings. At least ten people seem to have been killed in the massacre and as there were few men left for work, I think it unlikely that separate graves were dug.

The number of these rough head stones can be accounted for if other members of Vallentine Sevier's family died about that time and were buried there. Also it may contain some of the bodies of neighbors and friends, as all the settlement went to the Block House in time of trouble, according to the traditions of the neighboorhood now. Colonel Sevier died February 23, 1800, and it is possible that he is buried there also.

The bodies of the three sons, Valentine Sevier IV, Robert and William who were killed by Indians in 1792 were destroyed and therefore are not buried in this plot. It is possible that the body of Ann Sevier's first husband, Thomas Grantham, who was the first member of the family group to be sacrificed, may be in this plot.

Only eleven names of the fourteen children of Valentine Sevier III, and Naomi Douglass Sevier are known and if the other three died young they too may be buried in this graveyard.

After July 29, 1800 Valentine Sevier's son John Sevier who was administrator, removed his mother to East Tennessee where he married Susannah Conway. No more Seviers are therefore laid away in that plot of ground. The graveyard is plainly a part of the residence property and was probably included in the palisades. It lies in what was undoubtedly the rear of the premises.

The "Station" included the homes of the married daughters, Elizabeth Sevier, the eldest child who was married to Charles Snyder and Ann, the second daughter, who married first Thomas Grantham and married second John King. Probably both Elizabeth and Ann married before the removal from East Tennessee to the Clarksville site as Elizabeth was twenty-one years of age and Ann eighteen at that time. Thomas Grantham was killed shortly after the Seviers arrived in their new home. This was the first one of the dreadful calamities that befell the family. He was killed in 1790. Thus Ann was left a widow when she was nineteen.

Other heart breaking bereavements came in quick succession. General James Robertson had become alarmed at the war-like demonstrations of the Cherokees and he sent a call for volunteers "for spies

and rangers." Valentine IV, Robert and William Sevier desired to
offer themselves for this service and, despite the weakness of his own
station in the wilderness, Colonel Sevier gave them his permission and
his God speed. They were killed almost within sight of the home
and the father and mother never saw the three stalwart sons again.
They had not even the scant comfort of burial for their beloved as
the bodies were utterly destroyed.

The story is tragically short and details are few. They left their
home in January 1792 for the journey to Nashville, having been
joined by John Curtis, John Rice and two or three others. They started
up the river in canoes as horses were scarce in the settlement. The
Cumberland River above Clarksville makes a horseshoe curve to a
place called Seven Mile Ford. Double Head, the Indian Chief, having
discovered the purpose of the young men, crossed the country to
Seven Mile Ford and lay in wait or the party. As the boats came
around the bend the murderous Indians fired, killing John Curtis and
Robert and William Sevier. The remainder of the party got their
boats across the river and attempted to return to the station, hugging
the opposite shore. Seeing that he had failed to kill all the members of
the party, Double Head and his followers recrossed the isthmus made
by the river. The canoes by this time had been abandoned and Double
Head took the boats,clothes and other possessions. Early next morning Double Head found and killed John Rice and Valentine Sevier
and it was some time before the father knew of the terrible tragedy.
Robert and William Sevier were killed in the afternoon of January
15, 1792, and Valentine Sevier IV was killed January 16, 1792.

Scarcely had the family recovered from the shock of losing these
three young Seviers in the prime of their young manhood, when Nov.
11, 1794, without the slightest warning, the Station was attacked by
forty Creek Indians from a town called Tuskeya, and the rest of the
family was almost destroyed. Every history of Middle Tennessee
mentions this tragic story, but after all we have few details of the
massacre. Fifty years after, Dr. Draper secured interviews with
Hugh Bell, a neighbor; and a letter from Valentine Sevier III, to
Governor John Sevier telling the story very simply had been preserved. He had previously written to his brother telling of the loss
of his sons, Robert, William and Valentine, but saying that he had
other sons "small ones." at the massacre another son, Joseph, was
killed and two daughters, Elizabeth and Ann, were killed.

The letter to Governor Sevier is dated five weeks after the
massacre.

Clarksville, Tennessee
December 18, 1794

Dear Brother:

The news from this place is desperate with me. On
Tuesday 11th of November last,, about 12 o'clock, my
station was attacked by about forty Indians. On so sud-

den a surprise they were in almost every house before they were discovered. All the men belonging to the Station were out, except Mr. Snider and myself. Mr. Snider, Betsy, his wife, his son John and my son Joseph were killed in Snider's house. I saved Snider so the Indians did not get his scalp, but they shot and tomahawked him in a barbarous manner. They also killed Ann King and her son James, and they scalped my daughter Rebecca; I hope she will recover. The Indians have killed whole families about here this fall. You may hear the cries of some persons for their friends daily. The engagement commenced at my house, continued about one hour the neighbors say. Such a scene no man ever witnessed before; nothing but screams and roaring guns and no man to assist me for some time. The Indians have robbed the goods out of every house and have destroyed all my stock. You will write our ancient father this horrid news, also my son Johnny. My health is much impaired. The remains of my family are in good health. I am so distressed in my mind that I can not write.

Your affectionate brother until death,
Valentine Sevier.

Some historians in quoting this letter give Mr. Snider's name as William doubtless reading the "Mr." as "Wm." However there was no William Snider in the settlement at that time. Charles Snider's estate was settled two years after his death.

Two other contemporary letters give gruesome details of the event. Anthony Crutcher, a neighbor, wrote his brother William Crutcher, living in Nashville, and John Easton, a neighbor, wrote to General James Robertson. Both those letters were written the day following the massacre.

ANTHONY CRUTCHER'S LETTER

Clarksville, Tennessee

November 12 1794

Dear Brother:

Yesterday I was spectator to the most tragical scene that I ever saw in my life. The Indians made an attack upon Colonel Sevier's station, killed Snyder, his wife and child, one of Colonel Sevier's children and another wounded and scalped which must die. On hearing the guns four or five of us ran over. We found the poor old Colonel defending his house, with his wife. It is impossible to describe this scene to you. Mr. James, who goes to you was an eye witness, and can give you the particulars. The crying of the women and children in town, the bustle and consternation of the people, being all women and children but the few that went to Col. Sevier's, was a scene that cannot be described. This is a stroke that we have long expected, and from intelligence, we hourly expect this place to be assailed by the enemy. Col. Sevier is now moving, and the town will not stay longer than Mr. James' return. My wife

now lies on her bed so ill that it would be death to move
her; thus are we situated. This place will, no doubt,
be evacuated in a day or two unless succor is given by
the people of the interior part. Pray ask the influence
of Major Tatum, Douglass and all our friends, with
General Robertson, to guard us, or, at least, to help us
get away.

The discrepancy between Valentine Sevier's statement that forty
Indians were in the party of marauders and John Easton's "fifteen"
is easily accounted for. Colonel Valentine Sevier fought them alone
for sometime and they accomplished their murederous design before
men from the neighborhood arrived. They probably slipped quietly
away, one by one, as they saw help approaching.

JOHN EASTON'S LETTER TO BRIGADIER GEN. ROBERTSON:

Clarksville, Tennessee
November 12, 1794

Dear Sir:
I flatter myself that the contents of this letter will
be as seriously considered as the premises demand
Yesterday about eleven o'clock in the morning, a heavy
firing commenced at Colonel Sevier's by a party of
about fifteen Indians. The Colonel bravely defended
his own house and kept the savage band from entering;
but they cruelly slaughtered all around him. Three of
his own children fell dead. Charles Snyder and two
small children also fell. Unfortunately for us in this
place, we were not prepared to go to their assistance,
for the want of men. However, I was on the ground
the first man, and was the first spectator of the horrid
sight—some scalped and barbarously cut to pieces;
some tomawked very inhumanly, and the poor helpless
infants committed to the torturing flames. However,
without entering further into the horrors of this barbarous massacre, suffice it to say that, we consider
ourselves in most imminent danger. Indian signs in
almost every quarter, which lead us to think that we
stand in great need of protection. This is the object
of this letter, favored by Mr. Daniel Jones, who goes
mostly on this particular business, and I hope his journey, or the cause of his journey, will be attended to; if
not I am confident that Clarksville will be evacuated;
But I flatter myself a protection will be willingly and
speedily granted.

Charles Snyder was the husband of Valenntine Sevier's daughter, Betsey, or Elizabeth Sevier. Ann King was his daughter, married to John King, who escaped death. "Johnny" was Colonel Sevier's eldest son, who was then in East Tennessee. Rebecca, who was

---

The discrepancy in the spelling of the name Snyder will be
noted. Names were not unalterably spelled at the time and Snider
appears quite as often as Snyder, for the young man who married
Elizabeth Sevier. Colonel Sevier in his letter spells the name both
ways, as will be seen.

scalped, recovered as her father hoped she would. She wore a sort of tarred cap all of her life and was remembered by some of the elder people in the family because of that unusual distinction. She married John Rector and lived to a good old age.

Many historians in relating the story of the massacre say that the only surviving child of Colonel Valentine Sevier was the son "Johnny" who was in East Tennessee, but this is not correct as Rebecca survived, James survived, Alexander survived, and it is also believed another daughter, Joanna, survived.

James Sevier who was a lad of about seventeen, was working in the field with Ann King's husband, John King. They escaped, as before they heard the shots and screams and could reach the station the massacre was over. Hugh T. Bell told Dr. Draper that Colonel Valentine's son, Alexander Sevier, a child of about twelve, was out rabbit hunting and thus escaped the disaster.

At least one child of Charles Snider and Elizabeth Sevier Snider survived, though many children whose names are not recorded are said to have been killed.

In Dr. Draper's interview, Hugh Bell, who was the nearest neighbor, relates that he heard the noise and was among the first to reach the scene, though too late to be of assistance. In mentioning the survivors he speaks of a little boy, a grandson about four, whom Dr. Draper puts down with a question mark after his name—Alexander Green (?).

Colonel Valentine's son, Alexander Sevier, is said by Rebecca to have been almost twelve and out rabbit hunting, but as a matter of fact, he used G. as his middle initial. However, I have wondered if this child with the question mark after Greene might be a child of Ann King, whose first husband, Thomas Grantham, was killed by Indians in 1790. This is only supposition and could only be verified in case some descendants of this line have information. Dr. Draper it is understood, copied his notes after he returned to Michigan, many months after he made his historic trip through Tennessee, interviewing Tennesseeans. He was not seeking genealogical information primarily, but history, and moreover the interviews were secured fifty years after the massacre.

Hugh Bell says that the little four year old boy in the Block House, referred to in Dr. Draper's interview with Rebecca Rector, was a little grandson. Draper's notes of the interview seem to make him Colonel Sevier's son and that is the reason Draper seems uncertain of the name.

After the massacre Colonel Sevier removed his family to Nashville to live. After the killing and robbery, he had little left with which to withstand the winter. However he did not go immediately, as his letter is dated several weeks after the massacre, when he was still in the station. Several letters to his brother John written from Nashville are extant. In them he explains that he is making his home in Nashville. Later, 1798, in a letter to his brother, he says he is leaving Nashville to return to Clarksville to live. He did not, however, return to the station, as I understand, but to a town lot and house in Clarksville itself, fronting on what has been known for many years as the Square. There he lived and shortly afterwards, died.

Colonel Valentine Sevier III, while he was still in Virginia in 1767, when he was twenty years of age, married Naomi Douglas. She was called Amy. She survived him many years, dying in 1845. In her application for a pension she said that she was married to Valentine Sevier in Shenendoah County, Virginia, by a minister named Anderson. At her death in 1845, she was one hundred and one years of age. This would put her birth in 1744 and make her three years the senior of her husband who was born in 1747. In the Pension Record is the statement: "Naomi Sevier, living with John Rector (a son-in-law) aged 97," Pension List 1840. If Naomi was 97 in 1840, then she was born in 1743, and was four years her husband's senior. Her daughter, Rebecca Sevier Rector swore in her pension application that her mother, Naomi Douglas Sevier, who died July 17, 1845, was 101 years six months and ten days old. By that statement she was born Jan.. 7, 1744. In the Bible of a descendant, Charles Rector Sevier, her birth is recorded as April, 1743.

Colonel Valentine Sevier III, died February 23, 1800. He was only fifty-three years of age. His estate is inventoried by his son, John Sevier, who was his executor, July 29, 1800. The Inventory includes a lot in Clarksville and some household goods and a "house Bible," which I presume means a family Bible. In the sale of the effects the widow, Naomi Douglass Sevier, bought the Bible.

Naomi bought the Bible for fifty cents from which I conclude that she valued it very much as fifty cents was probably a great deal to her at that time. Her son John Sevier, bought for ten dollars, the brass blunderbuss which when discharged, the day of the massacre, knocked Valentine Sevier down and knocked out three of his teeth. It is a curious circumstance that the Bible, for which Naomi paid her pitiful little fifty cents is in existence now and has been a help in the preparation of this chronicle, whereas the blunderbuss for all its brass and its supposed ten dollar value is no more!

Colonel Sevier is buried in Clarksville. I visited the old City Cemetery in which there are many graves, but I am inclined to think that his body was interred in the plot on the Block House site, where his children were buried after the massacre.

The D. A. R. Chapter, of Clarksville, recently placed a handsome marker in the Court House Square to the memory of Colonel Valentine Sevier ,"The First Citizen of Clarksville." The bronze tablet calls attention to the massacre and the dreadful hard ships endured by this family and is a splendid testimonial to Colonel Sevier. Mrs. H.

A. Leach, of Clarksville, was chairman of the committee in charge of the work and it is largely because of her efforts that the testimonial was erected.

CHILDREN OF VALENTINE SEVIER

Valentine Sevier III, and Naomi Douglass Sevier had at least ten or eleven children whose names are positively known. It is said that he had fourteen children. So far as I am able to give the names are:

1. Elizabeth Sevier, born in Virginia, February 13, 1768, the eldest child.
2. John Sevier, born in Virginia, September 1769, named for his uncle, Governor John Sevier.
3. Ann Sevier, born March 23rd 1771.
4. Valentine Sevier IV, born 1772.
5. Robert Sevier, born 1775, twin to William.
6. William Sevier, born 1775, twin to Robert.
7. James Sevier, born August 31st, 1777. He was aged 17, November 11, 1794.
8. Joseph Sevier, born September 1778.
9. Alexander G. Sevier, born November 6, 1782.
10. Rebecca Sevier, born 1783.
11. Joanna Goode Sevier, born February 14, 1784.

The children of Colonel Valentine Sevier III will now be taken up under their individual names.

ELIZABETH SEVIER

(1.) Elizabeth Sevier, called Betsy, daughter of Colonel Valentine Sevier III and Naomi Douglass Sevier was born in Virginia, February 13, 1768, and was their first child. She accompanied her parents when they made their second migration to Middle Tennessee after the Revolution. As she was then past twenty she was possibly married at that time and probably her husband accompanied the party.

She married Charles Snider, or Snyder.

Some historians quote the letters from Colonel Valentine Sevier to his brother, Governor John Sevier, as saying that her husband was William Snider, but this is evidently a mistake on the part of the copyist who mistook the "Mr." for "Wm". Rebecca Sevier told Dr. Draper that her sister's husband was named Charles Snider and other evidence exists to show that he was Charles. John Montgomery Snider continually appears in land records with the Seviers, but he was probably a brother or perhaps the father of Charles Snider.

Elizabeth Sevier Snider was killed in the massacre, November 11,

1794. Her husband and little son John Snider were killed at the same time. No reference is made by Colonel Sevier, in his letter to his brother, to other children but Rebecca Sevier Rector says, "her son, John, and other little ones were killed." There must have been at least one surviving child for a descendant of Elizabeth has joined the D. A. R., giving the name of a surviving child, Susannah Snider, who married Thomas Stanley Warren. Their son Thomas Jefferson Warren maried Elizabeth Guthrie. Their daughter, Lelia Warren married Theodore A. Kline and joined the D. A. R. on this record.

The known children of Elizabeth Sevier Snider and Charles Snider therefore were:

(A) John Snyder, killed by Indians November 11, 1794
(B) Susannah Snider, married Thomas Stanley Warren.
Others killed in infancy.

JOHN SEVIER
Son of Colonel Valentine Sevier III

(2) John Sevier, son of Colonel Valentine Sevier III and Naomi Douglass Sevier, was born in Virginia, September, 1769. He was named for his uncle John Sevier. He accompanied his family to "the Mountains" when he was still a child and later, it is said, when the family moved to Middle Tennessee in the fall of 1769, he went with his parents, returning almost immediately for some reason to the home of his uncle, John Sevier, in East Tennessee. He thus escaped the Indian massacres. He seems, however, to have been in the Red River district at times. For instance, John Sevier and John Montgomery Snider bought land in Montgomery County in 1793 and 1749, showing that he was there at that time. He was apparently not in Clarksville when his three brothers, Valentine IV, Robert and William, were killed. Also he was absent when the dreadful massacre of November 11, 1794, took place. He served, however, as executor of his father's will, July 29, 1800. I imagine that his own marriage had taken place or was about to take place, for he completely closed up his father's affairs in Montgomery County, disposed of all the household possessions and moved his mother and the surviving children to East Tennessee. His only purchase in the sale of effects is the brass blunderbuss, for which he paid ten dollars.

He married and a large posterity traces through him. He was of a somewhat roistering disposition if his nick-name, "Devil Jack," is to be taken as evidence. The name distinguishes him from his uncle, Governor John Sevier, from his cousin, John Sevier, junior, and from the numerous other Johns. So I have adopted it in this record in places where merely "John Sevier" is not sufficiently distinctive.

His wife was Susannah Conway, born June 9, 1776; died May 4, 1816, the daughter of Colonel Henry Conway and Sarah Hundley Conway. The marriage took place in 1800. The name Hundley frequently appears in Sevier annals, as three sisters, Susannah, Nancy and Elizabeth, married Seviers. Nancy Conway married James Sevier, second son of Governor John Sevier. Elizabeth Conway married John Sevier, junior, third son of Governor John Sevier, and Susannah married "Devil Jack" Sevier. Susannah was called Susan by her father and Ann by her son, Senator Ambrose Hundley Sevier. In reading references to her therefore this fact of her seeming to have three names must be borne in mind.

The marriage bond of Devil Jack Sevier and Susannah Conway is dated 1800 and is now in Greeneville, Tennessee. They had seven children, but the marriage proved an unhappy one and Susannah Conway divorced her husband. This was at a time when divorce was uncommon and I imagine that Susannah's grievances were many before she took the step. Having secured her divorce she married September 30, 1812, Hugh Maloney. Hugh Maloney was born in Ireland in 1781, died in Tennessee, October 8, 1840. Hugh Maloney and Susannah Conway Sevier Maloney had two children, namely: William Conway Maloney and Thomas Fleming Maloney. Descendants of these Maloney children married, as will be seen, descendants of the first marriage of Susannah Conway. Susannah died in Greene County, Tennessee, in 1816. Her second husband survived her many years. Devil Jack Sevier volunteered for the War of 1812 and served with conspicuous bravery with General Jackson at New Orleans. It is said that on his way home he died and was buried at sea. He was General Jackson's color bearer at New Orleans.

The children of Hugh Maloney and Susannah Conway Sevier Maloney:

(A) William Conway Maloney, born July 13, 1813; died June 5, 1882. He married Louise Cureton. He had children: William Cureton Maloney, Hugh D. Maloney, born 1842, June 6; and Nannie Maloney. Nannie Maloney married Hal Herring as his first wife. William Cureton Maloney married ——————————— and had a daughter, Louise Maloney, who married Hal Herring as his second wife.

(B) Thomas Fleming Maloney, born January 3, 1815, died July 22, 1841.

The children of Devil Jack Sevier and Susannah Conway Sevier were:

(I do not know that they should be in this order).

(A) Ambrose Hundley Sevier, born 1801.

(B) Henry Sevier.

    (C)   Sarah Sevier.
    (D)   Mariah Sevier, born 1803.
    (E)   Narcissa Sevier.
    (F)   Nancy Sevier.
    (G)   A daughter, ——————— Sevier.

Ambrose Hundley Sevier

    (A) Ambrose Hundley Sevier, son of Devil Jack Sevier and Susannah Conway Sevier, was born in Greene County, Tennessee, November 10, 1801. He was named Hundley in honor of his mother's family. I do not know where Ambrose was obtained, although it was a frequently used name at that period, Ambrose being noted among several well-known families. Ambrose Hundley Sevier moved west while still a young man. At the time of his mother's death he was only fifteen and he may have decided then to emigrate to the western country. He became very prominent in his new home and was elected Senator from Arkansas. Later he was appointed by President Polk, Peace Commissioner to Mexico at the close of the war with Mexico. While he was in Mexico on this mission he contracted fever at Vera Cruz and died at his home in Arkansas, December 31, 1848, at the age of forty-seven years.

    He married August 26, 1827, Juliette Johnson, daughter of Judge Benjamin Johnson. Juliette Johnson was born October 12, 1812, and died March 16, 1845.

    The children of Ambrose Hundley Sevier and Juliette Johnson Sevier were:

    (a)   Mattie J. Sevier.
    (b)   Michael Sevier.
    (c)   Annie Maria Sevier.
    (d)   Elizabeth Sevier.
    (e)   Ambrose Hundley Sevier, Jr.

    (a) Mattie J. Sevier, daughter of Ambrose Hundley Sevier and Juliette Sevier, was born ——————————. She married John Shelby Williams, son of David and Priscilla Shelby Williams (see Shelby and Williams families in Notable Southern Families, Volume II).

    The children of Mattie Sevier Williams and John Shelby Williams were:

    (1)   David Shelby Williams.
    (2)   Juliette Sevier Williams, who died young.
    (3)   Maude Johnson Williams.
    (4)   Anna Fassman Williams.
    (5)   Ambrose Sevier Williams.

    Of the foregoing:

    (1)   David Shelby Williams married May Lawson McGhee, of

Knoxville, and had no children and married for his second wife ———.

(2) Juliette Sevier Williams died young.

(3) Maude Johnson Williams married Robert P. Bonnie, of Louisville, and had children: Shelby Williams Bonnie, Mattie Sevier Bonnie and Robert P. Bonnie, Jr.

(4) Anna Fassman Williams married Wentworth P. Johnson, of Norfolk, Virginia, and had Wentworth P. Johnson, Jr., and Shelby Williams, a daughter. Also there were three children who died in infancy.

(5) Ambrose Sevier Williams. Of him I have no record.

(b) Michael Sevier, son of Ambrose Hundley Sevier and Mattie Sevier, was born June 23, 1822. He married Sarah E. Bayless, October 14, 1854. She was born June 18, 1822. They had three children, Elbridge Gerry Sevier, born August 22, 1846, died 1923; Robert Edgar Sevier, born May 26, 1856, died December 30, 1898. He lives in Little Rock, Arkansas. He married Beulah Henderson and had two children, namely, Shelby H. Sevier and Mrs. Walter Morris. A daughter of Michael Sevier and Sarah E. Bayless was living in 1923.

(c) Annie Maria Sevier, daughter of Ambrose Hundley Sevier and Juliette Johnson Sevier, was born ———. She married, July 31, 1849, Thomas J. Churchill, Governor of Arkansas, born March 10, 1824, died 19—.

(d) Elizabeth Sevier daughter of Ambrose Hundley Sevier and Juliette Johnson Sevier, was born ———.

(e) Ambrose Hundley Sevier, Jr., son of Ambrose Hundley Sevier and Juliette Johnson Sevier, was born ———.

Henry Sevier

(B) Henry Sevier, son of Devil Jack Sevier and Susannah Conway Sevier, was born 18—.

Sarah Sevier

(C) Sarah Sevier, daughter of Devil Jack Sevier and Susannah Conway Sevier, was born 18—. It is said by some that she married ——————— Smith.

Mariah Sevier

(D) Mariah Sevier, called "Nannie," daughter of Devil Jack Sevier and Susannah Conway Sevier, married twice, her first husband being Lewis Broyles. They had a daughter, Mary Broyles, who married W. J. Mhoon. They had a daughter, Lucy Mhoon, who married M. Wilkerson. After the death of Lewis Broyles, Mariah Sevier Broyles married for her second husband, her cousin, Joseph Sevier, son of Valentine Sevier, of Greeneville, Tennessee, son of

Captain Robert Sevier, killed at King's Mountain. Joseph Sevier was killed in the War Between the States. Her children by Joseph Sevier were Dr. Robert Sevier, now deceased, Lewis Sevier, now living in Savannah, Tennessee, and Miss Nannie Sevier, living in Savannah.

Narcissa Sevier

(E) Narcissa Sevier, daughter of Devil Jack Sevier and Susannah Conway Sevier, was a twin to Nancy Sevier. They were born in Greene County, Tennessee, October 30, 1810. Narcissa Sevier married William J. Harding, whose mother was Esther Marian Herring, a sister of General Francis Marian. William Herring and Narcissa Sevier Herring had at least two children, namely:

(a)   Sarah Herring.
(b)   John Henry Herring.

Of these:

(a Sarah Herring married John Nelson Kendall and had two daughters, Blanche Kendall, who married J. W. Ridgeway and had a daughter, Mary Ridgeway, who married A. P. Wood and has a daughter, Anette Wood); and ——————— Kendall who married J. H. Happy and has five children, ——————— Happy, married Melvin Albutton; Miss Ina Happy, James H. Happy, J. Kendall Happy and Samuel Roberts Happy.

(b) John Henry (Harry) Herring, who married Julia Williams had a son, John Henry (Hal) Herring, who married twice, both times a kinswoman, descendants of his great-grandmother, Susannah Conway, by her second husband, Hugh Maloney. Hal Herring's first wife was Nannie Maloney, daughter of William Maloney and granddaughter of Hugh and Susannah Conway Sevier Maloney. By this marriage he had one son, Henry William Herring, who lives in Oregon. Hal Herring married for his second wife, Louise Maloney, granddaughter of William Maloney and great-granddauhter of Hugh and Susannah Conway Sevier Maloney. By this marriage Hal Herring has two sons, ——————— Herring and Lewis Broyles Herring.

Nancy Conway Sevier

(F) Nancy Conway Sevier, daughter of Devil Jack Sevier and Susannah Conway Sevier, was a twin to Narcissa. They were born on the Chucky River, near Warrensburg, Greene County, Tennessee, October 30, 1810. Shortly after their birth their mother divorced Devil Jack Sevier and when they were two years old, she married Hugh Maloney. When Nancy Sevier was eighteen years old, Dec. 18, 1828, she married James Irwin, of Murfreesboro, Tennessee.. In 1830 they moved to McMinnville to reside and a year later to Savannah, Tennessee, where Nancy Sevier Irwin died in 1885, being seventy-five years of age. Her death took place October 7, 1885. She had ten children, eight of whom lived to maturity and were living when she died.

The information of the family of Nancy Sevier was secured partly from the following obituary notice which appeared in the Savannah (Tennessee) Courier, October 22, 1885, a copy of which was recently sent me.

"Mrs. Nancy Sevier Irwin

"Mrs. Nancy Sevier Irwin, daughter of John Sevier and Susannah Conway Sevier, was born on the Chucky River, near Warrensburg, Greene County, Tennessee, October 30, 1810. Her father was a nephew of John Sevier, first Governor of Tennessee. Her paternal grandfather was Valentine Sevier, a Colonel in the Revolutionary War. She had three brothers and three sisters. Her brother Ambrose Hundley Sevier was for a number of years United States Senator from Arkansas and was sent to Mexico by President Polk as Peace Commissioner after the War of 1848. She married James Irwin, of Murfreesboro, Tennessee, December 18, 1828, and moved to McMinnville about 1830, and to Savannah, Tennessee, about 1831. She died October 7, 1885. Her ten children all grew up except the youngest, Hundley Irwin. Her daughter, Juliet, died March 22, 1861."

Children of Nancy Sevier Irwin and James Irwin:

(a) Anne Maria Irwin.
(b) Susannah Elizabeth Irwin.
(c) Juliett Sevier Irwin.
(d) Hattie Louise Irwin.
(e) Mary Dinwiddie Irwin.
(f) Cornelia L. Irwin.
(g) John Sevier Irwin.
(h) Dr. Louis B. Irwin.
(i) James William Irwin.
(j) Hundley Irwin.

Of the foregoing:

(a) Anna Maria Irwin, daughter of Nancy Sevier and James Irwin, married William H. Cherry, of Nashville. They had two children, Minnie Cherry (who married James M. Head, of Brookline, Massachusetts, and William Irwin Cherry (who married Florence Wilkes and lives in New York City).

(b) Susannah Elizabeth Irwin, daughter of Nancy Sevier Irwin and James Irwin, died unmarried.

(c) Juliette Sevier Irwin, daughter of Nancy Sevier Irwin and James Irwin, died unmarried.

(d) Hattie Louise Irwin, daughter of Nancy Sevier Irwin and

James Irwin, married William H. Cherry, of Nashville. They had
two children: Minnie Cherry, (who married James M. Head, of Brookline, Massachusetts.) and William Irwin Cherry, (who married
Florence Wilkes and lived in New York City.)

(b) Susannah Elizabeth Irwin, daughter of Nancy Sevier
Irwin and James Irwin, died unmarried.

(c) Juliette Sevier Irwin, daughter of Nancy Sevier Irwin and
James Irwin, died unmarried.

(d) Hettie Louise Irwin, daughter of Nancy Sevier Irwin and
James Irwin, married Dr. Robert A. Hardin. They have four children:
Nancy Elizabeth Hardin, who married R. Mahlen Stacey and lives
in Pulaski, Tennessee, and has one child Rebecca Louise Stacey, who
married Ernest Keller and lives in Knoxville; Robert A. Hardin, Jr.,
who married Irene Barlow and lives in Birmingham, Alabama. They
have four children, Hettie Louise Hardin, who married Robert Lee
Jordan and lives in Memphis, Tennessee. They have two chilren,
Elizabeth Irwin Jordan and Robert Hardin Jordan; and Charles W.
Hardin, who married Ida Isinger and lives in New York City. They
have one child, Mary Florence Hardin.

(e) Mary Dinwiddie Irwin, daughter of Nancy Sevier Irwin
and James Irwin, married Edgar Cherry, of Savannah, Tennessee, and
had four children, mong them Juliette Irwin Cherry, who married
Webb W. Crawford and lives in Birmingham, Alabama. They have
two sons, Webb W. Crawford, Jr., and Cherry Crawford.

(f) Cornelia L. Irwin, daughter of Nancy Sevier Irwin and
James Irwin, married Daniel A. Welsh. They had two sons who died
in infancy.

(g) John Sevier Irwin, son of Nancy Sevier Irwin and
James Irwin, married Fannie Church. They lived in Savannah, Ten-
nessee, and had three children, Dr. James Irwin, Annie Irwin and
Eliza Irwin.

(h) Dr. Louis B. Irwin, son of Nancy Sevier Irwin and James
Irwin, married Mary Bailey. They had no children.

(i) James William Irwin, Jr., son of Nancy Sevier Irwin and
James Irwin, married Cornelia Browles. They had four children:
Louise Irwin, Gertrude Irwin, James, Irwin and ———— Irwin.

(j) Hundley Irwin, son of Nancy Sevier Irwin and James Irwin,
died young.

(k) ————Sevier.

(G)————Sevier, daughter of Devil Jack Sevier and
Susannah Conway Sevier, was born 18———. I have no record of
her name or birth. In the obituary of Nancy Sevier who married
James Irwin is the statement that she had three brothers and three
sisters. I therefore have set down the number of seven children.
This daughter, was of course, older than the twins, who were the
youngest children of "Devil Jack."

ANN SEVIER

3. Ann Sevier, daughter of Colonel Valentine Sevier III and Naomi Douglass Sevier, was born in Virginia in 1771. She accompanied her parents to the mountains of Tennessee when she was very small and later in their second emigration to Middle Tennessee, near the present site of Clarksville. She married twice. Her first husband was Thomas Grantham. He was killed by Indians in 1790. Her second husband was John King. At the time of the massacre of the Valentine Sevier Station, November 11, 1794, John King was working in the fields some distance from the houses with Ann's brother, James, a lad of about seventeen. They heard the shots and screams but could not arrive in time to give assistance. Ann Sevier and her little son, James King, were killed in the massacre. She was but twenty years old. Several children were killed whose names are not recorded and also several survived whose names are not known. It is a matter of record, however, that several grandchildren of Valentine Sevier were in the station. It is a part of Rebecca's testimony and Hugh Ball's that Rebecca tried to rescue a child whom the Indians placed in a blazing fire and that because of this effort to save the child they scalped her. It is not known whether she saved the life of the baby. Hugh Ball, the nearest neighbor, who came to the assistance of Colonel Sevier when he heard the firing, in an interview with Dr. Draper, says that a little "grandson" about four years old survived, but does not mention his name. It is in notes of an interview with Rebecca Sevier that Dr. Draper calls him Alexander G. or Greene and seems uncertain which, but lists him as Colonel Sevier's son. This child was in the Block House with Naomi Douglas Sevier when Colonel Sevier shut the door and fired the blunderbuss which knocked him down and knocked out three of his teeth. This child, born in 1790, would not be Naomi's child, I imagine, but if Dr. Draper's "Greene," with a question mark, can be translated into Grantham, he could be Ann Sevier's child by her first husband, Thomas Grantham. In 1790 when this child was born, since he was about four in 1794, Ann Sevier was nineteen years of age and the wife or the recent widow of Thomas Grantham, who was killed by Indians in 1790. I know nothing, however, of this child Alexander and place him here merely on supposition. This cannot be Alexander who was about twelve and was out rabbit hunting.

The children of Ann Sevier Grantham King:

(A)   Alexander Grantham (?).

(B   James King, killed by Indians in infancy.

VALENTINE SEVIER IV

(4)   Valentine Sevier IV, son of Colonel Valentine Sevier III

and Naomi Douglas Sevier, was born in 1773, after his parents had removed from Virginia to the Mountains. He was the fourth Valentine Sevier in direct succession, and perhaps many times that number, as we have no record of the generations that preceded "Valentine Xavier" who fled from France to London and established the English branch of the family and the name as we know it: Sevier. Valentine Sevier IV is said to have been unmarried when January 16, 1791, he was killed by Indians near Clarksville, near the mouth of the Red River. His body and that of John Rice, who was killed at the same time, were burned by Captain Solomon White.

ROBERT AND WILLIAM SEVIER

(5 and 6) Robert and William Sevier, twin sons of Colonel Valentine Sevier III and Naomi Douglass Sevier, were born in "the Mountains" in 1775. They accompanied their parents to Middle Tennessee and were killed by Indians near the mouth of Blooming Grove Creek, January 15, 1791. They were on their way to join General James Robertson at Nashville. Hugh T. Ball found the body of William Sevier, but the body of Robert, who jumped into the water, was never found. A skeleton was found a year later a mile away and it was thought that Robert ran a mile before he died. They were just nineteen years of age and were unmarried.

JAMES SEVIER

7. James Sevier, son of Colonel Valentine Sevier III and Naomi Douglass Sevier, was born August 30, 1777, in the Mountains of East Tennessee. He accompanied his parents in their migration to Middle Tennessee and participatd with them in the dreadful hardships and sorrows that came to them. In 1794, when the massacre took place, James was a lad of seventeen. He was working in the fields at some distance from the houses when the Indians surprised the station. His brother-in-law, John King, was with him. They heard the noise and screaming but reached the house too late to be of any assistance.

In 1798, James Sevier married Susan or Susannah Warren, of Greene County, Tennessee. The marriage bond is dated November 29, 1798, and is signed by his brother, John Sevier. It is for $1,200. This is two years before his father died, but he was witness to a deed in Clarksville, July 30, 1798.

The marriage bond attracted quite a deal of interest when it was exhibited in 1924 by Judge J. T. Phillips, of Kingsport, who has kept it in his possession for many years.

The bond is signed by James Sevier as principal, and his brother, John Sevier, as security, and is given as a guarantee of the legal consummation of the marriage, and to insure that there is no impediment to the act existing. The bond is drawn in favor of John Sevier, Esq., Governor of Tennessee, and is for the sum of $1,200. It is witnessed by Dave Warren, clerk of the court, and the fee for its issuance is shown to be 75 cents.

The document is written in pen and ink, is perfectly preserved, and perfectly legible after a lapse of 136 years.

Senator Ambrose Hundley Sevier says that James Sevier moved to Kentucky and that when he last heard from it was 1843. Rebecca Sevier Rector testified that she was living at the time of their mother's death in 1845.

James Sevier died at his home in Kentucky in 1865.

James Sevier and Susannah Warren Sevier had twelve children:

- (A)   Elizabeth Sevier.
- (B)   Rebecca Sevier.
- (C)   Sarah Sevier.
- (D)   Mary Sevier.
- (E)   Charles Sevier.
- (F)   Thomas Sevier.
- (G)   Valentine Sevier.
- (H)   Alexander Sevier.
- (I)   John Rector Sevier.
- (J)   Martha Sevier.
- (K)   Robert Sevier.
- (L)   Samuel Sevier.

Of the foregoing:

(A Elizabeth Sevier, daughter of James Sevier and Susannah Warren Sevier, was born March 25, 1801. She married ————.

(B) Rebecca Sevier, daughter of James Sevier and Susannah Warren Sevier, was born March 27, 1803. She married ———— Brown and had one child, Douglas Brown, and he had one child, ———— Brown.

(C) Sarah Sevier, daughter of James Sevier and Susannah Warren Sevier, was born May 21, 1805. She married John Farris. They had a daughter, Martha Ann Farris, who married James Madison Adkin, and their daughter, Ella Nene Adkin, married James Edgar Lynch.

(D) Mary Sevier, daughter of James Sevier and Susannah Warren Sevier, was born July 27, 1807.

(E) Charles Warren Sevier, son of James Sevier and Susannah Warren Sevier was born July 21, 1810.

(F) Thomas H. Sevier, son of James Sevier and Susannah Warren Sevier, was born February 12, 1812.

(G) Valentine Sevier, son of James Sevier and Susannah Warren Sevier, was born Februaary 14, 1814. He married Margaret Smith.

(H) Alexander Sevier, son of James Sevier and Susannah Warren Sevier, was born March 15, 1816.

(I) John Rector Sevier, son of James Sevier and Susannah Warren Sevier, was born March 15 ,1818. He died 1865. He married Nancy Ewing and had five children: (a) Alexander Sevier; (b) James Sevier; (c) Douglas Sevier; (d) Charles Sevier; and (e) Susan Sevier. Of these (a) Alexander Sevier married Nancy Sawyers and has four children: Cora Sevier, Alexander Sevier, Jr., Marena Sevier and John Sevier.

(J) Martha Sevier, daughter of James Sevier and Susannah Warren Sevier, was born January 21, 1820. She married Tyre Gibson and had six children: James Gibson, Susan Gibson, Jane Gibson, Amelia Gibson, Ellen Gibson and Kitty Gibson.

(K) Robert Sevier, son of James Sevier and Susannah Warren Sevier, was born October 28, 1823. He married Margaret Beatty.

(L) Samuel Sevier, son of James Sevier and Susannah Warren Sevier, was born October 28, 1825. He married Amelia Hibbard.

JOSEPH SEVIER

8. Joseph Sevier, son of Colonel Valentine Sevier III and Naomi Douglass Sevier, was born in 1778 in East Tennessee. He accompanied his parents in their migration to Middle Tennessee and was killed by the Indians in the massacre November 11, 1794. He was very young, fifteen or sixteen at most, and was, of course, unmarried.

ALEXANDER G. SEVIER

9. Alexander G. Sevier, son of Colonel Valentine Sevier and Naomi Douglass Sevier, was born about 1782. At the time of the massacre in 1794 he was a lad of about twelve and was out rabbit hunting. He thus escaped the massacre. Hugh Bell, the neighbor who came to the help of the station, mentions Alexander, a lad of twelve, out rabbit hunting. He married about 18— Elizabeth A————. He is frequently mentioned in Governor Sevier's Journal. He died, according to Senator Ambrose Hundley Sevier, about 1828.

Senator Ambrose Hundley Sevier, in a letter dated 1843 (in the Draper manuscript), says, "My grandfather, Valentine Sevier, left three sons, John (my father), who died about thirty years ago; Alexander and James. Alexander died fifteen years ago. James went to Kentucky an I lost track of him."

He says at another time that in 1890, at the death of Colonel Valentine Sevier III, only three sons were living, John, James and Alexander. At the death of Naomi Douglass Sevier in 1846, her daughter says that only one son, James, was living.

Major Alexander G. Sevier in the War of 1812 and thus gained his title. He was commended for bravery and is mentioned many times in current histories and documents. He died in 1828. His widow, Elizabeth A. ———— Sevier, applied for a pension, and mentioned three children, but did not give their names.

REBECCA SEVIER.

10. Rebecca Sevier, daughter of Colonel Valentine Sevier III and Naomi Douglass Sevier, was born in East Tennessee in 1783. She was eleven years of age when, having accompanied her parents to Middle Tennessee, she suffered with other members of her family in the dreadful massacre. It is said that when the murdering Indians threw a child into the fire that Rebecca rushed to rescue the baby. For this deed she was scalped and left for dead. Some historians state that she was scalped three years earlier when her brothers were killed but Colonel Valentine Sevier's letter, quoted in full in the first part of this chapter, settles the question of the date. She wore a tarred cap all her life after this experience.

She married John B. Rector about the year 1800. Much of the information of this part of the Sevier history is obtained from her statements either in pension papers or in interviews with Dr. Lyman Draper. Her mother, Naomi Douglass Sevier, made her home for many years with Rebecca and drew a pension. One pension record shows Naomi Douglass Sevier living with John Rector (son-in-law), age 97, Pension List 1840."

Rebecca Sevier Rector, in her interview with Dr. Draper in 1844 in Greene County, Tennessee, tells him about the forty* Indians who surprised her father's station in 1794, killing her sister, Ann King and scalping her (Rebecca) and leaving her for dead. Ann King's husband escaped because he was in the field. (Ann's first husband, Thomas Grantham, had been killed by the Indians in 1790). In 1791 her twin brothers, Robert and William, were killed by the Indians near the mouth of Blooming Grove Creek and the next morning her brother, Valentine Sevier IV, was killed the same place.

She says that her sister, Elizabeth Snyder, born 1768, the first born, was killed, also her husband Charles, in the blacksmith shop, and "their son John and little ones." Rebecca's brother, Joseph, born 1788, was also killed under a work bench in the shop. Rebecca states that her brother James, a lad of 17 years (born 1777)

---

*Either Hugh Bell was mistaken in the number of Indians who carried out this frightful deed or Valentine Sevier and Rebecca were mistaken. Hugh Bell says that about fifteen Indians massacred the Station. Colonel Sevier and Rebecca say, forty, Indians.

was in the field pulling corn and that Alexander,† four years of age, born 1790, was in the block house with her mother when Colonel Valentine Sevier shut the door and fired the blunderbuss that knocked out three of his teeth.

Rebecca Sevier Rector and John Rector appear in the Greene County (Tennessee) census of 1850. John Rector's age is given as 86, establishing his birth in 1764. A descendant furnishes the exact date, March 10, 1764. This makes him much older than Rebecca, whose age is given in the census as 67, born in Tennessee. This agrees with the foregoing record of her birth in 1783 John Rector died February 5, 1856, according to entry in the Bible record of Charles Sevier Rector.

In 1851, Rebecca Sevier Rector applied for an increase of pension allowed her mother for her father's services in the Wars. She sets out that only she and her brother James were living at the time of her mother's death in 1845, (not 1844, she says, as the Pension Department had made a mistake).

The census of Greene County, Tennessee, of 1850 gives the names of John Rector and his wife, Rebecca Sevier Rector, and the names of four persons in their household, namely:

George Rector, age 33, born 1817.
Valentine Rector, age 16, born 1834.
Jane Rector, age 24, born 1826.
——————— Rector, age 7, born 1843. This last name could not be deciphered, but the child is too young to be a child of Rebecca and John Rector and may have been a grandchild.

In the census of Greene County, Tennessee, for 1870, Valentine Sevier Rector is given, aged 37. This puts his birth about 1833 and shows that he is the Valentine named above. Rebecca evidently gave him her father's full name. The census gives his children as:

a. Charles T. Rector, born 1859.
b. James Rector, born 1861.
c. Barbary E. Rector, born 1863.
d. Louisa Jane Rector, born 1865.
e. Frances Rector, born 1869.

Charles Sevier Rector, who is now (1924) living in Mohawk, Greene County, Tennessee, says he is the son of Jacob F. Rector, born January 29, 1844, died October 13, 1904, who was the son of John J. Rector, born ———————, died ———————, who was the son

---

†The Alexander mentioned by Rebecca as four years old was very evidently the little grandson mentioned by Hugh Bell, as her brother Alexander who was twelve was out rabbit hunting.

of John B. Rector and Rebecca Sevier Rector. Charles Sevier Rector has the Bible which the widow of Colonel Valentine Sevier III bought at the sale in Clarksville for fifty cents. He has given me many names and dates from this Bible, for instance, the birth of Naomi Douglass Sevier, April, 1743, and the birth and death of John B. Rector (March 10, 1764, February 5, 1856). These were not previously known to me.

From his record the only name we know positively as the child of Rebecca Sevier Rector and John B. Rector is John J. Rector, but I think from the dates of the people living with Rebecca and John in 1850 that George Rector, born in 1817, and Jane Rector, born in 1826, may have been their children. The other two, Valentine Sevier Rector and the child whose name is not given, are probably grandchildren.

The names, then, of the children of Rebecca Sevier Rector and John B. Rector:

a. John J. Rector.
b. George Rector.
c. Jane Rector.

a. John J. Rector, son of Rebecca Sevier Rector and John B. Rector, was born ————. He married Barbara Dearstone, born December 11, 1806, died July 17, 1872. They had a son:

Jacob F. Rector, born ————, died ————, married November 23, 185—, Louisa Jane Howell, born June 15, 1847, died March 15, 1879. Louisa Jane Howell was herself a descendant of the Sevier family. She was the daughter of ———— Howell and his wife, Sarah Jane Sevier Howell (born May 30, 1820, died March 29, 1896), whose father was "John Sevier," she said to her grandson, but I have not been able to determine which of the many Johns was her father. This was not Governor John Sevier, as her birth is given five years after his death.

Jacob F. Rector married after his first wife's death, Mary Kincer, December 9, 1879.

Their child was.

e. Charles Sevier Rector, born ————, 1878, in Greene County, Tennessee, now living in Mohawk, Tennessee.

JOANNA SEVIER

11. Joanna Goode Sevier, said to have been the eleventh child of Colonel Valentine Sevier and Naomi Douglass Sevier, was born ————. Miss Mary Ross Headman is authority for the statement that she was their eleventh child. In writing to Governor John Sevier in 1799, Colonel Sevier says, "the rest of my family is well, excepting Joanna, who is ill of a fever, but not serious."

Therefore, it may be accepted that Valentine Sevier III had a daughter, Joanna.

Whether this Joanna is the Joanna Goode Sevier who married Younger Landrum, Jr., November 8, 1800, I am unable to say.

See Part Four.

CHAPTER THREE

Captain Robert Sevier

CAPTAIN ROBERT SEVIER

ROBERT SEVIER, third son of Valentine Sevier II and Joanna Goode Sevier, was born about 1750, in Rockingham County, Virginia. He accompanied his father and four brothers to "the Mountains" in 1773. He there married, probably in 1777, Keziah Robertson, daughter of Charles Robertson and Sarah Nichols Robertson. They had two sons, Charles, aged two years, and Valentine, aged four months, when the call for the Mountaineers to assemble came and they marched to King's Mountain, where the British force engaged them. Captain Robert Sevier, commanding a company, was mortally wounded in the battle and was at first thought to be dead. He lived for a short time, however, and was carried from the battlefield toward his home. He died nine days after the battle, when he was almost within sight of his home, it is said. His contemporaries give him credit for being as brave and as handsome as his distinguished brother, Governor John Sevier, and it is thought by many that except for his early death he would have had a great part in the annals of Tennessee. As it is, his name remains one of the literal heroes of King's Mountain.

John Sevier was appointed administrator of Captain Robert Sevier's estate and guardian of the two children. Their mother married, shortly after the death of Captain Sevier, ——————— Tipton. The enmity existing between the Seviers and the Tiptons probably caused friction after this marriage, as it must have been awkward having a Tipton for a step-father and John Sevier for a guardian.

There is a tradition among the descendants of Charles Sevier that he and his brother, Valentine, ran away from home because their uncle, Governor John Sevier, was unkind to them and because he apprenticed them to a hatter! However Valentine's son, Charles Sevier, who is now living (1925), in Bristol, Tennessee, told me that the two boys were treated cruelly by their mother's second husband, ——————— Tipton. He did not mention any cruelty of his great-uncle, John Sevier, and as he is nearer in generation to the actual incidents than any other living person, his evidence is good. He had the information from many members of his family. He told me that Keziah Robertson Sevier Tipton joined her husband in unkindness and cruelty to the two orphan children of Captain Robert Sevier, and that the Seviers, all of them, including Governor Sevier, deeply resented her attitude and her husband's to the two orphan chil-

dren. Of course, the feud between the Seviers and the Tiptons is
well known and I can imagine that Governor Sevier would resent
any bad treatment of the orphans. Mr. Charles Lyman Sevier said
that the resulting family estrangement has lasted to the present
time. Keziah Robertson Sevier Tipton had children by her second
husband, but according to Mr. Sevier there has never been any
friendliness between the two branches of her descendants. I think
this story is more credible than the other and the evidence is certainly more direct. It is difficult to believe that Governor John
Sevier would be deliberately unkind to the fatherless children of his
favorite brother. I am inclined to think that if anything, he would
have aided them to escape from home and that he probably did!
The Sevier-Tipton feud, which was raging at this time, would lend
excuse to Tipton (Keziah's second husband)for disliking the Sevier
children.

    Captain Robert Sevier died nine days after the batttle of King's
Mountain, that is, October 16, 1780. He was about thirty years of
age.

    The children of Captain Robert Sevier and Keziah Robertson
Sevier were:

    1. Charles Robertson Sevier, born 1778, died 1855.
    2. Valentine Sevier, born June 1780, died March 24, 1854.

MAJOR CHARLES ROBERTSON SEVIER

    Charles Roberton Sevier, the elder son of Captain Robert Sevier
and Keziah Robertson Sevier, is known as Major Charles Sevier. He
was born in what is now known as East Tennessee, Greene County,
in 1778, two years before the Battle of King's Mountain. His father
was mortally wounded in that battle and died, leaving two infant
children. Charles, the elder, had evidently been named in honor of
Keziah's father. He is usually called Major Charles Robertson Sevier, but I
have seen his name given in full, Charles Robertson Sevier. He went
to Overton County when many of the Sevier family went there, early
in the years of 1800 and in the organization of the county he was
given in the military department of the county a commission as
Second Major. This was May 13, 1806. His cousin, Charles Matlock, received a commission as Captain at the same time. Charles
Matlock was, presumably, a son or grandson of Governor John
Sevier's sister who married William Matlock and was then living
in Overton County. A daughter of Governor Sevier, (Joanna) and
her husband, Joseph Hawkins Windle, were living in Overton County
at that time, where Joseph Hawkins Windle was keeping a store on
the John Sevier property. After the death of the Governor his
widow, Bonnie Kate, joined the rest of the family in Overton and
resided there until a few months before her death. Evidently, therefore, Charles Sevier was on exceedingly good terms with several

members of the John Sevier family. Although in 1806 he was twenty-eight years old and too old to be "running away," there is no evidence to show how long he had been in the county with other members of the Sevier family. Perhaps he did leave his step-father's house when he was a young boy.

It is said that Governor Sevier apprenticed him to a hatter about the year 1790 and that he did not like the job and left to go to live with his mother's brother, Charles Robertson, on the Chucky River. That shows friendliness with the mother's family.

Later he went to Overton County to make his home and there many of the Seviers gathered preceeding or follcwing Bonnie Kate's removal after the Governor's death. The fact that Charles Robertson Sevier joined them disposes of the story that he resented the cruelty and unkindness of his paternal relatives.

When West Tennessee was opened to settlers Charles Robertson Sevier went to Madison County and bought a farm four miles from the city of Jackson, Tennessee.

Charles Robertson Sevier married Elizabeth Witt, who was born about 1786. She was the daughter of Joseph Witt and Sarah Kimbrough Witt and the granddaughter of Charles Witt and Lavinia Harbor Witt, of Halifax County, Virginia. Elizabeth Witt was a first cousin to Preston Jarnagin, whose son, Dr. C. P. Jarnagin, married Catherine Anne Hale, also a descendant of the John Sevier family. See Chapter III, Part Six.

The marriage of Major Charles Robertson Sevier to Elizabeth Witt took place in 1802, in Greene County, Tennessee. In 1806, Charles Sevier was commissioned second major of Overton County. After a few years, the exact date not being known, he emigrated to Brownsville, Tennessee, where he reared a large family.

Major Charles Sevier served with General Andrew Jackson. It is said that he secured his military title in the War of 1812, and that he was promoted by General Jackson, but, as has been seen, he was commissioned Major in 1806, so he probably went into the war as a Major. He was living May 15, 1854, when his son, John Sevier, wrote to Dr. Lyman C. Draper that his father was "suffering from a bad memory due to old age."

Major Sevier was a very large man and was greatly interested in politics. It is told of him that he espoused the cause of James K. Polk and that on the day of the election in 1844, he rode into town on a white bull stained with poke berry juice.

In 1832, the sons of Major Sevier felt that General Jackson had not shown proper appreciation of their father's service. They declared, therefore, that they would not support him for President. This infuriated their father and he bade them never again darken his door! They voted for the opposition and left for Texas. This

story seems to account for the wholesale migration of the family to
the then new state of Texas, but evidently amity was restored, for the
father moved out to join his sons a few years later.   In 1854 he
came to this decision, but the long, hard trip (he was then seventy-
six years of age), seriously injured his health, and in a year's time,
1855, he died, at the home of his son Valentine Sevier, near Milford,
Ellis County, Texas. His wife's death occurred within a few weeks.

Children of Major Charles Sevier

Major Charles Robertson Sevier and Elizabeth Witt Sevier had
fourteen children, among them six sons:

(These are not given in the order of birth.)

A. Robert Sevier.
B. Valentine Sevier.
C. John Tinturff Sevier.
D. Mary Sevier.
E. Keziah Sevier.
F. Bathenia Sevier.
G. Catherine Sevier.
H. Elizabeth Sevier.
I.   Nancy Sevier.
J. ———— Sevier, a daughter.
K. Joseph Sevier.
L. Charles Wallace Sevier.
M. Elbridge Sevier.
N. Adam H. Sevier.

Robert Sevier

A. Robert Sevier, son of Major Charles Sevier and Elizabeth
Witt Sevier, married ———————— and had children, all of
whom died young.

Valentine Sevier

B. Valentine Sevier, son of Major Charles Sevier and Elizabeth
Witt Sevier, was in the Tennessee legislature for two or three terms.
He married Anna Murray. He moved to Texas in 1850 and lived to
be about ninety years of age. It was in his home in Milford, Ellis
County, Texas, that his father and mother died in 1856. He had eight
children, namely:

a. John Tinturff Sevier, Jr.
b. Bailey P. Sevier.
c. F. A. Sevier.
d. Mary F. Sevier, married ———— MacDonald.
e. Charles H. Sevier.
f. ———— Sevier.

g. ——————— Sevier.
h. ——————— Sevier.

Of the foregoing:

a. John Tinturff Sevier, Jr., son of Valentine Sevier and Anna Murray Sevier, was born October 29, 1831, at Brownsville Tennessee. He married and had thirteen children, namely: 1, George Wallace Sevier of Brandon, Texas, born at Milford, Texas 1871; 2, Oscar Sevier; 3, Charles Sevier; 4, Helen Norwood Sevier; 5, William Sevier; 6, Jane Sevier; 7, Lona Sevier; 8, May Sevier; 9, John Sevier; 10, Guy Sevier; 11, James Sevier; 12, Eddie Sevier and 13, Ernest Sevier.

b. Bailey P. Sevier, son of Valentine Sevier and Anna Murray Sevier, married ——————— and lived at Carter City, Mills County, Texas.

c. F. A. Sevier, son of Valentine Sevier and Anna Murray Sevier, married ——————— and lived at Cheatham, Texas.

d. Mary F. Sevier, daughter of Valentine Sevier and Anna Murray Sevier, married ——————— MacDonald and lived at Anson, Jones County, Texas.

e. Charles H. Sevier, son of Valentine Sevier and Anna Murray Sevier, married ——————— and lived at Sherman, Texas. He had a son, Charles S. Sevier, who was postmaster at Sherman.

John Tinturff Sevier

C. John Tinturff Sevier, son of Major Charles Robertson Sevier and Elizabeth Witt Sevier, was born January 23, 1807. He died 1866. He was sheriff of Haywood County for fourteen years. He married three times. His first wife was Maria Henderson, sister of Congressman Thomas J. Henderson, cf Princeton, Illinois. Six of the Sevier children left Major Charles Sevier's home, all going to Texas, as will be seen by reading their histories. John Tinturff Sevier, however, though leaving at the same time and perhaps for the same reason, did not go to Texas but to Brownsville, Tennessee, only twenty miles from Jackson. By his first wife he had one child, Mary Ann Amanda Sevier, who married ——————— Link and lived in Brownsville. By his second wife, ——————— Brickle, he had one son, Valentine Brickle Sevier, who moved back to Jackson and made his home with his grandfather, Major Charles Sevier. Valentine Brickle Sevier died 1905. He married first, ——————— Westbrook and had one son John Sevier, and married for his second wife, Mollie Whitehead, and had five children: Elizabeth Sevier, who married H. W. White and had a son, H. W. White, Jr.; Minnie Sevier, who married Finnis Lack, of Paducah, Kentucky, and has one son Frederick Lack; James Sevier, who married Pauline Houston and lived in Paducah, Kentucky; Charles William Sevier, who married

Nellie Steele and had a son, Charles Bertrand Sevier; and Robert Sevier, who married Gladys Spence and has three sons, Robert Sevier, Jr., James M. Sevier and Charles Wallace Sevier.

John Tinturff Sevier married for his third wife Sarah Sangster, by whom he had nine cildren, namely:

c. Charles Henry Sevier.
d. John Brickle Sevier.
e. James Sevier.
f. Robert Wallace Sevier.
g. ——————— Sevier, died in infancy.
h. Jane Sevier.
j. Mary Catherine Sevier.
k. William Sevier.
l. Laura Sevier.

Of the foregoing:

c. Charles Henry Sevier, son of John Tinturff Sevier and Sarah Sangster Sevier, was born in 1839, in Jackson, Tennessee. He died September 21, 1898. He married Cora Edwin Anderson, born July 26, 1839, died July 14, 1911. They had children namely: 1, Cora Amanda Sevier, born April 2, 1858, now living in Brownsville Tennessee, unmarried; 2, Dr. John Henry Sevier, born August 11, 1862, lives in Brownsville, Tennessee. He married Lee Wagner and has twin sons, both honor men at Johns Hopkins Medical School in Ba timcre, neither of whom is married. John Alston Sevier is located at Colorado Springs, Charles Edwin Sevier is in Lausanne, Switzerland; 3, Laura Sevier, died young; 4, Julia Sevier, married James M. Livingston and lives in Detrcit, Mich'gan. She has three children, Edwin Sevier Livingston, Cora Livingston and Charles Livingston; 5, Sue Sevier, died about 1910. She married Thomas F. Harolson and had children, Thomas Sevier Harolson, Hazel Sevier Harolson, William Harolson and Sallie Rose Sevier Harolson; 6, Charles A. Sevier, born August 13, 1870, lives in Jackson, Tennessee. He married Ida Matthews Sutherlin, of Paris, Tennessee, April, 1899. They have two children, Jane Sutherlin Sevier, born May 13, 1902, and Charles Henry Sevier, born September 20, 1906.

d. John Brickle Sevier, son of John Tinturff Sevier and Sarah Sangster Sevier, married Katherine Henderson, of Cedar Rapids, Iowa. He died without children, January 1, 1908.

e. James Sevier, scn of Jchn Tinturff Sevier and Sarah Sangster Sevier ———————

f. Robert Wallace Sevier, scn of John Tinturff Sevier and Sarah Sangster Sevier, married his cousin, Edith Anna Sangster. They left three children, Robert Wallace Sevier, Jr., Mary Sevier and Elder Sevier. Robert Wallace Sevier, Jr., is unmarried and lives in New York City; Mary Sevier married John A. Rose and has a daughter, Jeanne Adele Ross; they live in Clarksdale, Miss.; Elder Sevier married Hattie Yelovington and lives in Paris, Tennessee, and has two children, Gene Sangster Sevier and Mary Edith Sevier.

g. ——————— Sevier. This child died in infancy.

h. Jane Sevier, daughter of John Tinturff Sevier and Sarah Sangster Sevier, married Eph Clay. She died leaving no children.

i. Mary Catherine Sevier, daughter of John Tinturff Sevier and Sarah Sangster Sevier, married Dr. Thomas Potter, of Brownsville, Tennessee. They died leaving two children, a son, ——————— Potter, of Brownsville, and a daughter, Mary Potter, who married Fred Price, and has a daughter, Viola May Price.

k. Elizabeth Sevier, daughter of John Tinturff Sevier and Sarah Sangster Sevier.

l. Laura Sevier, daughter of John Tinturff Sevier and Sarah Sangster Sevier.

Mary Sevier

D. Mary Sevier, daughter of Major Charles Robertson Sevier and Elizabeth Witt Sevier, was born ———————. She married ——————— Anderson and lives in Missouri.

Keziah Sevier

E. Keziah Sevier, daughter of Major Charles Robertson Sevier and Elizabeth Witt Sevier, was born ———————. She married ——————— Simonton. The fact that Charles Robertson Sevier named a daughter for his mother, Keziah Robertson, seems to refute the statement that he resented her treatment of himself and his brother when they were children. Keziah Sevier Simonton lived at Purdy, Tennessee.

Bethenia Sevier

F. Bethenia Sevier, daughter of Major Charles Robertson Sevier and Elizabeth Witt Sevier, proves by her name that her father kept in close touch with his family, for the name Bathenia is identified with Sevier. It was borne by a sister of Governor John Sevier. Bethenia Sevier, daughter of Major Charles Sevier, married ——————— Brown and went to Texas to live.

Catherine Sevier

G. Catherine Sevier, daughter of Major Charles Sevier and Elizabeth Witt Sevier, was born ———————. She was also given a family name. She married ——————— Sanford and went to Texas

Elizabeth Sevier

H. Elizabeth Sevier, daughter of Major Charles Robertson Sevier and Elizabeth Witt Sevier, was born ——————. She was given her mother's name. She married —————— Holt and went to Texas.

Nancy Sevier

I. Nancy Sevier, daughter of Major Charles Robertson Sevier and Elizabeth Witt Sevier, was born ——————. She married Jesse Russell, of Jackson, Tennessee. They had two sons, Robert Russell and Jesse Russell, Jr. Robert Russell was in the Mexican War and later in the Confederate Army. Jesse Russell, Jr., married ———— —————— and had five children, namely: Charles Russell, Lucy Russell, Leighton Russell, Milborn Russell and Betty Russell.

—————— Sevier

J. —————— Sevier, a daughter of Major Charles Robertson Sevier and Elizabeth Witt Sevier, died young.

Joseph Sevier

K. Joseph Sevier, son of Major Charles Robertson Sevier and Elizabeth Witt Sevier, was born ——————. He went to California.

Charles Wallace Sevier

L. Charles Wallace Sevier, son of Major Charles Robertson Sevier and Elizabeth Witt Sevier, was born ——————. He went to Texas.

Elbridge Sevier

M. Elbridge Sevier, son of Major Charles Robertson Sevier and Elizabeth Witt Sevier, was born ——————. He went to Texas.

Adam H. Sevier

N. Adam H. Sevier, son of Major Charles Robertson sevier and Elizabeth Witt Sevier, was born ——————. He went to Texas.

VALENTINE SEVIER, SON OF CAPTAIN ROBERT SEVIER

Valentine Sevier, son of Captain Robert Sevier and Keziah Robertson Sevier, was born June, 1780. He was about four months old when Captain Robert Sevier fell mortally wounded at King's Mountain Valentine was the second child, his elder brother, Charles Robertson Sevier, being but two years of age in 1780. Their mother married —————— Tipton for her second husband.

The two Sevier children grew to maturity in East Tennessee.

where Valentine, reaching his majority, became Clerk of the Court at Greeneville, a position which he held fifty-two years until his death. He married twice and had fifteen children, thirteen by his first wife and two by his second wife. His elder son by the second wife, Charles Lyman Sevier, is now living in Bristol, Tennessee, and is one of the few men, if not the only man in America who is a grandson of a Revolutionary soldier who was killed in the Revolution. Mr. Sevier is also a grandson of a Colonial hero, as Captain Robert Sevier was an officer, as were his brothers, Valentine and John, in the Colonial Army.

Valentine Sevier married first Nancy Dinwiddie and second Vinerah Cannon. The first marriage took place when he was twenty-four years of age in 1804, in Greeneville, Tennessee. The second marriage took place April 26, 1846, also in Greeneville, Tennessee. Nancy Dinwiddie came of a Tennessee family. Vinerah Cannon, however, was of a Wallingford, Connecticut, family, and was visiting in Greeneville when she met and married Valentine Sevier.

Valentine Sevier died ———— 24, 1854.

The children of Valentine Sevier, son of Captain Robert Sevier, from a list found among his papers:

By his first wife:

A. Isabel Sevier, born January 10, 1805.
B. Keziah Sevier, born March 22, 1806.
C. Robert Sevier, born October 13, 1807.
D. Betsy (Elizabeth) Sevier, born October 13, 1809.
E. Susanna Sevier, born March 3, 1812.
F. James Sevier, born February 17, 1814.
G. Charles Sevier, born April 30, 1816.
H. Jane Sevier, born August 24, 1818.
I. David Sevier, born October 6, 1820.
J. William Robertson Sevier, born September 7, 1822.
K. Mary Sevier, born December 21, 1824.
L. Edward Sevier, born July 20, 1826.
M. Joseph Sevier, born March 30, 1830.

By the second wife:
N. Charles Lyman Sevier.
O. Henry Valentine Sevier.

Isabel Sevier

A. Isabel Sevier, daughter of Valentine Sevier and Nancy Dinwiddie Sevier, was born January 10, 1805. She married Frank A. McCorkle and had two children:

a. ———— McCorkle.
b. Nancy McCorkle.

a. ——————————— McCorkle, son of Isabel Sevier McCorkle and Frank A. McCorkle, married ——————— and had a son, Rev. Samuel McCorkle.

b. Nancy McCorkle, daughter of Isabel Sevier McCorkle and Frank A. McCorkle, married Cornelius Coffin and had Isabella Coffin who married Thomas Lanier Williams (see Williams Family, Vol. II, Notable Southern Families) and had Ella Williams, who is not married; Isabel Williams, who married William Gannaway Brownlow II (see Volume I, Notable Southern Families) and lives in Knoxville, Tennessee, and Cornelius Coffin Williams, who married ——— ——————— and has two children, Rose Isabella Williams and Thomas Lanier Williams II, and lives in St. Louis.

Keziah Sevier

B. Keziah Sevier, daughter of Valentine Sevier and Nancy Dinwiddie Sevier, was born March 22, 1806. She married George Jones, of Greeneville, Tennessee. She had at least one child, Mary Jones, born April 13, 1826 who, married August 7, 1852, Thomas A. Nelson, who died 1873. Their children are; Selden Nelson, of Knoxville; Lizzie Nelson, (who married John Williams and had a daughter, Mary Nelson Williams); Charles Nelson, (who married Mattie Chappell); Mary Nelson. (called Mollie, who married Charles E. McTeer); Lieutenant Commander Nelson, (who married Catherine McDonald); and Judge Thomas A. R. Nelson.

Robert Sevier

C. Robert Sevier, son of Valentine Sevier and Nancy Dinwiddie Sevier was born, October 13, 1807. He was educated at West Point. He entered West Point in 1824 and graduated in 1828 in the class with Jefferson Davis. He served for some years in the United States Army and participated in the Black Hawk War in 1837. He died in Missouri. He married Ann Hopkins Sibley.

Their children were:

(A) Charles Sevier, married Emma Denis and had Doctor Robert Sevier, born December 1, 1869; Reverend George F. Sevier; ——————————— Sevier, married Charles Zaeger; Ann Sevier married ——————————, Gras; M. ————Sevier, married George F. Maitland and Charles D. Sevier.

(B) Robert Sevier, M. D., married Virginia Elizabeth Woodson, June 14, 1893 and had Robert Woodson Sevier, born March 23, 1894 and Virginia Elizabeth Sevier, born April 27, 1905.

(C) Robert Sevier married Ann Sibley and had Charles Sevier, born September 30, 1832, at Fort Leavenworth, Kansas. Now living at 1481 Adams Street, Denver, Colorado.

Elizabeth Sevier

D.   Elizabeth Sevier, daughter of Valentine Sevier and Nancy Dinwiddie Sevier, born October 13, 1809, died June 14, 1882. She married Reverend John Whitfield Cunningham, of Kentucky, in 1831. John Whitfield Cunningham was a uncle of Martha Ellen Cunningham, who married William Robertson Sevier, and a brother of Samuel B. Cunningham. John Whitfield Cunningham and Elizabeth Sevier Cunningham had ten children, five of whom died in infancy. The surviving children were:

a.   Nancy Jane Cunningham, born 1834, died Minneapolis, Minnesota, 1909.   She married Herman Knickerbocker.

b.   John Cunningham married but had no children.

c.   Katherine Mitchell Cunningham, born 1835, died Fort Scott, Kansas, 1916. She married Cheney M. Castle, Minneapolis, Minnesota. She had no children.

d.   Jane Isaac Cunningham, died young.

e.   Lucy Isbell Cunningham, born 1845, Jonesboro, Tennessee, died Fort Scott, Kansas, 1909. She married Doctor William C. Porter, of English birth, in 1867.

Their children: Katherine Elizabeth Porter, born 1868, died 1884; John William Porter, born 1870, married Maud Taylor, of Chicago, and has four children: John William Porter, Jr., died young; Robert Taylor Porter, born 1903 in Chicago; Knight Cunningham Porter, born 1905 in Chicago; Alice Sarah Porter, born 1872, died 1916; Caroline Belle Porter, born 1874, married Dudley Feaherstone 1919 and has no children; and Lucy Porter, born 1886, married John Robinson McCurdy, in New York City in 1920. They have one child Jean McCurdy, a daughter born October 1924.

Susan Sevier

E.   Susan Sevier, daughter of Valentine Sevier and Nancy Dinwiddie Sevier was born March 3, 1812. She never married. She lived to a very great age.

James Sevier

F.   James Sevier, son of Valentine Sevier and Nancy Dinwiddie Sevier was born February 17, 1814. He married twice, first Jane Simpson, who died in 1863. He had a son Charles Sevier, who lived in Savannah, Tennessee, and a son George Jones Sevier, whose widow lived at one time in Oxford, Mississippi. James Sevier's second wife was Mrs. Eva Brewer Neil.

Mrs. Theodore Francis Sevier told me, (in 1924), that she and her husband Colonel Sevier, visited this cousin, James Sevier, in Rogersville, Tenn., in 1863 and that his wife had died three months earlier and that his sons were: Valentine, George and another who was in the Confederate Army. That there was another son, the youngest, named John, who was too young for military service. his father thought, but later he too joined the Confederate Army.

Charles Sevier

C. Charles Sevier, son of Valentine Sevier and Nancy Dinwiddie Sevier was born April 30, 1816. He married Elizabeth Briscoe and had two children, Thomas Sevier and Nannie Sevier. He died in Mississippi in 1844.

Jane Sevier

H Jane Sevier, daughter of Valentine Sevier and Nancy Dinwiddie Sevier, was born August 24, 1818. She married August 26, 1832, her second cousin, James Harvey Vance, of Kingsport, Tennessee, see Vance Family, Volume II, Notable Southern Families. The marriage took place at Warm Springs, North Carolina. James Harvey Vance died at Kingsport, Tennessee, July 7, 1893. James H. Vance and Jane Sevier were cousins, both being great-grand-children of Charles Robertson.

They had nine children, namely:

a. Charles Robertson Vance, who was born August 22, 1833, at Jonesboro, Tennessee. He married Margaret Newland, October 16, 1860 and had five children. James Isaac Vance, (born September 25, 1862 at Arcada, Tennessee, married December 22, 1866, at Yorkville, South Carolina, Mamie Currell. They have six children, Margaret Vance, Agnes Vance, James Isaac Vance, Jr., and Charles Robertson Vance); Dr. Joseph Anderson Vance, (born November 17, 1864); Charles Robertson Vance, Jr.; Margaret Vance, (born January 20, 1877); and Rebecca Vance, (born January 20, 1877.)

b. Maria C. Vance, who married Reverend John King, of Leesburg, Virginia.

c. Anna Elizabeth Vance, died young.

d. Keziah Vance, died unmarried.

e. James Harvey Vance, Jr., who married Easton or Faston Paddock.

f. William Kirkpatrick Vance, who married Fannie Miller, of Union City, Tennessee.

g. Nannie Vance, died unmarried.

h. Joseph Vance, who married Mattie Fain and had two sons, James Fain Vance and Charles Robertson Vance.

i. Jane or Jennie Vance.

David Sevier

I. David Sevier, son of Valentine Sevier and Nancy Dinwiddie

Sevier, was born October 6, 1820. He died May 22, 1890. He was
Clerk and Master at Greeneville, Tennessee, for many years. He
married Anne Netherland. They had six children, five daughters and
one son. He married a second wife, Annis Rutledge and had one
son by the second marriage. I have the names of only two daughters
and the one son by the second marriage who was David Rutledge
Sevier. One daughter Nellie Sevier, married William Roller, of
Kingsport, Tennessee and died several years ago. A daughter Nannie
Sevier, born August 6, 1849, married Reverend Alexander N. Carson
June 15, 1875. She died September 21, ——— in San Francisco. Her
four children were: Harry Carson, Frank Carson, Nannie Carson and
Charles Carson.

William Robertson Sevier

J. William Robertson Sevier, son of Valentine Sevier and Nancy
Dinwiddie Sevier, was born September 7, 1822, died August 22, 1882.
He married twice, first in 1844, Martha Ellen Cunningham, daughter
of Dr. Samuel B. Cunningham, first President of the East Tennessee
and Virginia Railway, now the Southern Railway, and married
second, in 1864, Lucy Evans. Lucy Evans was the daughter of Hamilton Evans, of Tazewell, Claiborne County, Tennessee. His mother
was a Holt and his grand-mother a Hampton. By the first wife
William Robertson Sevier had two children, a son Samuel D. Sevier,
who died young and a daughter, Nannie Sevier, who married Guy
Ellis Sabin, and by the second wife William Robertson Sevier had
a son, William Robertson Sevier, Jr., of the United States Navy.

Nannie Sevier, daughter of William Robertson Sevier and his
first wife, Martha Ellen Cunningham, was born in Jonesboro, Tennessee, in 1856. She married Guy C. Sabin, September 13, 1876. They
had six children, one of whom died in infancy. Mabel Sabin, the
only daughter, died at seventeen years of age. The sons: Albert
Sevier Sabin, born 1877, married Emily Maud Raysor, of South Carolina, and has seven children, six sons and one daughter, Archibald
Raysor Sabin, Albert Sevier Sabin, Katherine Margaret Sabin, William Robertson Sabin, Cornelius Ayre Sabin, Ellis Sabin and Donald
Gavin Sabin, Guy Earl Sabin, who is unmarried. William Robertson
Sabin, died unmarried, and Archibald D. Sabin, died unmarried.

Mary Sevier

K. Mary Sevier, daughter of Valentine Sevier and Nancy
Dinwiddie Sevier, was born December 21, 1824.

Edward Sevier

L. Edward Sevier, son of Valentine Sevier and Nancy Dinwiddie
Sevier, was born July 20, 1825. He married Mary Nelson Garrett and
resides in Asheville, North Carolina.

Joseph Sevier

M.   Joseph Sevier, son of Valentine Sevier and Nancy Dinwiddie
Sevier, was born, March 30, 1829.   He married his cousin Nannie
Sevier Broyles, widow of Lewis Broyles and a daughter of Devil
Jack Sevier and Susannah Conway Sevier.

They had children namely: Dr.   Robert   Sevier,   deceased;
Lewis Sevier, married and lives in Savannah, Tennessee, and has
three children and Miss Nannie Sevier, all of Savannah, Tennessee.

Joseph Sevier was killed in the War Between the States at Peach
tree Creek, Atlanta, July 22, 1864.

Charles Lyman Sevier

N.   Charles Lyman Sevier, son of Valentine Sevier and his
second wife, Venerah Cannon Sevier, was born 1847.   It will be noted
that the name Charles was used in the family of the first wife and
also in the family of the second. Charles Lyman Sevier married Julia
Brown.

Their children are:

a.   Wilbur Lyman Sevier, who married Leta Montague.
b.   Henry Brown Sevier, who married Etta ————.
c.   Dr. Joseph Ramsey Sevier, who married Edith Love.
d.   Eloisa Venerah Sevier, who married H. H. Shelton.

Henry Valentine Sevier

O.   Henry Valentine Sevier, son of Valentine Sevier and his
second wife, Vinerah Cannon Sevier, was born 1849. He died ————
He married Isabelle C. McGaughey, daughter of Samuel McGaughey.

Their children are:

a.   Samuel Valentine Sevier.
b.   Lyman Cannon Sevier.
c.   Victor Sevier.

CHAPTER FOUR

Joseph Sevier, Sr.

JOSEPH SEVIER, SR.

JOSEPH SEVIER, son of Valentine Sevier II, the Emigrant, and Joanna Goode Sevier, was born in Rockingham County, Virginia, in 1751. He moved to Tennessee in 1773, arriving on Chris'mas Day, 1773, accompanying his father and four brothers, to join Valentine Sevier III, who was al eady there. Three sisters were in the party and one sister had teen left in Virginia. Joseph Sevier was then twenty-one years of age. His father made a settlement in the Watauga District.

Joseph Sevier served in the Battle of King's Mountain and is mentioned in many histories, including Draper's Kings Mountain and Its Heroes. He is frequently confused with Governor Sevier's oldest son, Joseph Sevier, Jr., who was his namesake. Joseph Sevier, Jr., also served at King's Mountain and in the various Indian campaigns in which Joseph Sevier, Sr., participated. In addition to the service at King's Mountain Joseph, Sr., is men ioned in the Draper Manuscript as in the Indian campaign in the 'a'l of 1778 and he was one of the men who rescued Colonel John Sevier from the hands of General McDowell who held him under arrest, in the absence of the sheriff, at Morgantown, North Carolina. Joseph Sevier, Sr., and his nephew John Sevier, Jr., had a very exciting escape from Indians at one time.

It is said by some that Joseph Sevier, Sr., died in 1826, but even in death he may be confused with his nephew Joseph Sevier, Jr., who died in 1826.

He was only eleven years older than his nephew Joseph and the fact that they were so nearly the same age adds to the constant confusion concerning them. When only the name "Joseph Sevier" appears it is frequently impossible to know which Joseph is meant. Only other circumstances, text and date can solve the riddle, and it cannot always be solved.

Joseph Sevier, Sr., married Charity Keewood. This information as to his marriage was given me by his grandson, Alfred Windle Sevier. However, Bishop Hoss says that Joseph S v er, Jr., married Charity Keewood for his first wife. There is probably an error in this statement, as it seems incredible that two Joseph Seviers married two Charity Keewoods. And yet from various references I think it is quite possible that both of them married into the Keewood family. The Keewoods live not far from the home of Valentine

Sevier II, and were prominent people. Governor Sevier refers in his Journal to his brother Joseph and the Keewoods showing plainly that there was a close connection of some sort. And again in mentioning his son "Joseph and wife" he adds names of the Keewood family , as will be seen in the chapter in this book devoted to Joseph Sevier, Jr., Chapter One of Part Six.

It will be recalled that when the Sevier family moved from Virginia, they arrived in Tennessee, Christmas Day, 1773, at the Keewood Settlement. The family of Valentine Sevier II, remained in that neighborhood, though later John Sevier moved to another location.

Joseph Sevier, Sr., and his wife are buried three miles east of Willow Grove, Tennessee, on Obey River, in Clay County, Tennessee. I do not know whether there is a tombstone or whether there are dates upon it. I have seen his death date given as 1826, but I have no certain knowledge of this and he may have lived much longer. His father willed to Joseph and Abraham Sevier his estate after maintenance to the widow was paid.

Joseph Sevier and Charity Keewood Sevier had at least one son, namely:

Alfred C. Sevier.

Alfred C. Sevier, son of Joseph Sevier, Sr., and Charity Keewood Sevier, was born ———————. I do not know for what name his middle initial stood, but Keewood was as frequently spelled Cawood and Caywood as it is spelled Keewood. Alfred C. Sevier married his cousin, Mary Hawkins Windle, daughter of Joseph Hawkins Windle and Joanna Goode Sevier Windle who was the daughter of Governor John Sevier by his second wife Catherine Sherrill Sevier (See Chapter Fourteen of Part Six, this book).

Alfred C. Sevier and his wife, Mary Hawkins Windle Sevier, are buried at Monroe, Tennessee. They had at least two children namely:

A   Joseph Windle Sevier.
B   Amanada Sevier.

Joseph Windle Sevier

A   Joseph Windle Sevier, son of Alfred C. Sevier and Mary Hawkins Windle Sevier, was born ————. He is now living (1924) at Livingston, Tennessee. He married and has five daughters, namely:

Mrs. Lillian Sevier Stewart, Livingston Tennessee.
Mrs. A. E. Speck, Sheridan, Arkansas.
Mrs. J. S. Arms, Celina, Tennessee.
Mrs. John Lee Bowman, Crawford, Tennessee.
Miss Leuce B. Sevier, Livingston, Tennessee.

Amanda Sevier

B   Amanda Sevier, daughter of Alfred C. Sevier and Mary Hawkins Windle Sevier, was born _____. She married _____ Abston and lives at Willow Grove, Tennessee.

Joseph Windle Sevier gave me this information. He and his sister Amanda are by this record, grandchildren of Joseph Sevier, Sr., which is very close in gene:ation, and his information should therefore be reliable.

CHAPTER FIVE

Abraham Sevier

ABRAHAM SEVIER

ABRAHAM SEVIER, son of Valentine Sevier, the Emigrant, and Joanna Goode Sevier, was born in Rockingham County, Virginia, February 14, 1760. He died June 18, 1841. He went with his father and four brothers to the "Mountains" in 1773, where his elder brother, Valentine Sevier III, had preceded the family.

When he was just twenty years of age he fought in the Battle of King's Mountain and was the youngest of the five brothers who participated in that famous encounter. They were: John Sevier, Valentine Sevier III, Robert Sevier, Joseph Sevier, Sr., and Abraham Sevier. There were two other Seviers in the battle, namely: Joseph Sevier, Jr., and James Sevier, sons of Governor John Sevier.

Valentine Sevier II willed to his sons Joseph and Abraham Sevier his estate after maintenance to the widow was paid.

Abraham Sevier was living in Overton County, Tennessee, in 1832. His pension declaration was made there in 1832 and he died there in 1841. He is on the pension list of 1840, aged 80 years. That agrees with this record of his birth in 1760.

Abraham Sevier married about 1785, Mary Little, of Augusta County, Virginia. She was the daughter of Major-General Little and was born May 14, 1770. She died March 14, 1839.

Abraham and Mary Little Sevier had nine children. It is said they were all born in Overton County, Tennessee.

1. Elizabeth Sevier.
2. Mary Ann Sevier.
3. John Sevier, born January 13, 1795, died September 2, 1795.
4. Jemima Douglass Sevier.
5. Joanna Goode Sevier.
6. Valentine Sevier.
7. Rebecca Richards Sevier.
8. Abraham Rutherford Sevier.
9. Catherine Sherrill Sevier.

Of the foregoing children of Abraham Sevier:

ELIZABETH SEVIER

1. Elizabeth Sevier, daughter of Abraham Sevier and Mary Little Sevier, was born November 12, 1790. She died November 21,

73

1805. She married ——————— Scroggins and left no children, dying at the age of fifteen years, soon after her marriage.

MARY ANN SEVIER

2. Mary Ann Sevier, daughter of Abraham Sevier and Mary Little Sevier, was born December 9, 1792. She died November 21, 1813. She married ——————— Hatterman. She d'ed shortly af er her marriage, leaving no ch'ldren.

JOHN SEVIER

3. John Sevier, son of Abraham Sevier and Mary Little Sevier, was born January 13, 1795. He d ed in infanc , Sep'cmber 2, 1795.

JEMIMA DOUGLASS SEVIER

4. Jemima Douglass Sevier, daughter of Abraham Sevier and Mary Little Sevier, was born August 27, 1786. She died July 3, 1822. It is believed that she died unmarried.

JOANNA GOODE SEVIER

5. Joanna Goode Se ier, daughter of Abraham Sevier and Mary Little Sevier, was born April 5, 1799. She died December 29, 1839. She married Alfred C. Robinson and lived in Tennessee. She left children.

VALENTINE SEVIER

6. Valentine Sevier, son of Abraham Sevier and Mary Little Sevier, was born November 10, 1801. He died January 25, 1842. He married Elizabeth Arnett, in Tennessee, and is said to have had six sons, one of whom died young. The five who lived to maturity were:

A.   John Sevier.
B.   Annias Sevier.
C.   Abraham Sevier.
D.   George Sevier.
E.   Valentine Sevier, Jr.
F.   ——————— Sevier, died young.

Of these:

A. John Sevier, son of Valentine Sevier and Elizabeth Arnett Sevier, married ——————— and is said to have raised a family in Calhoun County, Illinois.

B. Annias Sevier, son of Valentine Sevier and Elizabeth Arnett Sevier, was born about 1827 and died in Illinois. He married Cornelia Caroline Gunnells, January 9, 1845, Morgan County, Illinois, and had children, among them:

a. Daniel A. Sevier, of Waverly, Illinois, who married ————
and had children, among them: 1 Marian E. Sevier (who married
Frederick E. Deatherage, son of Charles W. Deatherage, September
21, 1904, Morgan County, Illinois); 2, Elizabeth Caroline Sevier
(who married Wayne Leslie Carter, January 1, 1908, Morgan County,
Illinois); 3, John W. Sevier (who married Genevieve Peebles, daughter of William and Bertha Thomas Peebles, February 15, 1915, Morgan County, Illinois); 4, Nellie E. Sevier, of Rushville, Illinois
(who married Morris Hargrove Demaree Fe'ruary 21, 1917 Morgan County, Illinois, and had a son, born April 8, 1822).

b. John D. Sevier, deceased, who married Lizzie Clayton, daughter of Frank and Alpha Jane Clayton, and had several children, one
of whom was Edith Sevier (who married Peter Dawson, son of
Richard and Rebecca Kessler Dawson, November 20, 1901, Morgan
County, Illinois).

c. Charles D. Sevier, who married Margaret Carter, daughter
of N. and Nancy Masters Carter, December 9, 1880, Morgan County,
Illinois.

d. Nathan Sevier, who married Eliza McKay, November 24, 1878,
Morgan County, Illinois, and had several children, including: 1, Nora
Sevier (who married James M. Thompson, son of G. R. and Lydia
Hart Thompson, December 24, 1901, Morgan County, Illinois); 2,
Harriet Pearl Sevier (who married William Sitton, son of James
and Mary Patterson Sitton, November 25, 1905, Morgan County,
Illinois); 3, Vol (Valentine) Sevier (who married Maude Brown,
daughter of Charles and Lucretia Ryman Brown, August 30, 1911,
in Jacksonville, Illinois, and had a son, Charles Brown Sevier).

e. William Sevier, who married Mary Robson, August 3, 1892.

f. Don Manuel Sevier, who married Lilla B. Jones, daughter of
Albert and Luzetta Jones, November 8, 1893, Morgan County, Illinois.

g. Mary Sevier.

h. Nannie E. Sevier, born 1850, died May 12, 1924, Waverly,
Illinois, who married Charles Scott, April 28, 1874, Morgan County,
Illinois. Charles Scott died 1893.

i. Hattie Sevier, married William M. Miller, April 17, 1884, in
Morgan County, Illinois.

C. Abraham Sevier, son of Valentine Sevier and Elizabeth
Arnett Sevier, was born September, 1830, Overton County, Tennessee. He died in battle at Dallas, Georgia, May 25, 1864. He
served in the Union Army. Though born in the South, he had lived
for a long time in Illinois, where he had removed when he was a
boy, when he enlisted in the Union Army. He married Eliza Jane
Asbaugh, January 17, 1848, in Morgan County, Illinois. They had
two children:

a. Christopher Monroe Sevier, born May 19, 1856, married Madge Lee Cou tas, Apr l 29, 1885, and had: 1. Olive A. Sevier, born March 14, 1886; 2, Lois Aileen Sevier, born September 9, 1887 (known as Eva. She married Adolph Seymour, March 1904, Jefferson City, Mo., and had Lucile Seymour, born 1906, Jefferson City, Mo.); Annias Sevier, born January 11, 1890, (known as Nike G .Sevier. He married Margaret Freeman and had no children); 4, Lee Coultas Sevier, born March 8, 1891 (who married Nellie Wagoner in 1916 and had: Nellie Lee Sevier, born 1920); 5, Bertha Emma Sevier, born April 1, 1893, (who married first William Cook, 1909, who died in 1913, leaving William Cook, Jr., born 1911; and married second Ellis Elliott, in 1914, and had James Elliott, born 1916).

b. John H. Sevier, of Waverly, Illinois.

D. George Sevier, son of Valentine Sevier and Elizabeth Arnett Sevier, lived in Morgan County, Illinois.

E. Valentine Sevier, Jr., son of Valentine Sevier and Elizabeth Arnett Sevier, lived in Morgan County, Illinois.

REBECCA RICHARDS SEVIER

7. Rebecca Richards Sevier, daughter of Abraham Sevier and Mary Little Sevier, was born October 20, 1804. She died July 6, 1822, unmarried.

ABRAHAM RUTHERFORD SEVIER

8. Abraham Rutherford Sevier, son of Abraham Sevier and Mary Little Sevier, was born January 12, 1807. He died February 1ı, 1870, near Clinton, Henry County, Mo., at the home of his daughter, Elizabeth Jane Sevier. Abraham Rutherford Sevier marri.d about 1830 in Tennessee, Mary Colson, who was born 1808. She died November 16, 1861, in Clinton, Missouri.

Their children were:

A. Mary Susan Sevier.
B. Eliza Jane Sevier.
C. William Palmer Sevier.
D. George Allen Sevier.
E. Rebecca Catherine Sevier.

A. Mary Susan Sevier April 18, 1834, in Tennessee. She died 1917, in Nevada, Missouri. She married John Sartoricus, younger brother of the Earl of Sartorious. They had only one child, Anthony Sartorious, who lives at Rich Hill, Missouri. He is married and has children.

B. Eliza Jane Sevier was born December 16, 1835, in Tennessee. She died May 2, 1912, at Clinton, Missouri. She married three times. She married first ———— Sweet, by whom she had two children. She married second Henry Gragg, by whom she had four children. Henry Gragg was born January 27, 1820. He died May 12, 1892. She married third ———— Woods, by whom she had no children. He died shortly after their marriage. Her children were:

    a. William Sevier Sweet.
    b. Mary Sweet.
    c. Catherine Lee Gragg.
    d. George Washington Gragg.
    e. Dulcenia Gragg.
    f. Amos Gragg.

Of these:

a. William Sevier Sweet is unmarried.

b. Mary Sweet married William Walsh and has five chidren: 1, Belle Walsh (who married ————— M Daniel and lives at Rich Hill, Missouri, and has William McDaniel, Lorena McDaniel and John McDaniel); 2, Maggie Walsh (who married Dr. Joseph McDonald, lives at Rich, Missouri, and has four children); 3, Catherine Walsh, who married ———— Jenkins, lives in Oklahoma and has three children); 4, Ora Walsh (who married Roy Pulliam, lives in Sedalia, Missouri, and has three children); and 5, Jeffrey Walsh, who married ———— and has two children).

c. Catherine Lee Gragg was born January, 1865. She married Wylie Alexander and lives at Clinton, Missouri. She has six children, namely: 1, Naomi Elizabeth Alexander (who married ———— and has one child); 2, Mary Ann Alexander (who married ————————); 3, Herbert Alexander; 4, Nina Alexander; 5, Ralph Alexander; and 6, Margaret Alexander.

d. George Washington Gragg, was born December 20, 1867, in Missouri. He married Minnie Roach and had five children, namely: 1, Esther Gragg; 2, Emmett Gragg; 3, Edmund Gragg; 4, Ethel Gragg; and 5, Elbert Gragg.

e. Dulcenia Gragg, called Della, was born October 14, 1870, at Clinton, Missouri. She married Charles Otis Swift, June 16, 1897. They live in Jacksonville, Illinois, and have five children, namely: 1, William Frederick Swift, born August 21, 1900, and 2, Lillian Elizabeth Swift, born March 2, 1902. (She married Roy G. Blauvelt, June 14, 1924, at Springfield, Illinois).

f. Amos Gragg was born July 26, 1879, at Hutchinson, Kansas. He married Leona Waggoner and they live at Appleton, Mo. They have two children, namely: Herbert Gragg, born June 4, 1900, and Maurine Gragg, born November, 1902.

C. William Palmer Sevier, son of Abraham Rutherford Sevier and Mary Colson Sevier, was born February 17, 1843. He l ves in Bu ler Mo. He married Mary Lilly and had four children, namely:

(a) Lucille Sevier.
(b) Minnie Sevier.
(c) John Se ier.
(d) Charles Sevier.

Of these:

(a) Lucille Sevier, born 1860, lives at St. Joseph, Mo., and has been married twice. She has the Bible of Abraham Rutherford Sevior.
(b) Minnie Sevier, died in infancy.
(c) John Sev er, died in infan y.
(d) Charles Sevier, died at twenty-three.

D. George A len Sevier, son of Abraham Rutherford Sevier and Mary Colson Sevier, was born June 12, 1845, in Overton County, Tennessee. He died April 13, 1874, in Clinton, Missouri. He married Mary Frances Dunn, January 4, 1866. Mary Frances Dunn was born October 8, 1847. She and her husband were among the first settlers in Henry County, Missouri. She married, after George Allen Sevier's death, A. V. Clary and lives (1923) in Henry County, Missouri. George Allen Sevier had four children, namely:

a. James William Sevier.
b. Rose Ellen Sevier.
c. Dora Sevier.
d. Edward Franklin Sevier.

Of these:

a. James William Sevier, was born October 21, 1866, in Henry County, Missouri, died October 11, 1921, in Clinton, Missouri. He married February 15, 1892, Lucella Patt, daughter of J. M. and Martha Patt. Their children are: Walter Franklin Sevier, born January 2, 1894, died in infancy; Mary Sevier, (married Walter Goodman and has one child, Willard Sevier Goodman); Lee Sevier and Bessie Sevier.
b. Rose Ellen Sevier was born June 11, 1868, in Henry County, married William Williams and had two children, John Sevier Williams, deceased, and Sarah Williams, married ————— Wilson.
c. Dora Sevier, born October 23, 1870, in Henry County, Missouri, now living (1924) in Springfie d, mr rr ed November 3, 1897, W. G. Martin. Their children are Ray Paul Martin and Ruth Martin,

who married William Harbstreet and has William L. Harbstreet and Lula Ray Harbstreet.

d. Edward Franklin Sevier, born November 2, 1872, in Henry County, Missouri, lives in Urich, Missouri. He married Clara Barth. Their children are: Arlie May Sevier, born December 5, 1906; Wi l'am Harold Sevier, born October 4, 1908; Ruby Ellen Sevier, born May 21, 1910, and Paul Eugene Sevier, born April 4, 1912.

E. Rebecca Catherine Sevier, daughter of Abraham Rutherford Sevier and Mary Colson Sevier, was born April 6, 1848. She died 1918 in Gridley, California. She married three times. She married first Richard Watson. They had one ch ld, Harriet Wa'son, who was known by her step-father's name, Jeffrey. Harriet married George Daniels and had children. Rebecca Catherine Sevier married second ————— Jeffrey and had no children, and married th rd ————— Jaylor and had no children.

CATHERINE SHERILL SEVIER

9. Catherine Sherill Sevier, daughter of Abraham Sevier and Mary Little Sevier, was born March 17, 1809. She died September 18, 1861. She married ————— MacFarland. She lived in Tennessee. Once again the complimentary but confusing habit of naming children for the "in-laws" in the Sevier family has an example. Catherine Sherill Sevier was evidently named for her father's brother's second wife. Governor John Sevier married Catherine Sherill for his second wife and thereafter the Catherine Sherill Seviers are numerous.

MORGAN COUNTY, ILLINOIS, SEVIER MARRIAGES

So many Sevier descendants live in Illinois that the following list of marriages in Morgan County, which has been furnished me by Miss Lucy M. Ball, will prove of value. These persons doubtless are all descendants of Abraham Sevier and Mary Little Sevier.

Sevier, Annias and Mrs. Amanda Louise Weatherford, February 1, 1885.

Sevier, Albert Earl, son of Dan and Lela Jones Sevier, and Mary Bryan Morris, daughter of Richard and Lydia Dennis Morris, November 1, 1915.

Sevier, Mrs. Eliza J., and Wilson Mitchmer, October 14, 1871.

Sevier, Elizabeth, and Charles Hagen, August 9, 1872.

Sevier, Ella E., daughter of Valentine J. and Luvina Lassiter Sevier, and Ananias G. Thompson, son of Sylvester and Minerva Sample Thompson, January 14, 1892.

Sevier, Elizabeth Caroline, daughter of D. A. and Lillie Mills Sevier, and Wayne Leslie Carter, January 1, 1908.

Sevier, Ida, daughter of William T. and Delilah Johnson Sevier, and Frank Graham, son of John and Emily Sevier Graham, April 19, 1875.

Sevier, James, son of Archibald and Emily Medlen Sevier, and Lula Kidd, daughter of John and Mary Joiner Kidd, April 8, 1860.

Sevier, John A., and Amelia Burns. License granted August 28, 1841.

Sevier, John W. and Permelia A. Burns Sevier, and Mattie Timmons, daughter of William and Lucinda Burns Timmons, March 6, 1890.

Sevier, John M., and Charlotte Whitlock, February 21, 1866.

Sevier, John W., son of D. A. and Lillie Mills Sevier, and Bertha Thomas Peebles, February 11, 1915.

Sevier, Martha Ann. and James William Doulton, September 21, 1857.

Sevier, Mary E., and Henry Burch, November 23 ,1869.

Sevier, Laura, and John Austin, July 2, 1884.

Sevier, Nancy M., and James Brown, September 4, 1872.

Sevier, Roy D., son of N. S. and Mary Brown Sevier and Della Wetherbee, daughter of Walter and Nancy Dennis Wetherbee, March 9, 1905.

Sevier, Sarah Frances, and George W. Large, March 13, 1862.

Sevier, Valentine and Mrs. Lavinia Dennis, March 24, 1870.

Sevier, William T., and Delilah T. Johnson, June 4, 1874.

Sevier, W. A., son of John and Parmelia A. Burns Sevier, and Ella M. Ketcham, daughter of Samuel and Mary J. Osborn Ketcham, March 2, 1890.

CHAPTER SIX

Charles Sevier

CHARLES SEVIER

CHARLES SEVIER, son of Valentine Sevier, the Emigrant, and his wife, Joanna Goode Sevier, was born about 1768. I have found only two references to him by name. Mrs. Swift, of Jacksonville, Illinois, who has a copy of Abraham Sevier's Bible record, says that Abraham (son of Valentine II, the Emigrant) mentions a brother Charles. Otherwise the list which she has in the copy of Abraham's Bible record of the children of Valentine Sevier II corresponds with the list of children as given in other records I have found. Her list, however, does not mention either Rebecca or "G. Sevier," who is mentioned by Governor Sevier as being in Nashville, where he visited him. It is of course, possible that the transcriber from the original notes of Governor Sevier's Journal may have changed "C" to "G" and that the apparent reference to a brother named "G." in reality meant for "C." and means Charles.

Records show that Valentine Sevier, the Emigrant, was accompanied to the "Mountains" in 1773 by his five sons, to join his other son, Valentine Sevier III, who was already established there. Four of the five sons were John, Robert, Joseph and Abraham. The other son I have never seen mentioned by name. He was probably young, as Abraham, who was youngest of the five mentioned above, was only thirteen years of age in 1773. It is possible that Charles was the other brother and at that time, being only eight or ten years of age, was not important enough to mention by name. He was evidently too young in 1780 to serve in the Battle of King's Mountain.

February 8, 1794, Governor Sevier says in his Journal, "Charles lay here all night." This reference to an intimate member of the family circle suggests a brother.

In records of the Witt family, collected by Miss Lucy M. Ball, "Bathenia Witt, who was also called Thenia, married Charles Sevier, said to be a brother of Governor John Sevier." Miss Ball, however, has not been able to trace this couple or find whether they had any children. However, a marriage record in Grainger County, Tennessee offers possible clew to this family. The record is Thomas Hart to Nance Sevier, January 11, 1798, and the bond is signed by Charles Sevier. Bathenia is a family name.

As Governor John Sevier's daughter, Nancy, married Walter King, this "Nance" is without a doubt a niece of the Governor and very probably a daughter of Charles.

CHAPTER SEVEN

Catherine Sevier

CATHERINE SEVIER

CATHERINE SEVIER, daughter of Valentine Sevier the Emigrant and Joanna Goode Sevier, appears on some lists of Valentine's children and not on others. George Washington Sevier says that his "father's only sisters were Polly and Catherine," which seems to be sufficient proof that Catherine existed, although he palpably ignored the other sisters. This may be accounted for if he did not include "half-sisters" (for it is quite possible that Valentine Sevier II married and had children before his marriage to Joanna Goode) or he may have meant only living sisters at the time he wrote to Dr. Draper.

Also Catherine may have had a double name and may have been Catherine Elizabeth, for I find both Catherine and Elizabeth as married to William Matlock. (Certainly they may both have married him as first and second wife). William Matlock was living in Elizabethton in 1797. The April term of Court, Carter County, Tennessee. met in the home of William Matlock. In 1797, William Matlock applied for license to keep a tavern. The Matlocks moved to Overton County and were there in 1806.

Valentine Sevier II. in his will dated March 12, 1799, directs his sons, Abraham and Joseph, to pay, one of them forty pounds and one fifty pounds current money to Catherine. wife of William Matlock.

In the Life of Jefferson D. Goodpasture. written by his sons, mention is made of "Governor Sevier's sister, Mrs. Matlock, who was the mother of Valentine Matlock, one time sheriff of Overton County." She evidently named her son for her father, Valentine Sevier II.

The Borden Genealogy, states that John Borden married for his second wife in 1824, Catherine Sevier, daughter of Governor Sevier, (this is manifestly an error, as Governor Sevier's daughter was a generation older) and that his first wife was Catherine Matlock, daughter of William Matlock. It is probable that both wives were of the Sevier blood and that the first wife, Catherine Matlock, was a granddaughter of Catherine Sevier and William Matlock and that the second wife was a granddaughter or a grand niece of the Governor.

Catherine Sevier Matlock and William Matlock had probably four children whose names we know, namely: Valentine Matlock (the sheriff of Overton County); William Matlock, Jr., (whose daughter Catherine must have married John Borden); possibly George Matlock and Charles Matlock.

1. Valentine Matlock.

2. William Matlock, Jr.

3. George Matlock.

4. Charles Matlock.

VALENTINE MATLOCK

1. Valentine Matlock, born possibly about 1780, was sheriff of Overton County, Tennessee.

WILLIAM MATLOCK, JUNIOR

2. William Matlock, Jr., born about 1782, married ——————— and had a daughter, Catherine Matlock, who married John Borden as his first wife about 1818. (See Borden Genealogy below).

GEORGE MATLOCK

3. George Matlock was a deputy sheriff in Overton County.

CHARLES MATLOCK

4. Charles Matlock was a captain in the military department of Overton County at its organization, May 13, 1807.

FROM THE BORDEN GENEALOGY

The Borden Genealogy says:

John Borden, son of John and Mary Echols Borden and greatgrandson of Benjamin Borden (to whom Governor Gooch of Virginia granted the 100,000-acre tract of land known as Borden's Manor), married first, Catherine Matlock, daughter of William Matlock, and second, Catherine Sevier, daughter of Governor John Sevier.

They had nine children, namely:

1. Rebecca Borden, born June 26, 1817, married ——————— Alexander.

2. George H. Borden, born October 24, 1819, died 1865.

3. Ann Borden, born September 8 1821, died December 22, 1888, married ——————— Alexander.

4. Elizabeth Borden, born November 5, 1825, died September 5, 1851.

5. Euphemia Borden, born January 4, 1828, died September 16, 1866.

6. William Joseph Borden, born in Benton County, Alabama, May 14, 1830; married Emma Gabriel Gossom, of New Orleans.

Residence, Oxford, Alabama.   Their children were:

a. Edwin Gosson Borden, born August, 1858, married January 26, 1884, Caroline Moench.   Residence, San Francisco,   Their children are:

(1) Fredrick William Borden.
(2) Henry Forney Borden.
(3) Emma Claudine Borden.

b. Willie C. Borden, born August, 1859, married ————— Treadway, of Newman, Georgia.

c. Malbert Troupe Borden, married December 16, 1890, Mildred A. Harris, daughter of James M. and Mildred A. (McCulloch) Harris,, of Lynchburg, Virginia.   Residence, Cedartown, Ga.   They had Christine Borden.

d. Pelham Borden, born 1864, married ————— Harper, of Corsicana, Texas.

e. Ann Borden, married ————— Frey, of Newman,Ga.

f. Ermine B. Borden, married ——— Martin, of Newman, Ga.

g. Joseph Borden, born in·1871, died in infancy.

h. Francis Borden, born in 1871, died in infancy.

i. Benjamin Borden, born November 8, 1875.

7. Mary Catherine Borden, born May 2, 1833, married ————— Bacon (s. p.)

8. Andrew Campbell Borden, born November 15, 1835, married (1) January 1, 1856, Frances Knighten, (2 December 1, 1859, Frances Buford.   Residence, Dallas, Texas.   Their children were:

a. Lydia Catherine Borden, born April 26, 1858, died in infancy.

b. Henry Allen Borden, born October 25, 1860, married Martha Buckingham.   Their children are:

(1) Adelaide Louise Borden.
(2) Alberta Lake Borden.
(3) Henry Grady Borden.

c. Nancy Lorena Borden, born February 9, 1865, died May 5, 1865.

d. Lulu Ellen Borden, born March 19, 1866, died June 9, 1867.

e. Charles Lewis Borden, born June 21, 1868.

f. Dora Louise Borden, born January 29, 1871, married in Italy, Texas, J. M. D. Trammel.   They had Chesley Trammel.

g. Euphemia Tate Borden, born October 24, 1873.

h. John Pickins Borden, born August 30, 1876.

9. Joel E. Borden, married ——— —————, of Hope Arkansas, born August 12, 1838 died 1891.   They had Patrick Donnelly Borden.

CHAPTER EIGHT

Polly Sevier

POLLY SEVIER

POLLY SEVIER, daughter of Valentine Sevier the Emigrant and Joanna Goode Sevier, was born in Rockingham County, Virginia, in 1755. She possibly married Robert Rutherford. One of Governor Sevier's sisters married him, I believe.

In Madison, Wisconsin, are letters from George Washington Sevier, son of Governor Sevier, in which he mentions his aunts, "Polly and Catherine."

CHAPTER NINE

Bethenia Sevier

BETHENIA SEVIER

B ETHENIA SEVIER, said to be the daughter of Valentine Sevier, the Emigrant, and Joanna Goode Sevier, was born in Virginia about 17—. She is said not to be one of the three daughters who accompanied Valentine Sevier the Emigrant to "the Mountains" in 1773, but to have followed the family party "after 1773." She married James Hawkins, doubtless of the family of Sarah Hawkins, who was the first wife of Bethenia's brother, Governor John Sevier.

This information concerning Bethenia Sevier came from Mrs. Sophia Hoss French, of Morristown.

CHAPTER TEN

Elizabeth Sevier

ELIZABETH SEVIER

ELIZABETH SEVIER, daughter of Valentine Sevier the Emigrant and his first wife, Joanna Goode Sevier, was born in Rockingham County, Virginia, about 1757. She was possibly named Catherine Elizabeth, as I find both names listed as having married William Matlock. (Of course, two sisters may have married the same man as first and second wife).

In the life of Jefferson D. Goodpasture, written by his sons, mention is made of "Governor Sevier's sister, Mrs. Matlock, who was the mother of Valentine Matlock, one time sheriff of Overton County." She had evidently named her son for her father, Valentine Sevier II.

The Borden Genealogy (see Chapter Seven) states that John Borden married for his second wife in 1824, Catherine Sevier, daughter of Governor John Sevier, (this is manifestly an error, as the Governor's daughter Catherine was a generation older) and that his first wife was Catherine Matlock, daughter, of William Matlock. It is very probable that both wives were of the Sevier blood and that the first wife, Catherine Matlock, was granddaughter of Catherine or Elizabeth Sevier, sister to the Governor, who married William Matlock, and that the second wife was a granddaughter of Governor Sevier instead of a daughter, or possibly a grand-niece of the Governor.

Catherine or Elizabeth Sevier Matlock and William Matlock had, then, very probably, children as follows: Valentine, whom we know positively, and William Matlock, Jr., and possibly another, George Matlock. There was also a Charles Matlock.

1. Valentine Matlock, born about 1780.
2. William Matlock, Jr., ———————.
3. George Matlock, ———————.
4. Charles Matlock, ———————.

Valentine Matlock was born about 1780   He was Sheriff of Overton County.

William Matlock, Jr., married ——————— and probably had a daughter, Catherine Matlock, who was the first wife of John Borden, marrying him about 1818. See Borden Genealogy in Chaper Seven.

George Matlock was a deputy sheriff.

Charles Matlock was a captain in the military department of Overton County at its organization May 13, 1807.

"William Matlock" was a resident of Elizabethton in 1797. This was probably the husband of John Sevier's sister, either Catherine or Elizabeth.

It is an interesting fact that Valentine Sevier II in his will directed his two sons, Joseph and Abraham, who inherited the residue of his estate, to pay to Catherine Matlock, wife of William Matlock, one forty pounds and the other fifty pounds.

CHAPTER ELEVEN

Sophia Sevier

SOPHIA SEVIER

SOPHIA SEVIER, daughter of Valentine Sevier, the Emigrant, and Joanna Goode Sevier, was born in Rockingham County, Virginia, about 17—. She is said to have married —————— Peters.

PART FOUR
Joanna Goode Sevier
Who Married
Younger Landrum, Jr.

JOANNA GOODE SEVIER

Who Married Younger Landrum Jr.

JOANNA GOODE SEVIER was the name, according to several members of the family, of the eleventh child of Colonel Valentine Sevier III and Naomi Douglas Sevier. A descendant writes that she copied the list of children from the family Bible of Colonel Valentine Sevier III, then in possession of his granddaughter, and that Joanna Goode Sevier was the eleventh child. She gives her birth as February 14, 1784. She says, "I know nothing further concerning her." In a letter to Governor John Sevier in 1799, Colonel Valentine Sevier speaks of Joanna when he says. " The rest of my family is well, except Joanna, who is ill of a fever, but not serious."

In Greene County, Tennessee, November 8, 1800, a Joanna Goode Sevier married Younger Landrum, Jr. I have no positive information as to whether she is the Joanna who was the daughter of Colonel Valentine Sevier III. Possibly some other member of the family can give a connecting link that will establish her identity.

I will set down first all the facts relative to her birth and paternity, and then give her record from her marriage to Younger Landrum, from which point everything is clear concerning her.

Joanna is evidently a descendant of Joanna Goode, who married Valentine Sevier II, as she has that full name. Some of the Landrum descendants think that she was the daughter of Governor John Sevier, but that is not possible, as he had a daughter by that name who married Joseph Hawkins Windle and whose full history is given in Chapter Seventeen, Part Six, of this book. The other sons of Joanna, who married Valentine II, are Abraham, Joseph, Robert, Valentine III and a possible Charles. Abraham Sevier had a daughter, Joanna Goode, who married Alfred C. Robertson. Captain Robert Sevier, who was killed at King's Mountain, left two sons only. This leaves it possible that Joseph Sevier, Sr., Valentine Sevier III or Charles Sevier named a daughter Joanna Goode Sevier who grew to maturity and married Younger Landrum, Jr., in 1800. I know nothing of the children of Charles Sevier, if there were any. Of Joseph Sevier, Sr., I know of only one son, Alfred Sevier.

This leaves Colonel Valentine Sevier, who did have a daughter, according to some descendants. named Joanna, who was his eleventh child. As has also been noted, he mentions a Joanna who was a member of his household in 1799.

113

The Secretary of the Historical Society of Missouri, quoting a sketch of Judge Richard Hundley Landrum (1821-1915) by Walter B. Stevens, says that Richard Hundley Landrum's grandmother was Joanna Goode Sevier Landrum, a niece of Governor John Sevier.

However, Rebecca Sevier Rector, in her interviews with Dr. Lyman Draper, never seems to have mentioned a sister as having survived the massacre of 1794, or as living in the same county as Rebecca lived (Greene County, Tennessee), and there rearing a large family; but neither does Rebecca mention her brother John Sevier (Devil Jack), who was in East Tennessee at the time, so he can hardly be said to have literally survived it. Hugh Bell does not mention John and he does not mention Joanna.

Dr. Draper, who was evidently profoundly interested in the massacre and in securing information concerning it, makes no effort, apparently, to interview Joanna's sons and daughters who were living in Greene County when he interviewed Rebecca Sevier Rector. Hugh Bell, who gave a full account of the massacre to Dr. Draper, does not mention Joanna, but he also omits any mention of James, who is mentioned by Rebecca. Senator Ambrose Hundley Sevier, who gives the list of surviving sons when Colonel Valentine Sevier III died in 1800, does not mention either Rebecca or Joanna, although Rebecca was still living in 1848 when he wrote Dr. Draper.

Joanna, if born in 1784, would have been ten years old at the time of the massacre. If she had been merely out of the station, as James and Alexander were, it seems that fact would have been mentioned. If present and surviving that frightful calamity, it seems that she would have been mentioned by someone. Of course, there is the possibility that she was visiting some of the kinspeople, perhaps in East Tennessee, as was the eldest son, John, who is mentioned by Bell and others, though Rebecca, his own sister does not refer to him once in her interview with Dr. Draper.

Joanna's daughter, Elizabeth Landrum Scully, says her mother "died December 4th, 1841,, being in the fifty-fifth year of her age from the fourteenth of February last." This gives the same day of the month as indicated by other descendants, with a discrepancy of two years, an error which may have occurred in transcription.

She named her children some of the Valentine Sevier III family names. Of her six children, four were given names that suggest that family, for instance, "Elizabeth," "Rebecca," "Alexander Sevier" and "William Douglas." I have made an effort to locate among her descendants her family Bible which might give definite information.

Her children and grandchildren were familiar with the details of the massacre, which is an indicaton that Joanna was associated with it. Also her granddaughters, Rebecca Scully Adams and Sarah Turnbull, said their great-grandmother lived to be one hundred years of age. This seems to indicate Naomi Douglass Sevier. Also, Joanna's grandson, Charles K. Hale, said his mother said that her mother, Joanna Goode Sevier Landrum, was reared in Colonel Valentine Sevier's home.

Personally I have no doubt that she was the daughter of Colonel Valentine Sevier III and Naomi Douglass Sevier, but I have no proof to offer.

Joanna Goode Sevier was born February 14, 1784. She died at Warrensburg, Greene County, Tennessee, December 4, 1841, at the home of her daughter, Rhoda Landrum Turnbull. She is buried near by, in the Hawkins cemetery, and her daughter Rebecca Hale is buried beside her.

She married Younger Landrum, Jr., November 8, 1800. (That is the date of the marriage bond; sometimes the ceremony was delayed until later). The marriage took place at Lick Creek Church in Greene County, Tennessee. Younger Landrum, Jr., was the son of Captain Younger Landrum of the Revolution. Another son of Captain Landrum, James Landrum, served under him guarding prisoners of Burgoyne. James Landrum was afterwards a Presbyterian minister. Captain Landrum's company was in Lawson's Brigade of Colonel John Malcomb's Regiment, which assisted in the Guildford Expedition. This information is obtained from the pension declarations of Henry Caswell, Allen Blair and William Turner, who served under Captain Landrum. After the close of the Revolution Captain Landrum and his two sons moved from Amherst County, Virginia, to Greene County, Tennessee, to reside. Captain Landrum died in Greene County.

During the Revolution Younger Landrum Jr. became famous for an exploit that all his descendants know of through family legend. When his company was following the Indians in the Chickamauga Campaign and was located near where Chattanooga is now, several sentries were killed one after another, with apparently no enemy near at hand. Younger Landrum, Jr., volunteered to take the place of the next man assigned to the post. He declared before going out to his duty that he would shoot anything that moved. He kept his word and when a hog came rooting near him shot, with the result that an Indian warrior disguised in a hog's skin went to his happy hunting ground. The adventure made Younger Landrum famous, but his own death followed very soon. He left six children, the youngest being born in 1812, it is said the very year his father died.

The marriage bond of Joanna Sevier and Younger Landrum Jr., is now in the County Clerk's office in Greeneville, Tennessee, and in view of the discussion concerning her, is particularly interesting. It is dated November 8, 1800.

State of Tennessee:

Greene County

To any licensed minister of the Gospel regularly called, having care of Souls, or to any Justice of the Peace for said County, etc.

Whereas: Younger Landrum hath this day given bond and security agreeable to an act entitled "an act to establish rules to be observed in Solemnizing the Rites of Matrimony," by the same act being empowered and authorized, I do hereby License you, or any of you, to celebrate the Rites of Matrimony between the said Younger Landrum, and Joanna Sevier, of this County, according to the ceremonies of your respective Church, and agreeable to the rules prescribed in the said act.

Given under my hand at office the eighth day of November, 1800.

It is said that the marriage took place in Lick Creek Church. It is possible that records of that church, if they have been preserved, would yield further information.

The Greene County census of 1830 gives Joanna Landrum, widow of Younger Landrum, Jr., between forty and fifty years of age. This agrees with the record of her birth in 1784 or 1786.

She died December 4, 1841, and is buried a quarter of a mile from Warrensburg, Tennessee.

Joanna Goode Sevier and Younger Landrum, Jr., had six children, all of whom were born in Greene County, Tennessee. They were:

1. Elizabeth Landrum, born September. 1801.
2. Mary Landrum, called Polly, born January 22, 1803.
3. Rebecca C. Landrum, born December 9, 1805.
4. Rhoda Landrum, born September 7, 1810
5. Alexander Sevier Landrum, born October 24, 1811.
6. William Douglass Landrum, born 1812.

ELIZABETH LANDRUM

1. Elizabeth Landrum, daughter of Joanna Goode Sevier Landrum and Younger Landrum, Jr., was born in Greene County, Tennessee, September 1, 1801. She married October 21, 1824, in Greene County, William Scully. She died December 15, 1859, at Warrensburg, Tennessee. John Scully, the father of William C. Scully, moved from Virginia to Tennessee. William C. Scully died September 25, 1868, the year that his son, William A. Scully, died.

Elizabeth Landrum Scully and William C. Scully had six children, namely:

a. Rebecca Scully.
b. Naomi Scully.
c Ann Elizabeth Scully.

d. William A. Scully.

e. George Scully.

f. Robert Scully.

Of these:

a. Rebecca Scully, daughter of Elizabeth Landrum Scully and William C. Scully, was born about 18—, in Greene County, Tennessee. She married Ezekiel Adams. Their children were: Elizabeth Adams, who married William Francis Robinson and has Lula de Bush Robinson, Anna Mae Robinson, married W. D. Cobble; and Willie Emma Robinson.

b. Naomi Scully, daughter of Elizabeth Landrum Scully and William Scully, was born in Greene County, Tennessee, 18—. She married 18—, Jacob Luttrell. They had a son, William Luttrell, now living (1924) in Morristown, Tennessee.

c. Ann Elizabeth Scully daughter of Eilzabeth Landrum Scully and William C. Sculy, was born 18—.

d. William A Scully, son of Elizabeth Landrum Scully and William C. Scully, was born in Greene County, Tennessee, July 18, 1827. He died in Greene County in 1868, the same year his father died. He was a Confederate soldier. He married Donna M. Collier and they had at least one daughter. Mary (Mollie) Scully, who married ———————— Haworth.

e. George Scully, son of Elizabeth Landrum Scully and William C. Scully, was born in Greene County, Tennessee, in 18—.

f. Robert S. Scully, son of Elizabeth Landrum Scully and William C. Scully, was born in Greene County, Tennessee. 18—. He married twice, first Frances Murray and second Jane Williams.

Mary Landrum

2. Mary Landrum, daughter of Joanna Goode Sever Landrum and Younger Landrum, Jr., was called Polly. She married July 15, 1822, Nicolas Hayes Davis. (born in Jefferson County, Tennessee, 1797, died September 20, 1840) son of Nicolas Davis. Mary Landrum Davis died in Jefferson County Tennessee, April 26, 1862. Nicholas Hayes Davis was the son of Lieutenant Nicholas Davis, of Prince Edward County, Virginia, who served three and one-half years in the Revolutionary Army, enlisting twice. He was a British prisoner at Charleston for fourteen months. From Charleston he marched to old Jamestown, where an exchange of prisoners was made. He died in Tennessee in 1843. He married Mary Hayes and his son was given Hayes as a middle name in her honor. He made his pension declaration in Jefferson County in 1823. He came to Tennessee after the Revolution. His wife, Mary Hayes Davis, survived him.

The children of Nicholas Hayes Davis and Mary Landrum Davis were:

   a. Miranda Elizabeth Davis.
   b. Sarah Jane Davis.
   c. Elbert Sevier Davis
   d. Samuel Alexander Davis.
   e. Margaret Narcissa Davis.
   f. Mary A. C. Davis.
   g. Rebecca Landrum Davis.
   h. James Hayes Davis.

Of the foregoing:

   a. Miranda Elizabeth Davis, daughter of Mary Landrum Davis and Nicholas Hayes Davis, was born June 12, 1823. She married John McMillan in 1836. They had at least one son, Horace McMillan, who lives in Knoxville.

   b. Sarah Jane Davis, daughter of Mary Landrum Davis and Nicholas Hayes Davis was born November 11, 1824. She married ——————— Parker.

   c. Elbert Sevier Davis, son of Mary Landrum Davis and Nicholas Hayes Davis, was born January 23, 1827. He married——————— Campbell.

   d. Samuel Alexander Davis, son of Mary Landrum Davis and Nicholas Hayes Davis, was born June 27,1829, in Greene County, Tennessee. He married Sarah Chaney in 1854. He moved to Illinois to live in 1855 and died in Spring Garden, Illinois, January, 1902. His children were: James Davis, a Methodist minister, married Effie Hoskinson; Mary Davis, married Loyd Browning; Samuel Davis, married Ida Watson; Emma Davis, married Frank Springfield.

   e. Margaret Narcissa Davis, daughter of Mary Landrum Davis and Nicholas Hayes Davis, was born in Greene County, Tennessee, August 17, 1831. She died in Jefferson County, Tennessee, in 1918. She married Daniel Carter and had no children.

   f. Mary A. C. Davis, daughter of Mary Landrum Davis and Nicholas Hayes Davis, was born September 25, 1833. She married Martin Bennett and had two children who died in infancy.

   g. Rebecca Landrum Davis, daughter of Mary Landrum Davis and Nicholas Hayes Davis, was born March 17, 1836. She married in Jefferson County, Tennessee, in 1858, James Duncan Cox, born 1832 died 1889. She died March, 1876. They moved to Jefferson County, Illinois, to reside in 1860. They had six children, namely:

   Charles Andrew Cox.
   Mary Jane Cox.
   Sarah Lavinia Cox.
   William Martin Cox.
   Albert Franklin Cox.
   Samuel Walter Cox.

Of these: Charles Andrew Cox son of Rebecca Landrum Davis Cox and James Duncan Cox was born in Jeffe son County Tennessee, December 24, 1869. He married Alice Clinton, near Spring Garden, Illinois. Their children are Nettie Cox, who married Lycurgus Page and has Valora Page, married to William Cooper, Comaletta Page and Wastenia Page; Vivian Cox, who married Frank Fowler; Tarzel Zoe Cox, who married Asa Kelly and has one son, Stanton Kelly; Ivan Cox, who married Gertrude Wyrick, who died April, 1924, and left a daughter, Betty Jane Cox.

Mary Jane Cox, daughter of Rebecca Landrum Davis Cox and James Duncan Cox, was born February 5, 1861, near Spring Garden, Illinois. In this township she married Thomas Averett Turner, February 8, 1877. He was born in Henry County, Virginia, October 18, 1856. His father, Monroe L. Turner, was a Confederate soldier and died in the Confederate hospital at Richmond, December 24, 1863, at the age of 33. His widow, Martha Leah Turner, came to Belle-rive, Illinois, to her father, Archibald Grant, in 1865, with her family of five children.

The children of Mary Jane Cox (called Janey) and Thomas A. Turner are:

Alva Nola Turner, born February 1, 1878.

Lena Turner, died in infancy.

Rosa Lee Turner, born September 30, 1880, died at the age of twenty-two years.

Charles Andrew Turner, born October 22, 1883, in California.

Sadie Myrtle Turner, born December 1, 1886, in Illinois.

Theodore Turner, born August 11, 1889.

Eva May Turner died at the age of six years.

Evie Forest Turner, born April 3, 1894.

Vara Fay Turner, born August 10, 1896.

Duward Bellmont Turner, died in infancy.

Alva Nola Turner, son of Janey Cox Turner and Thomas A. Turner, was born February 1, 1878. He married Amy E. Neal, Frisco, Illinois, March 14, 1906, divorced November, 1919. Their children are: Mary Lee Turner, born Waco, Texas, May 5, 1907; Frank Theodore, born Spring Garden, Illinois, May 6, 1909.

Charles A. Turner, son of Janey and Thomas Turner, married Lois Hall at Effingham, Illinois, October 22, 1913. They have a daughter, Dorothy Jane Turner.

Sadie Myrtle Turner, daughter of Janey and Thomas Turner, married Fred Campbell, of Ewing, Illinois. They have one son, Clyde Campbell.

Sargeant Theodore Turner, son of Janey and Thomas Turner, married Ethel (Peggy) Daugherty. He served overseas in the World War.

Evie Forest Turner, daughter of Janey and Thomas Turner, married Dail Johnson.

Sarah Lavinia Cox, daughter of Rebecca Landrum Davis Cox and James Duncan Cox, was born 1867, near Spring Garden, Illinois. She married John Judson Monroe, of Mount Vernon, Illinois. Their children were: James Oliver Monroe, who married Fredda Kosch, and has children: John Judson Monroe, Oliver Monroe, Jr., and Thomas Warren Monroe; Blanche Monroe, who married Cleve Hester; Shelton Monroe, who died young; Raymond Monroe, who married Lucia Fisher; Floy Monroe, Ruth Monroe and Olive Monroe.

William Martin Cox, son of Rebecca Landrum Davis Cox and James Duncan Cox, was born 18—. He married Zettie Hammond. Their children are: Leo Cox, who married Ruth Dial; Otto Cox, who married Lura Lawson; Aline Cox, twin to Irene, married Joseph Kelly; Irene Cox, twin to Aline, married Dr. Harvey Wade; Aud Cox and Claude Cox.

Albert Franklin Cox, son of Rebecca Landrum Davis Cox and James Duncan Cox, was born —————. He married first Marie Hubbard and married second ————— Howard. He has two sons, Howard Cox and ————— Cox.

Samuel Walter Cox, son of Rebecca Landrum Davis Cox and James Duncan Cox, is in the regular army.

h. James Hayes Davis, son of Mary Landrum Davis and Nicholas Davis, was born February 23, 1839. He died in Jefferson City, Tennessee, in 1917. He married Belle Rannin. Among their children were: John Davis, Dr. Elbert Davis, Fanny Davis, Bert Davis and Christopher Davis.

REBECCA C. LANDRUM

3. Rebecca C. Landrum, daughter of Younger Landrum, Jr., and Joanna Goode Sevier Landrum, was born December 9, 1807, in Warrensburg, Greene County, Tennessee. She married Captain Joseph Hale, (born 1796,) of the War of 1812, as his second wife. They both died in the year 1873. Their children were:

a. James Hale.
b. George Sevier Hale.
c. Charles Keith Hale.
d. Younger Hale.
e. John Hale.

Of these:

George Sevier Hale who was a Confederate soldier, son of Rebecca Landrum Hale and Captain Joseph Hale, married first, Nancy Jones, and second, Catherine Smith. He has a son, Joseph Hale.

Charles Keith Hale, son of Rebecca Landrum Hale and Captain

Joseph Hale, married Margaret Evens. They had at least two children, Dr. Walter Keith Hale and Dr. Emma Hale. Charles Keith Hale died in Spartanburg, South Carolina, July 3, 1923.

Younger Hale, son of Rebecca Hale and Captain Joseph Hale, married Jennie Scruggs.

RHODA LANDRUM

4. Rhoda Landrum, daughter of Joanna Goode Sevier Landrum and Younger Landrum, Jr., was born in Greene County, Tennessee, September 7, 1810. She died May 7, 1889. She married Jam s Turnbull, called Turnbill by some of his descendants. They had five children:

a. John Turnbull.

b. Joseph Turnbull.

c. James Turnbull.

d. Rebecca Turnbull.

e. Sadie Turnbull.

ALEXANDER SEVIER LANDRUM

5. Alexander Sevier Landrum, son of Joanna Goode Sevier Landrum and Younger Landrum, Jr., was born 1811, in Greene County, Tennessee.

Alexander Sevier Landrum died in Tennessee in Jefferson County August 19, 1848, being only 37 years old. His wedding suit was made by Andrew Johnson, then a tailor of Greeneville, afterwards President of the United States.

Alexander Sevier Landrum married Anna Reams. Their children were:

a. William Bartl . Landrum, born 1832.

b. Richard Hundley Landrum, born 1834.

c. James Landrum, died young.

d. Durthulia Landrum, born 1842.

e. David Landrum, born 1844.

f. Rebecca Landrum, born 1847.

Of these: William Bartlett Landrum, son of Alexander Sevier Landrum and Anna Reams Landrum was born 1832, died 1903. He married twice, first ——————— and second Louisa Matilda Ryan. Their daughter, Olive Elizabeth Landrum, married Norman B. Pearman, who was a Major in the Army overseas, during the World War.

Richard Hundley Landrum, son of Alexander Sevier and Anna Reams Landrum, was born 1834. He died in Missouri, where he was very prominent, a Judge and for many years in the legislature.

WILLIAM DOUGLAS LANDRUM

6. William Douglass Landrum, son of Joanna Goode Sevier Landrum and Younger Landrum, Jr., was born in Greene County, Tennessee, March 1812. His name indicates descent from Naomi Douglass Sevier, and recalls also one of her twin sons, Robert and William, who were killed by Indians. William Douglass Landrum was only three months old when his father volunteered for the War of 1812. William Douglas Landrum married Martha Ann Owens. Both died and are buried in Nashville, Tennessee. Martha Ann Owens Landrum, died in 1866. Their children were:

a. Richard Alexander Landrum.
b. William Nicholas Landrum.
c. Thomas Irwin Landrum.
d. James Younger Landrum.
e. Cornelius Valentine Landrum.
f. George Henry Landrum.
g. Robert Houston Landrum.
h. Mary Catherine Landrum.

Of these: Richard Alexander Landrum, son of William Douglass Landrum and Martha Ann Owens Landrum, married —————— Rowe, in Talledega, Alabama. They had a large family.

Willam Nicholas Landrum, son of William Douglass Landrum and Martha Owens Landrum, married —————— Seahorn. His children live near Morristown, Tennessee.

Thomas Irwin Landrum, son of William Douglass Landrum and Martha Owens Landrum, served in the Confederate Army. He married —————— Morgan. After her early death he married Elizabeth Broadus, of Louisville, Kentuckey. They both died there in 1921. They had seven children:

(1) Henry Landrum, deceased; (2) Mattie Landrum, who married Reverend A. V. Sizemore; (3) John Thomas Landrum, who married Jennie Elizabeth Nenenirk and has one daughter Dorothy Landrum; (4) Robert Owen Landrum, who married first—————— Blankenbaker and had one son, Robert Owen Landrum, Jr., and married second —————— and has no children; (5) William Clarence Landrum, who married ———— Tigh, and has several children; (6) Oscar Broadus Landrum; (7) ———— Landrum, who married Robert S. Weaver in Sterling, California and has one child.

James Younger Landrum, son of William Douglass Landrum and Martha Ann Owens Landrum, never married.

Cornelius Valentine Landrum, son of William Douglass Landrum and Martha Owens Landrum, was born in 1844. He is the only living (1924) grandchild of Joanna Goode Sevier Landrum and Younger

Landrum, Jr. He married twice, first Annie E. Netherland, who lived three years only, leaving a son, Rufus E. Landrum, who lives in Nashville. Cornelius Valentine Landrum married for his sec nd wife Lovinia Parker, who lived less than five years. Her children were Mabel Landrum, married ————————————— and died at twenty-four, and George H. Landrum.

George Henry Landrum, son of William Douglass Landrum and Martha Ann Owens Landrum, married ———————————.

Robert Houston Landrum, son of William Douglass Landrum and Martha Ann Owens Landrum, married ———— Stone. They had two children, a son and a daughter. The son married and died. His widow and a daughter live in Missouri.

Mary Catherine Landrum, daughter of William Douglass Landrum and Martha Ann Owens Landrum, married ————————— Talbot and had two children.

PART FIVE

Governor John Sevier

His First Wife
Sarah Hawkins Sevier

and

His Second Wife
Catherine Sherrill Sevier

GOVERNOR JOHN SEVIER

P IONEER, soldier, statesman, and one of the founders of the Republic; Governor of the State of Franklin; six times Governor of Tennessee; four times elected to Congress; the typical pioneer who conquered the wilderness and fashioned the State; a projector and a hero of King's Mountain; thirty-five battles, thirty-five victories."

John Sevier, first child of Valentine Sevier I and Joanna Goade Sevier, was born September 23, 1745, in what was then known as Augusta County, Virginia, and is now Rockingham County, about six miles west of New Market on the old stage road between Staunton and Lexington, Va. He was sent to Staunton to school and there he acquired a fair education, and he learned also in his youth the outdoor sports and skill that stood him in good stead in after years. While he was still a youth at school in Staunton, he began the romantic career which he followed during all his years, for he fell into a mill race and was rescued by a young lady, Miss Anne Paul, who afterwards became the second wife of Governor George Matthews, of Georgia.

When he was sixteen, he left school, married and set up for himself. His wife was a school mate, Sarah Hawkins, and only fifteen years of age. They went immediately to housekeeping and very soon after their marriage John Sevier purchased land and laid out a village which he called New Market. He resided there for a period of ten years. At the close of the French and Indian War he saw military service and was given a Captain's commission in 1772, by Lord Dunmore, the last royal Governor of Virginia. He is said to have survived, with his usual romantic good fortune, death in an ambuscade at this time.

With a gift for success in any line, John Sevier prospered as a merchant in the town which he had built, and had accumulated a comfortable fortune when he felt the lure of the "Mountains" and, after two trips to the country we now know as Tennessee he decided to move his family to the new land. He made his first trip in 1770. In 1772, he attended a horse race at Wautauga Old Fields. His brother, Valentine Sevier III, was already settled in the "Mountains" and enthusiastic about the country. After the trip of 1772, John

Sevier decided to settle in the new country and he persuaded his father's family to journey with him. I imagine that Joanna Goode Sevier had passed away before this time, as no mention is made of her in the wholesale removal of the two families. She was alive in August 1773, however, as she is mentioned as a witness in the Augusta County, Va., Abstracts.

The group included John Sevier, his wife and several children, Valentine Sevier II and four other sons, Abraham, Joseph, Robert and Charles (?) and four daughters whose names are not recorded. The statement is made that one of Valentine's daughters remained in Virginia. One son, Valentine III, was already in the "Mountains."

The caravan arrived in Keewood settlement in the "mountains" on Christmas day, December 25, 1773, after a tiresome wagon trip of three hundred miles. Keewood is variously spelled, Keewood, Keywood, Cawood, and Caywood. Francis Turner's Life of John Sevier says that upon arrival each family went to its own cabin. The settlement was six miles from Shelby's. Later the Seviers abandoned the Keewood Settlement and moved to Washington County.

Sarah Hawkins Sevier lived just a few weeks more than seven years in the new country. She died in January or February 1780. Several historians, including Wheeler of North Carolina, give 1779 as the date of her death, but I believe 1780 is right. George Washington Sevier, the first son by John Sevier's second marriage, says that she died in "Washington County, (East Tennessee) 1780."

In 1776 John Sevier moved his family to the north bank of the Watauga, three miles above Elizabethton, and in 1778 to the south bank of the Nolichucky, about ten or twelve miles from Jonesboro.

John Sevier was at the time of his removal to Tennessee, comparatively a rich man for the period and place. He might have continued his successful business career. Instead he gave himself almost wholly from that time to public service, and though he died a poor man, he died a great man, and he gave to us, who follow after, a great state, and to his country a great territory, for all historians unite in yielding him great credit for the Winning of the West.

Even before his permanent settlement in the new country he had been chosen as one of the leaders, for in 1772 he was elected one of the thirteen commissioners of the Watauga Aassociation and one of the five judges. This was the first free organized government in the world.

In the first military movements in which Tennesseans took part, the expedition to Point Pleasant, 1774, John Sevier was not present. His brother, Valentine Sevier III, was conspicuous, and his brother Robert Sevier was also a participant.

The first general outbreak of the Cherokees occurred in midsummer, 1776. The Battle of Long Island Flats, near Kingsport, Tennessee, took place July 20, 1776, and Fort Lee was assaulted July 21, 1776. Fort Lee is near Elizabethton. It was at Fort Lee and on this date that the famous incident of Catherine Sherrill having a hairbreadth escape from the Indians took place, when she leapt the stockade and was caught in the arms of John Sevier.

In 1776, the inhabitants of the Watauga District, after repelling the Indians, but having suffered severe losses, prayed the Government of North Carolina to annex the district. The petition was received at Raleigh, August 22, 1776. John Sevier prepared the paper according to Dr. Ramsey, who found the document in the North Carolina archives. He says: "It appears to be in the handwriting of one of the signers, John Sevier, and is probably his own production."

November 12, 1776 the Provincial Congress of North Carolina met at Halifax and among other delegates were John Carter, John Haile and John Sevier as elected delegates from the "across the Mountain" territory, already called Washington district, though it received later the formal title of the County of Washington. A year and a half later the first session of the Court of Washington County was held, February 23, 1778, with twenty-three justices present. Colonel John Carter was elected chairman. Valentine Sevier III (he is called Jr. in the record, but in this history, owing to there being many Valentines he is distinguished as Valentine III) was elected Sheriff and John Sevier clerk. John Sevier retained the clerkship of Washington County until he was elected Governor of Franklin, when his second son, James Sevier, became the Clerk of Washington County and retained that office for the extraordinary term of fifty-seven years. Some records say that he was clerk for forty-seven consecutive years but either number establishes a record.

John Sevier was the first citizen in the community. He was the leader in all enterprises and his Indian warfare was making him famous. In the summer of 1780, a part of his regiment, under the command of Major Charles Robertson, Captain Valentine Sevier III, and Captain Robert Sevier, accompanied Colonel Isaac Shelby to the aid of the patriots in South Carolina. This regiment served in the Battles of Thicketty Fort and Musgrove's Mills. Major Patrick Ferguson of the British Army was incensed by this action on the part of the Mountaineers and he sent word to them that if they did not immediately lay down their arms he would burn the country clean and hang the leaders!

The message served but to inflame them against the British commander instead of intimidating them as he had intended. The word was carried by Samuel Phillips, a paroled prisoner, to Shelby, who was living in Sullivan County. Shelby rode at once forty or fifty miles to John Sevier's residence to consult with him, and the result of that conference was the assembling of the Mountain men at Sycamore Shoals and the march to King's Mountain.

The credit of the first plan for the campaign of King's Mountain is due to Shelby and Sevier. All historians unite on this point.

The story of King's Mountain fills us with unspeakable admiration. Every man in the mountains responded to the call of Shelby and Sevier and the first draft in American history had to be resorted to, not to determine which men should go to battle, but to decide which men should stay at home as the women and children could not be left unprotected.

Of the battle itself we have not space here to tell the story in full. Campbell, Shelby and Cleveland made an official report of it a few days later, Sevier leaving immediately after the battle for a raid against the Indians who took that opportunity of course to threaten the settlement. The report says that the right wing of the American forces commanded by Col. Sevier was first to reach the summit of the Mountain and "obliged the enemy to retreat along the top of the mountain to where Col. Cleveland commanded."

Whole families participated in the King's Mountain Battle. It is not surprising that there were seven Seviers in it when one thinks of the military spirit of their blood and the history of their participation in war and military operations for centuries. John Sevier was a Colonel; Robert Sevier was a Captain and was mortally wounded; Valentine Sevier III was a Captain. Abraham Sevier was a private and Joseph Sevier Sr., brother of Governor Sevier, was a private. John Sevier's two eldest sons, Joseph Sevier, Jr., and James Sevier were privates. In addition John Sevier's brothers-in-law were present and several of the young men who were either then or later married to his daughters, were present. So King's Mountain for the Seviers was quite a family party!

After the successful close of that engagement John Sevier went out immediately on an Indian campaign. Upon arriving at his home from King's Mountain, he had only one hour's rest out of the saddle! His sons and many of the men of the regiment followed him in this campaign, also.

In August, 1781, Sevier and Shelby and their men crossed the Mountains again, at the insistence of General Nathaniel Greene, who sent a request for help. They joined Francis Marion and participated in the military operations in South Carolina for several months. Ramsey's Annals says:

"A large number of negroes and a vast amount of other property were taken from Georgia and South Carolina and carried away. But to the honor of the troops under Sevier and Shelby no such captives or property came with them into the country of their residence; their integrity was as little impeached as their valor. They came home enriched by no spoils, stained with no dishonor, enriched only by an imperishable fame, an undying renown and an unquestionable claim to the admiration and gratitude of their countrymen and posterity. This has been accorded to them by a consent almost unanimous. The authorities of the states in whose service they were employed conceded it to them. The officers who commanded them asserted it for them."

John Sevier's Indian Campaigns are a part of Tennessee history; their full story would require a volume, and it required for him almost his whole time for twenty years. This includes the time of his arrival in "the Mountains." to permanently reside at the close of the year 1773, to the Etowah Campaign, in 1793. He was always victorious. There is no other commander in any war who was always victor. He served in so many campaigns that it would be impossible to really name or number them and he actually fought thirty-five battles with the Indians and never lost a battle. His plan was to be always aggressive, to strike quick and hard. Roosevelt says of him:

"For many years he was the best Indian fighter on the border. He was far more successful than Clarke, for instance, inflicting greater loss on his foes and suffering much less himself, though he never had anything like Clarke's number of soldiers. His mere name was a word of dread to the Cherokees, the Chickamaugas and the upper Creeks. He combined a cool head with a dauntless heart; he loved a battle for its own sake, and was never so much at ease as when under fire; he was a first class marksman and as good a horseman as was found upon the border. He was almost the only commander upon the frontier who ever brought an Indian War of whatever length to an end, doing a good deal of damage to his foes and suffering very little himself."

Tradition is authority for the belief that John Sevier was the handsomest man on the frontier. His son, George W. Sevier, describes him to Dr. Draper: "He was five feet, nine inches high, well proportioned and straight. He weighed one hundred and ninety pounds. He had a long face, and a broad, high forehead. He had deep blue eyes, an aquiline nose and a fair complexion.

He had the extraordinary power of winning the multitude and was simply adored in the Mountain country. He made few enemies; those few, however, were powerful and mighty: Andrew Jackson, Archibald Roane, John Tipton. Someone writing of him says: "He knew how to be gracious and condescending, but he possessed at the same time a reserve of personal dignity upon which no one ventured to tresspass. His courage was indisputable; he fought every fight to a finish. But for all that he was essentially a man of peace, hating strife and loving quietness and ease. From his youth up, in spite of all statements to the contrary, he was strictly temperate in his habits, never touching tobacco in any form and rarely making use of any liquor."

The historian Phelan has thus summed up Sevier's attainments: "John Sevier is the most prominent name in Tennessee history. And within these limits and upon this field he is the most brilliant military and civil figure the state has ever produced. Jackson attained a larger fame in a broader field of action, and perhaps his mental scope may appear to a wider horizon to those who think his statesmanship equal to his generalship. But the results he accomplished affected the history of Tennessee only in so far as it formed a part of the United States. Sevier, however, was purely a Tennessean. He fought for Tennessee, he defended its boundaries, he watched over and guarded it in its beginning, he helped form it and he exercised a decisive influence on its development. The basis of Sevier's character was laid in sincerity, in truth, and in honor. He was loved because he had a loving heart. The gentle word, the quick sympathy, the open hand, the high purpose, the dauntless courage, the impetuosity, the winning suavity, were the wings and the turrets and the battlements of a magnificent and harmonious structure. Energy, ability, and determination can accomplish many feats, and cunning can simulate many effects. But the tender and the true and the loyal heart is beyond their power. This may not be counterfeited, and its deficiency cannot be supplied. The most beautiful trait of Sevier's character was the exquisite sweetness of his disposition."

Roosevelt, who is not too enthusiastic about Sevier, nevertheless pays him a remarkable tribute which deserves to be quoted in full. He says:

"Sevier, who came to the Watauga early in 1772, nearly a year after Robertson and his little colony had arrived, differed widely from his friend in almost every respect save high-mindedness and dauntless, invincible courage. He was a gentleman by birth and breeding, the son of a Huguenot who had settled in Shenandoah valley. He had received a fair education, and though never fond of books, he was, to the end of his days, an intelligent observer of men and things, both in America and in Europe. He corresponded on intimate terms and equal terms with Madison, Franklin, and others of our most polished statesmen; while Robertson's letters, when he had finally learned to write them himself, were almost as remarkable for their phenomenally bad spelling as for their shrewd common sense and straight forward honesty. Sevier was a very handsome man; during his lifetime he was reputed to be the handsomest man in Tennessee. He was tall, fair-skinned, blue-eyed, brown haired, of slender build, with erect military carriage and commanding bearing; his lithe, finely proportioned figure being well set off by the hunting shirt which he almost invariably wore. From his French forefathers he had inherited a gay, pleasure-loving temperament that made him the most charming of companions. His manners were polished and easy, and he had great natural dignity. Over the backwoodsmen he exercised an almost unbounded influence, due as much to his ready tact, invariable courtesy, and lavish, generous hospitality as to the skill and dashing prowess which made him the most renowned Indian fighter of the South West. He had an eager, impetuous nature, and was very ambitious, being almost as fond of popularity as he was of Indian fighting. He was already married and the father of two children when he came to Watauga, and, like Robertson, was seeking a new and better home for his family in the West. So far his life had been as uneventful as that of any other spirited young borderer; he had taken part in one or two unimportant Indian skirmishes. Later he was commissioned by Lord Dunmore as Captain in the Virginia Line."*

To detail the history of John Sevier would require volumes and involve the whole history of Tennessee, and indeed all of that history so aptly called by Roosevelt "The Winning of the West." Only a few opinions of the Great Tennessean and a few salient facts in his life can be recorded here. A leader, the foremost citizen in the community, he was elected Governor of the State of Franklin at its inception and remained its guiding influence throughout its life. As its term of existence shortened and a lesser domain was included in its boundaries he became Captain General of Franklin. When Franklin no longer existed and he was an outlaw and debarred by the great State of North Carolina from holding office, the people elected him to the North Carolina Legislature, a piece of bravado which must have shocked the North Carolinians, though it was justified when the Legislature repealed its former act and permitted the late Captain General and Governor of the Lost State of Franklin to take his seat.

He was elected to Congress and served two terms.

When Tennessee became a state in 1796, John Sevier was looked upon by the whole populace as the coming Governor. He was elected and was twice re-elected, serving three terms of two years each. Being then ineligible by the constitution to another term he retired to private life. Archibald Roane served a term of two years as Governor. At the close of Governor Roane's administration,

---

*Roosevelt is in error regarding the number of children, for John Sevier and Sarah Hawkins Sevier had five or six children at this time. The date of Lord Dunmore's commission to John Sevier, was given in 1772, before he removed to "The Mountains," not afterwards.

John Sevier, having become eligible again, was re-elected to the office and once again served three terms—six years, making twelve years in the chair as Governor of Tennessee, with a previous administration of the Governorship of Franklin for a period of four years. Few men have received such an extraordinary mark of the appreciation and confidence of a people.

He was re-elected to Congress in 1811 and served four years. In 1815 he was re-elected to his seat in Congress without his knowledge, being then in Alabama as a Commissioner to establish the Creek Boundary Line.

President Madison had appointed him one of the Commissioners for the Creek Boundary Line in 1815 and on that service he died. He was buried where he died on the east bank of the Talapoosa River near Fort Decatur, with honors of war, by Captain William Walker.

John Sevier was never wounded in all his remarkable career, but at Boyd's Creek he had what might be called a close shave, for a lock of his hair was cut off by a rifle ball, at the Battle of Boyd's Creek.

John Sevier is identified with the religious and educational life of the South as well as with its military history and civil government, for he contributed to Church and School in a large way. He gave three acres for the site for a Baptist Church in the new town of New Market, which he established, and built the Church. He was then scarcely more than a boy in years, for he established the town of New Market shortly after he was sixteen years old. In Tennessee he built a Presbyterian Church near the site of his home.

He was one of the incorporators of Blount College, now the University of Tennessee, and introduced the bill for its establishment. He was a trustee of Washington College. These two institutions were the first institutions of learning west of the Allegheney Mountains.

He died in 1815, September 24, in Fort Decatur, Ala., being one day past his seventieth year. He was buried there but later his body was removed to the Court House Square in Knoxville, where a tall shaft stands to mark the spot for all time.

CHRONOLOGY
LIFE OF
John Sevier

1745 September 23, born in Virginia.

1761 Married Sarah Hawkins.

1761 Established town of New Market, Virginia.

1772 Lord Dunmore gave him a Captain's Commission.

1772 Elected one of thirteen Commissioners and one of five judges of Watauga Association, though not then a resident of Watauga.

1773 Christmas Day. Arrived in Watauga to make his home in what we now know as Tennessee.

1776 July 21. Fort Lee was assaulted. He saved Catherine Sherrill. The famous incident resulted in her nick-name, Bonny Kate.

1776 August. Watauga Association prayed North Carolina to annex the territory. John Sevier prepared the paper.

1777 Represented Watauga in North Carolina Territory.

1779 Aggressive Indian Campaigns.

1780 January (or February) Sarah Hawkins Sevier died.

1780 August 14, Married Catherine Sherrill.

1780 October 7. Battle of King's Mountain.

1780 Important Indian Campaigns, Chickamauga, Lookout Mountain.

1784 August 23. Presided at Jonesboro Convention.

1784 November. Appointed Brigadier General of Militia for Washington District.

1784 State of Franklin organized.

1784 Elected Governor of Franklin.

1785 March 1. Took Oath as Governor of Franklin.

1785 Fall of year. Concluded Indian Treaty

1786 September. United with Georgia against Creeks.

1787 Made member of Society of Concinnati.

1787 June 24. Asks mediation of Georgia between North Carolina and Franklin.

1788 Warrant issued by North Carolina for High Treason. Arrested at Jonesboro. On trial at Morgantown, North Carolina. Dramatic rescue at Morgantown. Returned with his rescuers to Tennessee.

1788 November 21. Debarred from Office by the North Carolina Assembly.

1788 Captain-General of State of Franklin.

1788 Fall of the State of Franklin.

1789 Elected to Assembly of North Carolina.

1789 November. North Carolina repealed act of November 1788 and Sevier took his seat in Assembly and was reinstated Brigadier General.

1790 March. Elected to Congress from Washington District, embracing all present State of Tennessee.

1790 April 2. United States having accepted deed from North Carolina, what is now Tennessee ceased to be a part of North Carolina.

1790 June 17. John Sevier took his seat in Congress.

1790 William Blount having been appointed Governor of the United States Territory South of the Ohio, recommended Sevier as Brigadier General of Washington District and President George Washington made the appointment.

1796 May 6. He was admitted to the Bar by Gov. William Blount.

1796 Tennessee becomes a State.

1796 Sevier having been elected Governor of Tennessee takes Oath March 30. Serves three terms, (six years) all that is allowed by Constitution.

1803 Re-elected Governor of Tennessee; again serves six years, limit of Constitutional eligibility.

1811 Elected to Congress. Serves four years.

1815 Re-elected to Congress without his knowledge.

1815 Appointed by President Madison one of the Commissioners to establish the Creek Boundary line.

1815 September 24, died at Fort Decatur, Ala.

CHAPTER TWO

Sarah Hawkins

SARAH HAWKINS

Sarah Hawkins, who was the first wife of John Sevier, was born about 1746 in Virginia. She was the daughter of Joseph Hawkins and his wife, Anneke Jane Edwards Hawkins.

She married John Sevier in 1761 when she was only fifteen years of age. They went immediately to housekeeping and John Seiver soon established a township called New Market. Their first child, Joseph Sevier, was born in 1762. He was named for Sarah Hawkins' father. John Sevier's brother, Joseph Sevier, was only ten or eleven years older. Much confusion has resulted because of the similar names of these two young Seviers.

After they had lived in the village of New Market for about ten years, John Sevier became interested in the new country to which his brother, Valentine Sevier I.I, had removed and he made two trips to visit this brother and inspect the country. In 1772 on the second of these trips he had evidently decided to make his home there for he was elected a Commissioner of the Watauga Association in that year. In 1773 he removed his family and they arrived in the new settlement, Christmas Day, 1773. Roosevelt says they removed with two children, but there were then more than two children, perhaps five or six.

Sarah Hawkins lived a short seven years in the new country, dying in January or February, 1780, in Washington County. Several historians give her death in 1779, and some historians say she never moved to Tennessee from Virginia, but George Washington Sevier, her stepson, said she died in January or February 1780, in Washington County, in what is now East Tennessee. I imagine that she is buried in one of the old graveyards near Jonesboro, though it would be impossible at this time to identify the grave.

When the dust of Bonny Kate was removed from Alabama where she had lain for nearly ninety years, to lie beside her husband in the Knox County Court House grounds, where were many who thought that Sarah Hawkins should also be moved and the same honor paid to her. The circumstances, however, were very different, for Bonny Kate's grave had been marked at her death and her grave place was well known. Sarah Hawkins died more than fifty years earlier than Bonny Kate, and the grave was not known. Removal under the circumstances would have been literally impossible.

The following interesting data concerning the early history of the Hawkins family has been compiled by Mrs. Sessler Hoss (Irene Ewing Morrow) of Muskogee, Okla. Mrs. Hoss found this valuable information in the course of her research work. She calls attention to the fact that the record as here printed gives Joseph Hawkins' daughter who married John Sevier as "Susan" Hawkins, whereas, all Sevier records mention her as Sarah. In this record Sarah is mentioned as having married Mr. Graham, of Winchester, Virginia. This is quite probably an accidental transposition made by the early chroniclers. It is somewhat curious that Mr. A. W. Putnam, the eminent historian, who was a grandson-in-law of Governor John Sevier, (having married the daughter of George W. Sevier,) gives the name of Governor Sevier's first wife as Susan Hawkins. Otherwise all historians agree upon her as Sarah Hawkins. He may have had a copy of this Hawkins genealogy and have been misled by it.

The marriage of Jane Hawkins to Col. Richard Campbell is interesting as it gives the parentage of Richard Campbell, who married Catherine Sevier, daughter of Governor John Sevier by his second wife, Bonny Kate Sherrill. Richard Campbell Jr., was thus first cousin to Catherine's half brothers and sisters, and they were first cousins also to Tennessee's famous hero, who gave his life in the Alamo, Davy Crockett.

The record supplied by Mrs. Hoss is as follows:

Three brothers, Joseph, Benjamin, and Samuel Hawkins came to America from England in 1658, settling in Gloucester and Matthew Counties, Va., which were then a part of Maryland. Another brother, John, followed in 1691 and settled in Massachusetts. The fifth came the same year but died shortly afterwards.

Samuel Hawkins had three sons:

Joseph
Benjamin
Samuel

Joseph (son of Samuel, the emigrant) was born in 1712 and married the Quakeress, Anneke Jane Edwards, in 1739. All four of their sons served in the Revolution.

Their children were:
Benjamin
Joseph
Richard
Samuel
Jane, married Col. Richard Campbell.
Susanna, married John Sevier, first Governor of Tennessee.
Rebecca, married John Crockett. "Davy" was their son.
Sarah, married Mr. Graham, of Winchester, Va.
Mary, married John Byrd, of Virginia.
Caroline, married Mr. Wyndall, of Virginia.

Samuel, son of Joseph and Anneke J. Edwards Hawkins, married Christian Worthington and had nine children, all five of the sons serving in the War of 1812.

Joseph
Benjamin
Samuel
Byrd
John J.
Lydia
Sara
Rebecca
Eleanor

John J. Hawkins, son of Samuel and Christian W. Hawkins, had six children:

Samuel, born 1811
Benjamin, W., born 1816
Christiana, born 1816
Joseph C., born 1818.
Nathan B., born 1812.
Elizabeth Caroline, born 1819

Philemon Hawkins was born in England in 1690. Came to Virginia and settled at Todd's Bridge, about 1815. Married 1815, Ann Eleanor Howard, daughter of Col. Howard, of Plymouth, England. Children:

Philemon, II.
John, moved to North Carolina, and then back to Virginia.
Ann, died unmarried.

Philemon II married Delia Martin in 1743 and had the following children:

John
Philemon III
Benjamin
Joseph
Ann
Delia

Philemon Hawkins III married Lucy Davis in 1775 and had the following children:

Eleanor, married Sherwood Haywood.
William, married Ann Boyd.
John D. married Jane Boyd.
Delia, married Stephen Haywood.
Sarah, married Col. William Polk.
Joseph, married Mary Boyd.
Benjamin, married Sally Pearson.
Lucinda, married Louis B. Henry.

Another correspondent says that Sarah Hawkins, daughter of Joseph Hawkins, was a descendant of Sir John Hawkins and his wife, Katherine Conson. Sir John Hawkins was Admiral of the Port during the fight with the Spanish Armada.

A very interesting account of the Hawkins family appears in Wheeler's Reminiscences. This is too long to quote here. Hawkins County, in Tennessee is not named for Sarah Hawkins, first wife of Governor Sevier, as many have supposed, but for Benjamin Hawkins, who appears in the foregoing table as the son of Philemon Hawkins. So far as I know, Governor William Blount's wife, Mary Grainger Blount, is the only one of our early Tennessee women pioneers for whom a county is named. Grainger County bears her family name, and she has the additional honor of having Maryville named for her.

Sarah Hawkins Sevier had ten children, all of whom lived to maturity. One, Richard Sevier, died a young man, however, and he was then unmarried. Each of her other nine children was married and left children, and the descendants of these are literally thousands of well known people, residing now in all parts of America.

George Washington Sevier, the first son of Governor John Sevier by the second wife, Bonny Kate Sherrill Sevier, gave the full list of Governor Sevier's children to Dr. Lyman C. Draper, in a letter which is now on file in the Draper Collection in Madison, Wisconsin. Other authorities agree on the list, although we have no knowledge of the exact order in which these children were born. In the chapter concerning each of these children I will give the date of birth where it is known, and I have arranged the names in the order that seems probable from the information at hand. George Washington Sevier, in his letter, groups them, giving first the five sons and then the names of the five daughters of the first marriage.

James Sevier also mentions his brothers and sisters in his letters and they are mentioned in Governor Sevier's Journal. Though no list is given in the Journal, he refers many times to his children, even mentioning Richard, the young boy who died, giving in full the dream of seeing in Heaven "my son Dickey."

This statement is made because several early historians say that John Sevier had only six children by his first wife. Roosevelt follows these historians and says particularly that in 1793, at the close of the year, they moved to the new country, "then having two children." As a matter of fact they then had several children (the dates of birth of the three sons, Joseph, James and John, are a matter of record), probably three sons and two daughters. The rest of ten children were born between Christmas Day, 1773, and January or February, 1780, when Sarah Hawkins Sevier died.

It is a remarkable fact, showing a patriotic spirit that probably has not an equal, that all of her five sons, all under age, served in the Revolution and the campaigns that immediately followed.

Joseph and James Sevier at eighteen and sixteen were in the Battle of King's Mountain and the Indian Campaigns. James says that he was in "all of his father's campaigns except one." John Sevier, Jr., is said, upon good authority, to have served in the Revolution, although he was too young (fourteen) to go to King's Mountain. He joined his father later, before the Revolution was over. Valentine Sevier, at fifteen, in 1788, was serving in the Indian campaigns. He was, of course, entirely too young for Revolutionary service. Richard Sevier, her fifth son, is also said to have seen military service with his father, although very young.

THE CHILDREN OF SARAH HAWKINS SEVIER

Joseph Sevier

James Sevier

John Sevier

Elizabeth Sevier

Sarah Hawkins Sevier

Mary Ann Sevier

Valentine Sevier

Richard Sevier

Rebecca Sevier

Nancy Sevier

Catherine Sherrill
"Bonny Kate"

CATHERINE SHERRILL

Catherine Sherrill was born in 1754, in North Carolina. Her family resided on the Yadkin and with other pioneers moved to the Mountains we now know as East Tennessee. Her father was Samuel Sherrill and the family consisted of several sons and two daughters. One of the daughters, Susan Sherrill, married Col. Taylor, "a gentleman of considerable distinction," to quote the account in Mrs. Elizabeth F. Ellett's book, Pioneer Women of the West. Mrs. Ellett, in the preface of this book, says that the article on Catherine Sherrill was prepared by A. W. Putnam, the distinguished historian of Middle Tennessee. A. W. Putnam married Catherine Sevier, daughter of George Washington Sevier, who was the eldest son of Catherine Sherrill Sevier and Governor John Sevier. The account of "Bonny Kate" in Mrs. Ellett's book is the fullest known of the vivacious lady who so greatly influenced her state and time, and I have therefore relied upon Mr. Putnam's statements for the detail of this sketch. The one or two small errors in his article are such as might easily occur in setting type from hand-written manuscript. The book was published in 1852 and the article was prepared probably some time before that date. This was less than twenty years after Bonnie Kate's death, and, as Mr. Putnam knew her well and talked to her many times I conclude his statements are correct.

Samuel Sherrill settled upon the Nollichucky, and his home was called "Daisy Fields." He was "well to do in the world for an emigrant of that day." He served in the Revolution and he was in the Battle of King's Mountain. Three of his sons. Adam, George and Samuel, Jr. were also in the Battle of King's Mountain. George Sherrill was very young. Adam Sherrill was born on the Yadkin, in North Carolina, in 1758. He died in Russellville, Ala., where he had accompanied his sister, "Bonny Kate." Adam Sherrill married Mary McCormack, or Carmack. It is said that the other sons of Samuel Sherrill were Uriah Sherrill and John Sherrill. Someone has written me that Bonny Kate's father was Uriah Sherrill, but practically every historian gives her father as Samuel Sherrill. Governor Sevier in his Journal speaks once of Acquila Sherrill and several times of William Sherrill.

Although the Sherrills came to Watauga Settlement quite early and the Seviers in 1773, it is said that John Sevier and Catherine Sherrill had not seen each other until the historic occasion in June, 1776, when the Fort was attacked and the famous incident of his christening her "Bonny Kate" took place. Old Abraham and a party of braves besieged the station Fort, into which the people of the settlement had gathered for protection, as for some weeks the Indians had been threatening the settlers. James Robertson and John Sevier were in the Fort and in command with some thirty fighting men. Some of the women went out of the enclosure thinking the Indians had withdrawn. The savages, however, approached stealthily and attacked the party. The women screamed and ran toward the Fort, some of them reaching it in time to enter. Catherine Sherrill succeeded in almost reaching the gates, but the Indians intercepted her direct path, and she made a circuit, resolving to scale the palisades in the rear. Someone inside the wall tried to help her, but slipped, falling within the enclosure while she fell to the ground without. The savages were almost upon her, firing and shooting arrows at her. She said, in telling the story: "The bullets and arrows came like hail. It was now—leap the wall or die! For I would not live a captive." She managed to get to her feet and then leapt to the edge of the palisades into the arms of Captain John Sevier, who was calling to her "Jump! My Bonny Kate Jump!" He reached toward her, caught her and swung her to safety.

The Sherrill family had moved into the Fort only the day before the attack by the Indians, according to A. W. Putnam's account, which makes it quite possible that historians are correct in saying that John Sevier had never seen Catherine Sherrill until she started toward the enclosure. Some of the men within the Fort had desired to sally forth to the protection of the women, when the attack was first discovered, but the commanders advised against this, as it would endanger the entire group and it was already too late to be of any assistance. Some of the other women in the party reached the Block House safely, one was killed, one or two were captured.

The incident is one of the most famous in Southern History, and any one will acknowledge that the introduction of the intrepid girl and the soldier was romantic. Four years later, after the death of his wife, Captain Sevier married Bonny Kate, whom he had saved and christened.

Catherine Sherrill is credited by tradition and written history as being the handsomest young woman of her time, at least in her vicinity. A writer declares that she could "out run, out jump, walk more erect, and ride more gracefully than any other female in the mountains 'round about or on the continent at large."

She certainly gave ample proof of her ability to run and jump, and as for her carriage, "she bore herself jauntily even in old age."

It is rather an interesting fact that Putnam does not once in his account of her in Mrs. Ellett's book refer to her sobriquet, Bonny Kate, or tell the story of Captain Sevier so calling her or of his actually saving her on that day, although every other historian of that time gives the story in full. Putnam says she was over and within the defences and quotes her as saying she found herself 'by the side of one in uniform,' and "I could gladly undergo that peril and effort again to fall into his arms and feel so out of danger, but then it all of God's good Providence." So perhaps he simply neglected to tell the story merely through too great familiarity.

I think she proved her courage by her marriage, quite as much as by the many feats attributed to her, for she became stepmother to ten young Seviers of ages varying from eighteen years to not as many months. She was equal to the emergency however, and raised them all to maturity. Richard Sevier, a young boy when she married his father, died at eighteen, unmarried.

Catherine Sherrill Sevier and Governor John Sevier had eight children, all of whom survived to maturity and marriage, and they evidently also raised four of the Governor's grand-children, as Elizabeth Sevier, the eldest daughter by the first marriage, died early and left four children to the care, apparently, of Governor and Mrs. Sevier. Also several of Catherine's nephews and nieces were raised by her, and in my research into Sevier records, I am continually finding a niece or nephew of John Sevier, who claims to have been raised in the Governor's home by Bonny Kate. She must have had a heart of gold and she certainly had her hands full. Some one may say that a stepson of eighteen—Joseph Sevier was eighteen—could not have been of much care to the bride, but in the few weeks between her marriage and the Battle of King's Mountain, (seven in all) Catherine is said to have made the homespun suits which her husband and his two sons wore to the Battle. So the honey-moon was evidently not an idle one. It is said that when some one complimented her on this she answered that if all of Governor Sevier's ten children had been boys and all of them old enough to go to the Battle she could have outfitted them all!

Her athletic habits must have stood her in good stead, after her marriage, for she managed her husband's estate, farmed it and marketed the products.

Modern wives express resentment sometimes when husbands bring home "a friend to dinner." "Bonny Kate's" husband was apt to bring his whole company home, as he says, "to dine and lodge!" And it is gravely said in history that he never let an old comrade leave in the morning on an ancient, tired nag, but always urged him to go to the stables and choose one of the blooded horses in exchange!

We can imagine that Bonny Kate must have been sorely strained to retain her title as "Bonny" under such circumstances, that is, if "Bonny" described her disposition as well as her beauty. General Sevier did not confine his hospitality apparently to his friends, for it is told that on one occasion, having taken thirty Indian prisoners, he had no place to take them, so he took them to his home! They loved that and settled down to stay and thereafter nothing could make them stir from the plantation. They seem to have been there for years; at least no one has set down the time of their departure, if it ever happened. They did nothing, and Bonny Kate, with her energetic disposition, must have been tried by the arrangement, however much the Indians enjoyed it. Their only contribution to life, I gather, was the teaching of their language and other Indian languages to Catherine's second daughter, Ruth Sevier. The result of this teaching, which was probably more the effect of companionship than actual intention, was that before she was ten, she could chatter like a magpie in several tribal tongues. This ability served her afterwards on many occasions, for she acted as official and unofficial interpreter several times. In the meanwhile the little tribe of thirty adopted her and made her a princess, and prophesied that she would marry a great chief of their people, which was little enough to promise in return for overlong hospitality. How this prophesy was fulfilled is an interesting part of the history of Ruth Sevier, which appears in Chapter XII, Part Six of this volume.

Bonny Kate's step daughters were all married from her home, each of them, it is said, being married by Dr. Doak. John Sevier mentions the minister, Dr. Doak, in giving accounts of the weddings of his daughters.

Putnam says that Governor Sevier's first wife died in 1779, that date being given also by Wheeler's History of North Carolina and several others. Other historians say that she died in January or February, 1780. It is also a rather curious fact that Putnam says her name was Susan Hawkins. This coincides with a genealogy of the Hawkins family, although every other authority gives her name Sarah Hawkins.

The marriage of John Sevier and Catherine Sherrill took place August 14, 1780, and was performed by Joseph Wilson.

Bonny Kate was left alone, often for weeks at a time, to manage the estate and take care of the children and servants, for the grown sons by the first marriage were with their father in practically every campaign—James Sevier in his pension declaration

says he was in every campagn with his father except one—but she
seems not to have been afraid. She refused to go to the Block
House in time of danger, saying, "The wife of John Sevier knows
no fear," and "I neither skulk from duty or danger." The Indians
seem to have respected this fearlessness and perhaps to have ad-
mired her and protected her because of it; but the Tories were serious enemies. It is said that at one time some Tories came to her
demanding to be told her husband's whereabouts, intending to hang
him, but offering her and her childen safety in return for information. When she refused to give them any information one man
drew his pistol and threatened to kill her. "Shoot, shoot!" was
her answer, "I'm not afraid to die." The leader of the party told
the man to put up his pistols, saying. "Such a woman is too brave
to die."

Since no picture survives to tell of Catherine Sherrill's beauty,
this quotation from Putnam is particularly interesting:

"We have seen her in advanced age—tall in stature, erect
in person, stately in walk, with small piercing blue eyes, raven locks,
a Roman nose, and firmness unmistakable in every feature. She
was able to teach her children in the exercises conducive to health
and usefuless, to strength of nerve and of action. None could,
with equal grace and facility, placing a hand upon the mane of
a spirited horse, and standing by his side, seat themselves upon his
back or in the saddle. She had the appearance and used the language of independence, haughtiness and authority, and she never laid
these entirely aside. Yet was not her pride offensive, nor her words
or demeanor intended heedlessly to wound. It could be said of her
without any question, that she 'reverenced her husband,' and she
instilled the same scriptural sentiment into the minds of his children. The very high respect and deference which one of her digni-
fied appearance ever paid him, no doubt had a favorable influence
upon others; for though he was a man of remarkable elegance of
person, air and address, and of popular attraction, yet it must be
confessed that she contributed much to all these traits, and to his
usefulness and zeal in public service. She relieved him of his
cares at home, and applauded his devotion to the service of the
people.

"Her reply to those who urged her 'to fort,' or to take protection in one of the station, was 'I would as soon die by the tomahawk
and scalping knife as by famine! I put my trust in that Power
who rules the armies of Heaven, and among men on earth. I know
my husband has an eye and an arm for the Indians, and the Tories
who would harm us, and though he is gone often, and for weeks at
a time, he comes home when I least expect him, and always covered
with laurels. If God protects him whom duty calls into danger,
so will He those who trust in Him and stand at their post.'

"This was the spirit of the heroine—this was the spirit of Catherine Sevier. Neither she nor her husband seemed to think there could be any danger or loss when they could encourage others to daring to duty, and usefulness.

"She embraced the religious sentiments of the Presbyterians, and her life throughout was exemplary and useful. In this faith she lived and died. A favorite expression of hers was 'I always trust in Providence.' She always taught her children that 'Trust in God, with a pure heart, is to be rich enough; if you are lazy your blood will stagnate in your veins, and your trust will die.' She would never be idle. Knitting often engaged her fingers, while her mind and tongue were occupied in thought and conversation. She always wore at her side a bunch of very bright keys."

"During the twelve years in which he officiated as Governor of Tennessee, his wife made his home delightful to him, his children, and his friends. It was the rest of the weary, the asylum of the afflicted, well known as the 'hospitable mansion of the First Governor, the people's favorite.'

"After the death of Governor Sevier in 1815, his widow removed to Overton County, Tennessee. where Governor Sevier had 57,000 acres of land. Several of her children and other kinspeople had preceded her to this location and practically all her family resided there. She selected a romantic and secluded spot for her residence and named it 'The Dale.' It was on a high bench or spur of one of the mountains a few miles from Obed River. Her sons erected log cabins for bedroom, dining-room, and kitchen, and others for stable and crib. Here she resided for years attended by the Governor's body servant, Toby, who had accompanied him in all his Indian campaigns; Toby's wife, Rachel, and one other female servant, Susy, and a boy. Seldom did she come down from her eyrie in the Mountain. The aged eagle had lost her mate."

Among the treasures she had transported from the Governor's mansion was a carpet which admirers had presented to Governor Sevier. This was the first article of its kind west of the Alleghanies, and it was an object of greatest curiosity. When distinguished company was expected it was carefully spread upon the floor, only to be dusted and re-rolled, boxed and put away, when the visitors departed. It is said that only one one occasion was it ever left on the floor over night, and that was during the visit of the Princes of Orleans It can be easily imagined that its splendor failed to impress the palace bred youngsters!

"She was remarkably neat in her person, tidy and particular, and uniform in her dress, which might be called half-mourning—a white cap with black trimmings. She had a hearth rug the accompaniment of the favorite carpet, which was usually laid before the fireplace in her own room, and there she was commonly seated, erect as a statue, her feet placed upon her rug, her work-stand near her side, the Bible ever there or on her lap, the Governor's hat upon the wall; such were the striking features of that mountain hermitage."

Late in her life, June 10, 1836, her favorite son, Samuel Sevier, removed to Alabama to reside, and Bonny Kate decided to go to him to spend her remaining days. She was then already eighty-two and but a few months were vouchsafed to her in that son's society, for she passed away, October 2, 1836, in his home at Russellville, Ala. She was buried there and her body lay for many years beside that of her son and other members of the family. In June, 1922, it was determined by patriotic Tennesseans to bring back her ashes to the home of her youth. Mr. Samuel Heiskell, of Knoxville, secured permission from the authorities and relatives. July 27, 1922, he brought the remains to Tennessee to re-inter her ashes beside her husband in Knoxville. The occasion was made a patriotic one and hundreds of people gathered from all parts of the South.

THE CHILDREN OF CATHERINE SHERRILL SEVIER

Catherine Sevier

Ruth Sevier

George Washington Sevier

Samuel Sevier

Polly Preston Sevier

Eliza Conway Sevier

Joanna Goode Sevier

Robert Sevier

PART SIX
Descendants of
Governor John Sevier

CHILDREN OF GOVERNOR JOHN SEVIER

By the First Wife, Sarah Hawkins Sevier:

By the Second Wife, Catherine Sherrill Sevier:

It is not possible to give the foregoing names in the exact order of birth, as authorities differ widely regarding this. In the chapter devoted to each child the date of birth when known will be given, or the approximate date and the reason for considering it the approximate date.

The list of children has been carefully compiled from statements by George Washington Sevier and James Sevier, checked carefully with Governor Sevier's Journal, other historical documents and later statements by descendants, Bishop Hoss, Mrs. Sophia Hoss French, Mr. Charles Bascom Sevier, Mr. Samuel Sevier, and many others.

CHAPTER ONE
Joseph Sevier

JOSEPH SEVIER

Joseph Sevier, Jr., son of Governor John Sevier by his first wife, Sarah Hawkins Sevier, was their eldest child. He was born in Rockingham County, Virginia, in 1762, as shown by the fact that at the Battle of King's Mountain, October 7, 1780, he was eighteen years of age. Joseph was named for his mother s father, Joseph Hawkins, and his uncle, Joseph Sevier, Sr.

Joseph Sevier went with his father to "the Mountains" in 1773. At the Battle of King's Mountain he was the last man to cease firing, disobeying the order to cease, crying out, "They have killed my father, they have killed my father!" He was mistaken, however, as it was Captain Robert Sevier, his uncle, who fell mortally wounded. This same story is told of James Sevier, who was sixteen years of age, and evidently happened to one or both of them.

Joseph Sevier, when he was only nineteen years of age, was employed to keep watch on hostile movements of the Indians. This probably began the long association with the Indian people which he later cemented by marrying an Indian girl. He was almost continually employed to conduct Indian affairs from the time he was nineteen years of age and during the entire administration of Governor Blount he was a trusted agent. Like several other Seviers he was fluent in the Indian tongues and this made his services very valuable. His second marriage took him evidently entirely from his own people, for Governor Sevier, in writing to George Washington Sevier, alludes to Joseph rather sadly when he begs his son Washington not to go West, as so many young men were doing. He says, "I have already lost one son to the savages."

This Joseph Sevier is frequently confused with his uncle, for whom he was named, and many historians are misled by the name "Joseph Sevier." There is, indeed no way of distinguishing them when so named except by the date or the text of the article, and frequently no way whatever.

They were nearly the same age, at least the difference was not radical, a matter of eleven years at most. Joseph Sevier, Sr. was the fourth son of his father and that indicates his birth about 1751, though if daughters were born to Valentine Sevier II and Joanna Goode Sevier before Joseph Sr., was born, then his birth was later than 1751 and he was even nearer the age of his nephew and name-sake. Joseph Sevier, Jr., who was born in 1762.

Even in the matter of marriage they are almost hopelessly confused by the family historians. Each of them is said to have married "Charity Keewood" and certainly one of them did marry Charity Keewood, but the oc-incidence of two Joseph Seviers marrying two Charity Keewoods seems too extraordinary! Bishop Hoss gives the information that Joseph, Jr., married Charity Keewood, but I am inclined to think that he, too, was confused by the Joseph Seviers. The descendants of Joseph Sevier, Sr., give his marriage positively to Charity Keewood.

It is very probable they both married into the Keewood family and perhaps they married cousins of the same name. Many references indicate the possibility of two Keewood marriages. The Keewood plantation was not far from the Seviers' and the exchange of visits and courtesies was frequent. It will be recalled that when the Sevier family moved from Virginia they arrived at the Keewood Settlement Christmas Day, 1773. The intimacy with the Keewoods evidently continued. Governor Sevier in his Journal makes mention of the Keewoods in connection with his brother, Joseph, denoting some relation, and again mentions his son Joseph and the Keewoods. He several times sets down the visit of Mr. and Mrs. Joseph Sevier (son) and Miss Sallie Keewood.

Governor Sevier in his Journal dated February 2, 1794, mentions "son Jo., wife and Sally Keewood came here."

February 4, 1794, "Self, wife, Jos., wife, Miss Sallie Keewood Mary Ann and Ruth went to Jonesboro."

Therefore Joseph, Jr., was married before 1794.

Joseph Sevier, Jr., married evidently rather young as did his father, and there is a record that he had two sons by his first marriage. Their names were John Finley Sevier and Richard Cunningham Sevier. John is evidently named in compliment to Governor Sevier. Joseph, Jr., had a brother, Richard and that name is perhaps a compliment to that brother who died about the time the younger Richard was born. This leaves the names Finley and Cunningham unaccounted for and it may be that the mother of these two sons was a Finley or a Cunningham. A John Findlay, or Findley, served in the Revolution and is given as one of the participants in the Battle of King's Mountain. The name may have been in compliment to him, whether he was a relative or friend only. I have no record of their descendants, and little mention of them except in documents in Washington giving power of attorney to their uncle George Washington Sevier, to collect their inheritance of their father's part of Governor John Sevier's estate.

They testify that they are the only heirs of their father, Joseph

Sevier, Jr. Their Uncle, George Washington Sevier, also so testifies.

William Matlock, their great uncle by marriage, also so testifies. This document is dated 1826. This statement plainly ignores the second marriage of Joseph Sevier, Jr., and the children by the second marriage.

Joseph Sevier's second wife was Elizabeth Lowry, the Indian girl, and it is because of this Indian connection that the sons Richard and John refused to recognize the marriage.

Of John Finley Sevier and Richard Cunningham Sevier I have no further information after their declaration in 1826 that they are the only heirs of their father, Joseph Sevier, son of Governor John Sevier.

It is the irony of fate that the descendants of John Finley Sevier and Richard Cunningham Sevier, if there are any, are not known, whereas the descendants of the other children are known.

Joseph Sevier, Jr., married for his second wife, Elizabeth Lowry, daughter of George Lowry, a Scotchman, and Ocatlootsa, who was a daughter of the great chief Oconstoto. A few years after this marriage Joseph Sevier died, and his widow, Elizabeth Lowry, married for her second husband, John Walker, supposed to be an Englishman, although Governor Blount calls him a half-breed. A son of this marriage was John Walker, Jr., who became famous for his elopement with Elizabeth Meigs.

THE CHILDREN OF JOSEPH SEVIER
By the First Wife, Charity Keewood (?) Sevier:

1. John Finley Sevier
2. Richard Cunningham Sevier

By the Second Wife, Elizabeth Lowry Sevier:

3. Margaret Sevier
4. Eliza Sevier

MARGARET SEVIER

Margaret Sevier, daughter of Joseph Sevier, Jr., and Elizabeth Lowry Sevier, was born about ————. She married Gideon Morgan about ———— and had at least three children:

(a). Gideon Morgan, II
(b). Elizabeth Lowry Morgan
(c). Cherokee America Morgan

(a). Gideon Morgan, II, son of Gideon Morgan and Margaret Sevier Morgan, was living in 1920, in Tip, Oklahoma. I know nothing further of him.

(b) Elizabeth Lowry Morgan, daughter of Gideon Morgan and Margaret Sevier Morgan, married Hugh McDowell McElrath.

They had a son, John Edgar McElrath, who married Elsie Ann Alden. They had a daughter, Bertha McElrath Alden, who married Benjamin Bakewell.

(c). Cherokee America Morgan, daughter of Gideon Morgan, and Margaret Sevier Morgan, married Andrew Lewis Rogers. They had seven children, namely:

    A.   Andrew Lewis Rogers, Jr.
    B.   Connell Rogers
    C.   Hugh Morgan Rogers
    D.   John Otto Rogers
    E.   ucy Rogers
    F.   Paul Rogers
    G.   Clifford Rogers

A. Andrew Lewis Rogers, Jr., married Josephine Howard and has four children, namely: Andrew Lewis Rogers III, Partricia Rogers, Josephine Rogers and Kenneth Rogers. Paul Rogers died in infancy. Andrew Lewis Rogers and his family live on Garrison Hill, Fort Gibson, Okla.

B. Connell Rogers, married for his first wife, Florence Nash, and had Ella Nash Rogers and Gertrude Whitman Rogers and married for his second wife Kate Cunningham and had Marion Sevier Rogers, Lewis Byrne Rogers, Howard Cunningham Rogers, and Connell Rogers, Jr. Of these: Gertrude Rogers married a Persian, Dr. Georgivus Shimoon, a prominent dentist of Muskogee, and had one daughter. Mrs. Shimoon died in the summer of 1916. Ella Nash Rogers married David Castle and had two sons, David Castle, Jr., and Connell Rogers Castle, who live in Kansas City. Marion Sevier Rogers married ————.

C. Hugh Morgan Rogers married twice but had no children by his first wife. He married for his second wife, Bertha ————. They had one daughter, Bertha, who was born January, 1919, two weeks before her father's death.

D. John Otto Rogers married ———————— and has two children, Lucy Rogers and John Otto Rogers, Jr. He lives at Eagle Lake, Texas.

E. Lucy Rogers.

F. Paul Rogers.

G. Clifford Rogers married ———————— and has two sons, Clifford Rogers, Jr., and ————————Rogers. He lives at Fort Gibson, Okla.

Mrs. Cherokee America Morgan Rogers made her home with

her eldest son, **Andrew Lewis Rogers, Jr.**, and died in the spring of 1919.

ELIZA SEVIER

Eliza Sevier, daughter of Joseph Sevier, Jr., and Elizabeth Lowry Sevier, was born about ———. She married about ——— Templin Ross, of Pennsylvania, and had two children, Hugh Ross and Joseph Ross. Templin Ross and Elizabeth Sevier Ross died of cholera at the time of the Indian emigration in 1838. Their children were cared for by some people in Arkansas.

JAMES SEVIER

James Sevier, second son of Governor John Sevier by his first wife, Sarah Hawkins Sevier, was born in Virginia, in Rockingham County, October 25, 1764. He was still a small boy when his father moved to the "Mountains." He participated in Governor Sevier's Indian Campaigns, writing to Dr. Lyman Draper, in a letter which is now in the Draper Collection in Madison, Wisconsin, that he was in every Indian Campaign with his father except one. His elder brother, Joseph, was only a little elder and the two lads went with their father to the Battle of King's Mountain, as many histories testify. James was not quite sixteen when the forces were gathering for the King's Mountain Campaign. He was too young to be included in the list of men to go or stay to protect the homes and women and children, a vitally important duty, but his stepmother, Bonny Kate, called out, "Mr. Sevier, here is another of your sons who wants to go with you." The Governor then decided to permit him to accompany the party and found a horse for the boy. He was thus one of the two youngest participants in the Battle, the other being William Isbell, who was only fifteen. James Sevier was within three weeks of being sixteen. Bonny Kate, whose marriage had taken place a few weeks before, made the homespun suits which Joseph and James wore in the Battle.

The story is told of him and of his brother Joseph that he was the last man to cease firing, disobeying the order to cease firing when the Battle of King's Mountain was over, crying, "They have killed my father, they have killed my father." It was, however, his uncle, Captain Robert Sevier, who was mortally wounded. The incident may have occurred to both boys as a matter of fact, and evidently did occur to one or both. Governor Sevier gave the field glass which Patrick Ferguson, the English Commander, carried, to his son, James Sevier. The glass remained in the family for some years and was presented to the Tennessee Historical Society by a grandson of James Sevier, who was also James Sevier. During the World War, when a request was made by the Government of the United States for field glasses, this historic instrument was loaned to the government. I do not know its present location.

James Sevier, starting so early in life upon a successful career of war, followed his distinguished father and was in all but one of the thirty-five battles with Indians. He had a long and honorable life in the service of his state and country. He was Clerk of the Court of Washington County, Tennessee, for forty-seven years, some histories even say fifty-seven years. He lived with his father and stepmother, Catherine Sherrill Sevier until his own marriage in 1789 and then established his own home a few miles from theirs. This was near Jonesboro, Tennessee. He died on his place, January 21, 1847, aged eighty-two years.

JAMES SEVIER'S PENSION DECLARATION
Draper Mss. 100247-254

James Sevier—Washington County, Tennessee: Declaration— 11th Sept. 1832: aged 68 years served in 1780, in his uncle Robert Sevier's Company, in his father, Col. John Sevier's regiment, in the Battle of King's Mountain—that Capt. Robert Sevier was mortally wounded in that battle and died a few days after—that immediately after, the regiment collected at a place called the Swan Ponds, now in Greene County—Col. John Sevier commanded, Jesse Welton & Jonathon Tipton were the Majors: Affiant was in Captain Landon Carter's Company: Left home the last of Nov.— met the Indians in force on the South side of French Broad, on Boyd's Creek, & had a pretty severe engagement with them, in which we were pretty successful—must have been more than two months on this tour.

Shortly after Gen. Green's battle with the British at the Eutaw Springs, there was a request made for men from this side of the mountains—who were to serve three months—after they joined Gen. Greene. My father, Col. John Sevier, & Lt. Colonel Charles Robertson, commanded the Washington troop—Valentine Sevier & Jonathon Tipton were Majors—commenced our march for South Carolina in September, 1781, we passed through Morgantown & Charlotte, N. C. & through Gen. Gates' battle ground—joined Gen. Greene, at the High Hills of Santee, where he was recruiting his men after the severe service at Eutaw: we were sent on to join Gen. Marion in the Swamps of Santee; while with Gen. Marion, declarant was one of a party that took a British post below Monk's Corner, consisting of about a hundred men. They had fortified a large brick tenement, belonging to a Mr. Colleton: The officers commanding the Americans were Cols. Sevier, Mayhem, Oree (Horry) or Horre, & Maj. Valentine Sevier. We made some attempt to take more of their outposts, but found them all evacuated—I suppose called in by the British General. Having served out the time, we returned home, although Gen. Marion expressed a great desire that we remain a few weeks longer. My father, Capt. Carter, and most of his company, did stay for some considerable time longer & were then discharged; believes he was upwards of 4 months from home on this service.

Shortly after his return home from S. C.,—he thinks in Feb. 1782, there was an Indian alarm, & call for men; that himself & an elder brother who had returned from Virginia that fall, equipt themselves as volunteers & went about 50 miles to the place of rendezvous on Holston River; that shortly after they got there, & before many men had collected, the weather became extremely cold & a deep snow fell, so that it was thought the Indians would not disturb the frontier people at that time, & that it would be advisable to break up and return home—we did so. Who was the officer that ordered the men out at that time. I do not recollect, unless it was Col. Charles Robertson, as my father and Capt. Carter had not returned at that time from S. C. My brother and myself joined no company, & I think were not more than two weeks from home. That through the summer of 1782, the lower Cherokees near the Lookout Mountain & on Coosa River were very troublesome: As soon as their crops were matured, my father raised an army of men—set out the last of August or first of September & went & destroyed all the Lower Towns on the the waters of the Tennessee, & two towns on Coosa River—one called Estanaula, the other called Spring Frog's Town; two villages on the waters of Coosa. On this campaign we had no fighting. The body of Indians kept out of our way. We took some 7 or 8 prisoners (warriors)—with a number of women & children. After remaining some length of time in the Nation, & having destroyed everything that came within our grasp, on which they could support. An Indian countryman by the name of Rodgers came in with a flag for peace—the Indians were requested if they wanted peace to go up to Old Chota town, on Tennessee River, & there a peace talk would be held with them. They did so; a peace was made & the prisoners restored to their friends. Maj. Valentine Sevier was all the Major that was out at that time, as I believe. Declarant served in Capt. Alex Moore's company—there was Capt. Sam Weare & Capt. Robert Bean who commanded companies—the other captains now forgotten. I believe we were upwards of two months on that campaign.

In August, 1780, a campaign was ordered against the Middle Settlements Indians—the place of meeting was beyond the limits of the settlements, on a creek called Indian Creek, that he was one of the men that met to go on said tour. While at the place of rendezvous, & waiting for others to collect, a man by the name of Hull went into the mountains to hunt, & was shot at by an Indian before he discovered him, but being missed, & seeing the Indian, he fired on & killed him. This circumstance caused a mutiny amongst the men. They were afraid their families would be killed in their absence, broke for home, & the campaign fell through. I mention this to show that I was twice called out to go on campaigns that fell through. My father, in this atter instance, was to have commanded—there was no major that I recollect. I believe we were not more than 10 days or 2 weeks from home.

Early in the summer of 1781, the frontier inhabitants became much alarmed about the Indians. My father, who was Colonel of the County, ordered out a company of Rangers—or what was then called a scouting party—this declarant was one of that party, & went out, & James Hubbard was the Captain, as well as he recollects—were out about 2 weeks.

Was born in 1764. Col. Richard Campbell, who was killed at Eutaw Springs was said declarant's uncle.

March 29, 1789, James Sevier married Nancy Conway, whose sisters, Elizabeth and Susannah also married into the Sevier family. Elizabeth marrying James' brother, John Sevier, Jr., and Susannah marrying their first cousin, "Devil Jack Sevier," son of Valentine vier III. The three Conway sisters were daughters of Colonel Henry Conway, who was also a distinguished Revolutionary soldier. Nancy Conway, who married James Sevier, was born March 22, 1772. She died July 15, 1743, aged seventy-one years.

James Sevier and Nancy Conway Sevier had eleven children, namely:

1. Elizabeth Conway Sevier, born July 9, 1790.
2. Sarah Hundley Sevier, born July 22, 1792.
3. Maria Antoinette Sevier, born May 12, 1794, died two years later.
4. Minerva Grainger Sevier, born May 30, 1796.
5. Pamelia Hawkins Sevier, born March 15, 1798.
6. Susannah Brown Sevier, born June 25, 1800.
7. Elbert Franklin Sevier, born September 17, 1802.
8. Elbridge Gerry Sevier, born March 19, 1805.
9. Clarissa Carter Sevier, born April 9, 1807.
10. Louisa Maria Sevier, born December 16, 1811.
11. Mary Malvina Sevier, born April 14, 1814.

ELIZABETH CONWAY SEVIER

1. Elizabeth Conway Sevier, first child of James Sevier and Nancy Conway Sevier was born, July 9, 1790. She was named in honor of her mother's sister, Elizabeth Conway, (who married John Sevier, Jr., and died in a very short time after the marriage). Elizabeth Conway Sevier married March 8, 1810, James S. Johnston.

SARAH HUNDLEY SEVIER

2. Sarah Hundley Sevier, second child of James Sevier and Nancy Conway Sevier was born July 22, 1792. She married January 11, 1810, Hugh Douglas Hale, born August 12, 1787, in Far-

quahr County, Virginia. He was a son of Phillip and Catherine Douglas Hale. The children of Hugh Douglas Hale and Sarah Hundley Sevier Hale were:

a. James W. Hale
b. Phillip Perry Hale
c. Eliza Jane Hale
d. Catherine Anne Hale
e. William Dickson Hale
f. Lemuel Johnson Hale
g. Sarah Amanda Hale
.h. Laura Evelyn Hale
i. Hugh Douglas Hale, II.
j. Franklin Sevier Hale.

Of the foregoing:

a. James W. Hale, son of Hugh Douglas Hale and Sarah Hundley Sevier Hale, died September 9th, 1842, unmarried. It is told that he was engaged in his young manhood to Miss Taylor, an aunt of Robert L. Taylor, former Governor of Tennessee, and that she was struck by lightning at a Camp Meeting and instantly killed. This is said to have grieved him so deeply that shortly afterward he died.

b. Phillip Perry Hale, son of Hugh Douglas Hale and Sarah Hundley Sevier Hale, married Caroline Susan Gullege. Their children were: (1) Sarah Hale, who married L. B. Snyder and died without issue; (2) Thomas Hale, who died young; (3) Elizabeth Hale, who died young; (4) Franklin Sevier Hale, who died young; (5) Laura Hale, who married Lieutenant Hundley Maloney and died without issue; (6) Fred Douglas Hale, who married first Theodosia Bell and had: Fred P. Hale, Harriet Susan Hale, John Weller Hale, Josephine Hale and Annie Lee Hale; and married second, Mary Neal and had: Ruth Sevier Hale, Annie Lee Hale and Elizabeth Hale, and married third Minnie Edwards and had: Phillip Hae, Mildred Hale, Hugh Douglas Hale and James Hale; (7) Anna Eliza Hale, who married Frank Gottsseilig; (8) Joseph Hale, who married Laura Beaucamp and had children: William Hale, Joseph Hale, I'. and Carolina Susan Hale; (9) Hugh Lemuel Hale, who married Emma Wilkinson and had three children: Phillip Hale, Douglas Hale and Eugenia Hale; (10) Phillip Thomas Hale, who married Lena Lyle Bolinger and had six children: Thomas Farris Hale, William Roy Hale, Phillip Theodore Hale, David Ward Hale, Earl Douglas Hale and Franklin Sevier Hale.

c. Eliza Jane Hale, daughter of Hugh Douglas Hale and Sarah Hundley Hale, married David Wendel Carter and had eight children: (1) James William Carter, who married Mary Lou Tindal and had among other children, Mary Carter, who married Robert Augustine

Burne; Mary Weller Carter, Janie Carter and John Tindal Carter;
(2) Alfred Moore Carter, who married first Chassie King and had
one daughter, Maud Carter, who married Ellis Crymbel and had two
sons, Carter Crymbel and Ellis Crymbel, II; Alfred Moore Carter
married for his second wife, Nannie Zimmerman, by whom he had
no children; (3) David Wendal Carter, II, who married Cornelia
Keith and had children: Lieutenant Keith Carter, David Wendal
Carter, III, Annie Frazier Carter, Hugh Sevier Carter, Stanley
Carter, who married Nettie Lee Hill; (2) Franklin Alexander Car-
ter, who married Annie Laird and has three children: Annie Laird
Carter, David Wendell Carter and Robert Cowden Carter; (3 Ella
Douglas Carter, who married Dr. Samuel W. Rhea and has two
sons, Joseph Carter Rhea, (who married Troupe Davis and has
Ellen Douglas Rhea and James Wendel Rhea, who married Helen
Haynes and has two sons, James Wendel Rhea, II, and Haynes
Rhea).

(d) Catherine Anne Hale married Dr. Charles Tenant Porter
Jarnagin, in Jefferson County, Tennessee. Dr. Jarnagin was born
April 6, 1812, died about 1894. He was born and died in Jefferson
County, Tennessee. Dr. Charles Tenant Porter Jarnagin was the
son of Preston Bynum Jarnagin and his wife, Elizabeth Conway
Jarnagin, who were married December 20, 1810. Preston Bynum
Jarnagin was born August 13, 1791, near Witt's Foundry, then in
Jefferson, now Hamblen County, Tennessee, died July 28, 1828,
in Jefferson County. He was the son of Captain Thomas and Mary
(Witt) Jarnagin. Thomas Jarnagin was born July 25, 1747, in
Virginia, died February 26, 1802, near Witt's Foundry, Tennessee.
He was the son of Capt. John and Mary Jarnagin. Mary Witt, born
April 4, 1753, Virginia, died December 14, 1829, near Witt's Foun-
drey, Tennessee, the daughter of Charles and Lavinia Witt,
who lived in Halifax, Virginia.

Elizabeth Conway Jarnagin married, December 20, 1810, Preston B. Jarnagin, and died July 14, 1816. She was the daughter of
General Joseph Conway.

The children of Catherine Anne Hale Jarnagin and Dr. Charles
Tenant Porter Jarnagin were: (1) Ann Eliza Jarnagin, who died
young; (2) Charles Jarnagin; (3) Douglas Jarnagin, who married
——————— and had at least one child, Beatrice Jarnagin;
(4) Catherine Jarnagin, who married Dr. Britt Watkins; (5) Mary
Jarnagin, who married David Swaggerty and their child, Katie
Swaggerty, married Lon McSwain; Mary Jarnagin married for her
second husband, Joseph Carty, and had no children; (6) John Sevier
Jarnagin, married Kate D. Hubbard May 23, 1872, at Jefferson City,
Tennessee. They had four children, (Estelle Jarnagin, married
Blair Neff; Mary Kate Jarnagin, married Walter Harris; Henry

Porter Jarnagin, died young; and Ruth Jarnagin, died young);
(7) Dr. Joseph Conway Jarnagin, married Ida Bass, July 4, 1876, in
Montezuma, Georgia. Their children were: Mamie Vinson Jarnagin, who married Clifford Corbin Farmer and has, Mary Farmer,
Joseph Jarnagin Farmer, Clifford Corbin Farmer, Jr., William
Hawes Farmer, and Catherine Hale Farmer; Annie Kate Jarnagin,
who married Daisy Cason; Caroline Chapman Jarnagin, who married William Edward Markwalter, and has Edward Markwalter, Jr.,
and Rebecca Markwalter; Joseph C. Jarnagin, who died young; and
Ida Bass Jarnagin, who married Milton Randolph Lufborrow and
has Carolina Lufborrow and Charmion Lufborrow; (8) —————
Jarnagin, a daughter, who died in Georgia. She married ————
Yates and left two children, William Yates and Eliza Yates. By
the will of Dr. Jarnagin she is mentioned as a child of his first wife,
Catherine Anne Hale and therefore a Sevier descendant. There are
some people, however, who say she was the daughter of Dr. Hale's
second wife.

(e). William Dickson Hale, son of Hugh Douglas Hale and
Sarah Hundley Sevier Hale, married Martha Powell and had children: Mary Hale, Catherine Hale, Sarah Hale, and Leila Hale, who
married Joseph Green.

(g) Sarah Amanda Hale, daughter of Hugh Douglas Hale
and Sarah Hundley Sevier Hale, married Charles W. Meek. Their
children were, James Hale Meek, who married Jennie Hensley and
had one son, James W. Meek, who married Caroline Corinne Mc-
Williams and has one son, James W. Meek, Second; Daniel Kenny
Meek, who died young; William Blain Meek, who married Martha
Powers and has two daughters, Vesta Sevier Meek, who married
Robert Lee Davis and has one child, Katherine Davis; Iva Douglas
Meek, who is unmarried; Florine Cornelia Meek, who married
Jams P. Evans and has one son, Hubert Evans, who married
Clara Theresa Hill, and a daughter, Lula Evans who married Wi-
liam James for her first husband and for her second husband mar-
ried Dr. Paul Gheering and died at the birth of a daughter; Ida
Sevier Meek, who married Jacob Orville Lotspeich and had children:
Claude Meek Lotspeich, (who married Helen Gibbons and has five
children, Henry Gibbons Lotspeich, Margaret Sevier Lotspeich, Ed-
gar Hale Lotspeich, William Douglass Lotspeich, and James Fulton
Lotspeich); Roy Douglass Lotspeich, who married Ethel Weir and
has children, Katherine Mildred Lotspeich, Jacob Orville Lotspeich,
Second, Helen Sevier Lotspeich, Douglass Weir Lotspeich; Edgar
Sevier Lotspeich married Ruth Moore and has children: Caroline
Lotspeich, Edgar Sevier Lotspeich and Robert Orville Lotspeich;
Ella Douglas Meek married Charles E. Lothrop and has two chil-
dren, Ida Meek Lothrop and Douglass B. Lothrop, who married Ruth

Dooley and has two sons, Douglass B. Lothrop Second and Clinton Dooley Lothrop; Charles W. Meek married Adah Jariel and had two children: Joseph Meek and Sarah Meek. Franklin Hale Meek married Almena McG. Smith and had two children, Charles W. Meek, who died young, and Bathurst Lee Meek (who married Grace Tarver and has Bathurst Lee Meek, Jr.; Joseph M. Meek married Alma Burt Hughes and has two children, James Hughes Meek and Sarabel Meek.

(h). Laura Evelyn Hale, daughter of Hugh Douglas Hale and Sarah Hundley Sevier Hale, married Thomas E. Gosnell and had children: Lemuel Ward Gosnell (who married Mary Elizabeth Hill and had children: Myroyn Aydlett Gosnell, Katherine Lisserand Hill Gosnell, Clara Douglass Gosnell and Munsey Ward Gosnell. Kahrine Lisserand Gosnell, married Dr. Sterling P. Martin, Second, and had two daughters; Clara Douglass Gosnell, married first Samuel McLaughlin, and second William Silverthorne, and has two sons, Harry Douglass Silverthorne (who married Caroline M. Roes) and Carl Douglass Silverthorne.   Lemuel Ward Gosnell married for his second wife, Mrs. Cullie Oglesby; Matthew Gosnell, who died young; and Franklin Gosnell, who is unmarried.

(i). Hugh Douglas Hale, Second, son of Hugh Douglas Hale, First, and Sarah Hundley Sevier Hale, married Sarah Vance, a sister of Governor Zebulon Vance, of North Carolina, and had three children: Margaret Hale, Sarah Hale and Franklin Hale.

(j). Franklin Sevier Hale, son of Hugh Douglas Hale and Sarah Hundley Sevier Hale, was killed in the Battle of Franklin in The War Between the States.

MARIA ANTOINETTE SEVILR

3. Maria Antoinette Sevier, daughter of James Sevier and Nancy Conway Sevier, was born May 12, 1794. She died 1796.

MINERVA GRAINGER SEVIIR

4. Minerva Grainger Sevier, daughter of James Sevier and Nancy Conway Sevier, was born March 15, 1796. She married April 30, 1816, John Nelson, who died in 1830.

PAMELIA HAWKINS SEVIER

5. Pamelia Hawkins Sevier, daughter of James Sevier and Nancy Conway Sevier, was born March 15, 1798. She died in 1842. She married May 6, 1817, Alexander M. Nelson, who was probably a brother to John Nelson, who married her sister, Minerva. She had a son, Alexander M. Nelson, Jr., who was born July 23, 1820.

SUSANNAH BROWN SEVIER

6. Susannah Brown Sevier, daughter of James Sevier and Nancy Conway Sevier, was born June 25, 1800. She married, November 26, 1818, Richard Purdom. They had a son, Alexander Purdom, who was born, November 12, 1819.

ELBERT FRANKLIN SEVIER

7. Elbert 'Franklin Sevier, son of James Sevier and Nancy Conway Sevier, was born September 17, 1802. He married twi e. He first married Matilda Powell. The marriage took p'ace August 9, 1832. They had two children, Elbert Powell Sevier, who married and had a son, James Sevier; and Sarah Sevier, who died with her mother in Knoxville of cholera in 1854. Elbert Frank'in Sevier married for his second wife, Eliza James, a daughter cf Reverend Jesse James, of Chattanooga. They had a son, James Sevier, who became a minister.

ELBRIDGE GERRY SEVIER

8. Elbridge Gerry Sevier, son of James Sevier and Nancy Conway Sevier, was born March 19, 1805. He married November :3, 1827, Mary Caroline Brown, born February 27, 1810, died ————. daughter of Thomas Brown and his wife, Mary McElwee Brown.

Elbridge Gerry Sevier and Mary Caroline Brown Sevier had twelve children, namely:

    a. Thomas Brown Sevier
    b. Henry Clay Sevier
    c. Rowena Jane Sevier
    d. James Sevier
    e. Elbert Franklin Sevier, born January, 1836, lived a few days only.
    f. John Elbridge Sevier
    g. Elbert Franklin Sevier, (second child by this name).
    h. Mary Caroline Sevier
    i. Charles Bascom Sevier
    l. William Hazleton Sevier
    j. Conway Sevier, and   (twins).
    k. Ann Elizabeth Sevier

a. Thomas Brown Sevier, son of Elbridge Gerry Sevier a d Mary Caroline Brown Sevier was born September 16, 1828. He was never married.

b. Henry Clay Sevier, son of Elbridge Gerry Sevier and M ry Caroline Brown Sevier, was born July 16, 1831, died in Liberty, Mo., 1918. He married, December 19, 1853, Mary Jennie Tipton, born Mobile Alabama, 1831, died Liberty, Mo., 1920. Their children were:

    A. Elizabeth Sevier
    B. William James Sevier
    C. Robert E. Sevier
    D. Charles Sevier
Of these:
    A. Elizabeth Sevier, born 1856, died ————.

B. William James Sevier, born 1858, Bates County, Mo. He married Mary McGuinness, born Missouri City, Mo.,1864. They had eight children: (1) Herbert Eugene Sevier, born 1885 (who married Grace Muir and lives in Windham, Mont. They have six children, Jean, Alice, May, John Woodrow, Mary Elizabeth, Hazel, Madeline and Parker Sevier); (2) Roy Sevier, born 1887 (who married Lois Froman and lives in Liberty, Mo.); (3 Oscar Sevier, born 1899, (who married Vivian Ritter and lives in Liberty, Mo. Oscar Sevier served in the 91st Division 316 Military Police in France); (4) Ethel Sevier, born 1891 (who married Keller Bell and has two children, Keller Bell, Jr., and Anna Margaret Bell, and lives in Liberty, Mo.); (5). Stella Sevier, born 1892 (who married Frank Jackson and lives in Edgerton, Mo.); (6) Robert Earl Sevier, born 1895 (who married, 1920, Virginia Isabell Kendrick, born 1898, daughter of Edgar and Effie Kendrick. They live in Liberty, Mo., and have one child, Marilyn Sevier, born 1924. Robert Earl Sevier enlisted December 5, 1917 in Coast Artillery Corps and was in Camp at Fort McArthur, Calif., until May 13, when he was sent to France, where he served in 52nd Ammunition Train. He was discharged February 14, 1919); (7) Anna Bernice Sevier, born 1897; (8) Hazel Madeline Sevier, born 1899.

C. Dr. Robert E. Sevier, born 1860, married May Waddell. They have two children, (1) Helen May Sevier, and (2 Roberta Ann Sevier.

D. Charles Sevier, born 1865, married Elizabeth Taboy. They have two sons, (1) Charles Henry Sevier; and (2) Robert Fields Sevier.

c. Rowena Jane Sevier, daughter of Elbridge Gerry Sevier and Mary Caroline Brown Sevier, was born May 14, 1832. She married H. W. Von Aldehoff. They had five children: Florence Caroline Von Aldehoff, Alice Eugenia Von Aldehoff, John Sevier Von Aldehoff, Blanche Von Aldehoff, and John Sevier Von Aldehoff. Florence Caroline Von Aldehoff, daughter of H. W. Von Aldehoff and Rowena Jane Sevier Von Aldehoff, was born July 2, 1851. She married Thomas Augustus Hurt and had at least one child, Augusta Hurt, who married Frederick Trabue Mosely. John Sevier Von Aldehoff first son of H. W. Von Aldehoff and Rowena Jane Sevier Von Aldehoff, was born September 2, 1852. He died October 23, 1859. Alice Eugenia Von Aldehoff, daughter of H. W. Von Aldehoff and Rowena Jane Von Aldehoff, was born January 13, 1855. John Sevier Von Aldehoff, second son of H. W. Von Aldehoff, and second son to bear the name, was born September 14, 1855 Since he was born four years before his older brother of the same name died, I conclude that his name was changed after that brother's death. He is married and lives in Dallas, Texas. Blanche

Von Aldehoff, daughter of H. W. Von Aldehoff and Rowena Jane Sevier Von Aldehoff, was born April 10, 1859.

d. James Sevier, son of Elbridge Gerry Sevier and Mary Caroline Brown Sevier, was born August 1, 1835. He made his home in Kingston, Tennessee, and was a distinguished and learned man. He never married. He died in 1908.

e. Elbert Franklin Sevier, son of Elbridge Gerry Sevier and Mary Caroline Brown Sevier, was born in January, 1836, and lived only a few days.

f. John Elbridge Sevier son of Elbridge Gerry Sevier and Mary Caroline Brown Sevier, was born January 24, 1839.

g. Elbert Franklin Sevier, son of Elbridge Gerry Sevier and Mary Caroline Brown Sevier, was born December. 25, 1843. He was the second child to be given the name as the first child of the name died in infancy. He married Bettie Taylor and had five children, one son and four daughters, namely: Taylor Sevier, Evelyn Sevier, Edith Sevier, Ethel Sevier and Hazel Sevier. Of these: Evelyn Sevier married Gray Gentry, son of Fenton Allen Gentry and has one son, Fenton Allen Gentry, Jr.; Taylor Sevier is unmarried. Edith Sevier, Ethel Sevier and Hazel Sevier died young.

h. Mary Caroline Sevier, daughter of Elbridge Gerry Se ier and Mary Caroline Brown Sevier, was born July 18, 184—.

i. William Hazleton Sevier, son of Elbridge Gerry Sevier and Mary Caroline Brown Sevier, was born October 15, ————.

j. Conway Sevier, son of Elbridge Gerry Sevier and Mary Caroline Brown Sevier, was a twin to Ann Elizabeth Sevier and was born November 7, 1848. He was christened Conway, but as a child was nicknamed Samuel, and lived and died known by that name. He died in 1923. He never married.

k. Ann Elizabeth Sevier, daughter of Elbridge Gerry Sevier, and Mary Caroline Brown Sevier, was a twin to Conway (known as Samuel) and was born November 7, 1848. She married Noah Lybarger and had no children. Being left a widow she returned to the family home in Kingston and kept house for her bachelor brothers James Sevier and Samuel Sevier, until her death, about 1915.

l. Charles Bascom Sevier, son of Elbridge Gerry Sevier and Mary Caroline Brown Sevier, was born November 12, 1856. He married Alice Zedder and lived in Harriman, Tennessee, until his death in 1920. He had one daughter, Mary Katherine Sevier, who married Thomas Francis Reimer

CLARISSA CARTER SEVIER

9. Clarissa Carter Sevier daughter of James Sevier and Nancy Conway Sevier, was born April 9, 1807. She married May 7, 1822,

John Jones, and had at least one son, ————— Jones, who married ————— and had a son, Thomas E. Jones, of Knoxville, Tennessee. He married and has a son, Derrell E. Jones.

Carissa Carter Sevier Jones and John Jones had probably several children. In the family Bible, (from which I secured most of the information in this chapter), which is now in possession of Mrs. Gray Gentry, two children are entered as "Jones" but it is not stated which of these children are Clarissa's and which her sister's, for it will be noted that her sister, Louisa Maria Sevier, also married a J nes. However, by the date of birth of two of her children, ! evier James Elbridge Jones, born February 20, 1823, and S rah Ann Jones, born January, 1825, they were evidently Clarissa's ci....i.en, as Louisa Maria Sevier was not married until 1827.

LOUISA MARIA SEVIER

10.   Louisa Maria Sevier, daughter of James Sevier and Nancy Conway Sevier, was born Decen'ber 16, 18 1. She married James Houston Jo.es, O tober 16, 1827. They had childr:n, namely:

    a.   Sue Purdom Jones

   .b.   Ann E i a Jones

    c.   George Jones

    d.   Mary Louise Jones

    a.   Sue Purdom Jones, daughter of Louisa Mar'a Sevier Jones and James Houston Jores, married in 1841, Gibson Allen Duckworth. They had thirteen chidren, only six of whom survived to maturity, namely: E la Louise Duckworth, who was their first child; (9) Susan Duckworth; (10) Harry Duckworth; (11) Maria Duckworth; (12) Minnie Duckworth and (13) Kate Duckworth. Ella Louise Duckworth, the first child cf Sue Purdom Jones Duckworth and Gibson Allen Luckwcrth, married December 16, 1879, Valentine John K ndel E la Louise Duckworth Kind l and Valentine John Kindel had five children, namely: Eva Lcis Kindel, married 1907, John Robert Boxley and has John Robert Boxley, Jr.; William Allen Kindel, married September 1, 1905, Lineta Rogers and has Wil iam Allen Kindel. Jr.. and Martha Louise Kindel; Cher y Maud Kindel married Carey C. Orr, 1914, and has Dorthy Jane Orr and Cherry Sue Orr.

    b.   Ann Eliza Jones, daughter of Louisa Maria Sevier Jones and James Houston Jones, born July 5, 1829, marri d Felix G. Lee.

    c.   George Jones, son of Louisa Maria Sevier Jones and James Houston Jones, born September 7, 1838, died April 11, 1922.   He married Catherine ———————.   They had a daughter, Nannie Sevier Jones, who married John M. Bishop.

    d.   Mary Louise Jones, daughter of Louisa Maria Sevier Jones and James Houston Jones, married Thomas J. Lane. Their children were Annie Lane, who married Clarence Carter Trim and has an only child, Louise Trim, who married Charles Donaldson, and has an only child, Geraldine Trim Donaldson; Jessie Lane, who married twice, first —————— Drummond, and second —————— Stamps, and has two sons, Fleming Drummond and Bowie Drummond; and Henry Lane, who is not married.

THE JONES CHILDREN ENTERED IN THE JAMES SEVIER FAMILY BIBLE

There are five children named Jones whose births are recorded in the Family Bible belonging to Major James Sevier, now in possession of his great-grand daughter, Mrs. Gray Gentry. There is no indication as to the parents of the five Jones children, but as noted above by the date two of them, Sevier James Elbridge Jones and Sarah Ann Jones are evidently children of Clarissa and John Jones, whose marriage preceded that of Louisa Maria and James H. Jones.

The five entries are:
Sevier James Elbridge Jones, born February 20, 1823.
Sarah Ann Jones, born January 1825.
Ann Eliza Jones, born July 5, 1829.
William Elbert Franklin Jones, no date given.
James Sevier Jones, born September 1830.

MARY MALVINA SEVIER

11. Mary Malvina Sevier, daughter of James Sevier and Nancy Conway Sevier, was their youngest child. She was born April 4, 1814. She married James Stuart July 2, 1829. She had a daughter, Mary Stuart, who married John Howard, of Knoxville.

John Sevier, junior

JOHN SEVIER, JUNIOR

Major John Sevier, Jr., as he was known, was third son of Gov John Sevier and his first wife, Sarah Hawkins Sevier. He was born June 20, 1766, at New Market, Virginia, and given his father's full name. He died April 26, 1845.

John Sevier, Jr., was too young to participate in the Battle of King's Mountain, though he accompanied his father on several of the later Indian Campaigns, and it is said by his daughter, Mrs. Thomas Price, (Martha Ann Sevier, that he fought in the Revolution. He was only seventeen when the war was over, but his brother, James, was fighting at sixteen. It is probable that he accompanied his father in the campaigns of the last two years of the Revolutionary war and later in the Indian warfare.

He was elected recording and engrossing clerk of the first Convention held in the State of Tennessee.

He married three time and had eighteen children. He married first Elizabeth Conway; second, Sarah Richards, and third, Sophia Garoutte.

His first wife, Elizabeth Conway, was the daughter of Colonel Henry Conway, of the Revolution. Her sisters, Nancy and Susannah Conway, also married into the Sevier family. Nancy married James Sevier, (John Sevier, Jr.'s, brother) and Sussnnah married John Sevier, son of Valentine, called Devil Jack to distinguish him among the Johns. He was first cousin to James and John.

The marriage bond of John Sevier Jr., and Elizabeth Conway, is dated July 8, 1788. He was just twenty-two years of age. His bond was for $1,250, and it was signed by his father. It is said that his wife died in childbirth with her first child. A list of the children of John Sevier, Jr., prepared by his grand-daughter, Mrs. George French, a sister of Bishop Embree Hoss, from whom she secured her material, does not show the name of any child by the first wife. She gives seventeen children, beginning with the first child by the second wife. She told me that if there was a living child by Elizabeth Conway Sevier that she never heard of it. On the other hand, Bishop Hoss himself says there were eighteen children.

John Sevier Jr., married for his second wife Sarah Richards, of Philadelphia. They had seven children:

1. William Sevier
2. Samuel Sevier
3. James Sevier
4. Eliza Sevier
5. Sarah Sevier
6. John Sevier, III.
7. Thomas Sevier

John Sevier, Jr., married for his third wife Sophia Garoutte, of a French family of distinction. They had ten chi'dren, namely:

8. John Garoutte Sevier
9. Elizabeth Conway Sevier
10. Sophia Smith Garoutte Sevier
11. Louisa Rebecca Sevier
12. Michael Robert Sevier
13. George Washington Sevier
14. Anna Maria Sevier
15. Sarah Hundley Sevier
16. Archibald McAfee Sevier
17. Martha Ann Sevier

Sophia Garoutte was the daughter of Michael Garoutte, a Frenchman and his wife, Sophia Smith Garoutte. They had thirteen children, of whom Sophia, who married John Sevier, was the sixth. Michael Garoutte was born April 12, 1750. He married October 23, 1778. His parents were Antoine Garoutte and Lady Anne De Lascour. Antoine Garoutté was born January 19, 1695 He llved in Marseilles, Frances, and was Attorney General for that section of France. His son, Michael Garoutte, was a Captain of many vessels, and was very wealthy and was an admiral in the French Navy.

WILLIAM SEVIER

1. William Sevier, son of John Sevier, Jr., by his second wife, Sarah Richards Sevier, is given as their first child. No information.

SAMUEL SEVIER

2. Samuel Sevier, son of John Sevier, Jr., and his second wife, Sarah Richards Sevier. No information

JAMES SEVIER

James Sevier, son of John Sevier, Jr., by his second wife, Sarah Richards Sevier, was evidently named for his father's bother. He went to Indiana. In an old letter, now in possession of the family, written by Robert E. Sevier (son of Michael) to his uncle, John Garoutte Sevier, he says: "I have found some new kinspeople, James Thompson Sevier, son of your brother James who went to Indiana." This letter is dated 1871. This James Thompson Sevier lived at Russellville, Ark.

ELIZA SEVIER

4. Eliza Sevier, daughter of John Sevier, Jr., by his second wife, Sarah Richards Sevier, married Joseph W. Threckmorton, of Philadelphia. No further informatioh.

SARAH SEVIER

5. Sarah Sevier, the daughter of John Sevier, Jr., by his second wife, Sarah Richards Sevier, received her mother's name and her grandmother's name, as John Sevier, Jr., was the son of Sarah Hawkins Sevier.

JOHN SEVIER, III.

6. John Sevier, III, was the son of John Sevier, Jr., by his second wife, Sarah Richards Sevier. He received his father's and his grandfather's name. I have no further data.

THOMAS SEVIER

Thomas Sevier, son of John Sevier, Jr., and Sarah Richards Sevier, was born about 1803. He never married. He lived almost all his life with a sister, probably Eliza, in Philadelphia. In 1860 Thomas Sevier came South to visit his niece, Elizabeth, in Union City, Tennessee. He was too old for service in the Army but he sympathized strongly with the South. He was about sixty years old when he went to Corinth to see his friend of many years, General Albert Sidney Johnston. This was just before the Battle of Shiloh. General Johnston sent him up the Tennessee River in charge of Commissary boats. The boats were captured by Federal troops, and he was never seen or heard of again.

JOHN GAROUTTE SEVIER

8. John Garoutte Sevier, son of John Sevier Jr., and his third wife, Sophia Smith Garoutte Sevier, was born April 28, 1810. It will be observed that a son by the second wife is also named John Sevier. To add to the confusion, each of these is referred to at times as John Sevier, III.

John Garoutte Sevier was educated for a lawyer. In 1831 when he was twenty-one years of age he married Mary N. Mayfield. They had ten children, only five of whom lived to maturity, namely:

    a. Elizabeth Evelyn Sevier
    b. Henry DeCab Sevier
    c. William J. Sevier
    d. John Michael Sevier
    e. James J. Sevier

John Garoutte Sevier and his family, including his brother,

Michael Sevier and his sister, Martha Ann Sevier, who had made
her home with her brother, John Garoutte Sevier, since the death
of their father, John Sevier, Jr., moved about 1845, to Obion County
Tennessee, near Union City, Tenn. In 1859 John and Michail
again felt the call of the frontier and they went to Conway C unty,
Arkansas. They were there only a few years when John Garoutte
Sevier lost his wife and a young daughter. The War Between the
States divided his family, one son going to the Northern Army.
The remaining three sons joined the Confederate Army. After the
War he went back to Union City to make his home with h's on'y
surviving daughter, Elizabeth Evelyn Sevier, who had married in
1854 Thomas Ransom Curlin, son of Samuel Curlin. Thomas Ran-
som Curlin was descended from the Curlins and Coopers, of North
Carolina, the Coopers being descended from Sir Ashley Cooper, the
first Earl of Shaftsbury.

    a. Elizabeth Evelyn Sevier Curlin and her husband, Thomas
Ransom Curlin had eight children, one of whom died in infancy. The
seven surviving children were:

    A. Robert T. Curlin, born April 22, 1852.
    B. Sarah Eliza Elizabeth Curlin, born August 5, 1854.
    C. Laura Sophia Curlin, born July 21, 1857.
    D. Mary Rebekah Joanna Curlin, born December 12, 1858.
    E. Nancy Alida Curlin, born September 11, 1861.
    F. John Edward Allen Curlin, born July 4, 1864.
    G. James Lemuel Curlin, born January 27, 1867.

    Of these:

    A. Robert Curlin married Virginia Watson, and had one child,
who died in infancy. He has made his home in Union City, Tenn.

    B. Sarah Eliza Elizabeth Curlin married Lycurgus Hall. They
had five children, one dying in infancy. The other four are (1) Dr.
Horace Curlin Hall, born September 12, 1873, residence Laredo, T_xas,
married Carmilla Scott. They have three children, Mary Hall (who
married Captain William H. Colburn, U. S. A., and has one daughter,
Mary Beverly Colburn; Horace Curlin Hall, Jr., and Beverly Scott
Hall. (2). Ioma Hall, born August 5, 1876, married George DeBoe
Lauderdale, resides in Dallas Texas and has one child, Edward Kirk
Lauderdale. (3). Nell Kirk Hall, born 1887, married first James
Merrin, and had one daughter, Minda Merrin. Her second mar-
riage was to William B. Kellogg. Their residence is at Houston,
Texas. (4). Elizabeth Sevier Hall, born 1890, married Jack M. Litt'e
and has two children, Jack M. Little, Jr., and Mary Elizabeth Litt'e,
residence, Dallas, Texas.

    C. Laura Sophia Curlin married George B. Sower, of Christian-
burg, Va. They resided at Wanchula, Florida, and had two children
one dying young. The remaining son, Curlin Brook Sower, married

Harriet Edwards, and has one son, George Bruce Sower, born September 30, 1907.

D. Mary Rebekah Joanna Curlin married James E. George and had two children, one dying in infancy and the remaining one, Gertrude Sevier George, residing at Union City, Tennessee.

E. Nancy Alida Curlin married Martin Walker Barney. They have two children, Earle Sevier Barney, born July 17, 1890, and Pauline Curlin Barney, born Jan. 9, 1890, residence Union City, Tenn.

F. John Edward Allen Curlin married Dorothy Bain, residence Dallas, Texas. They have four daughters: (1) Laura Earl Curlin (married first Lucius Earl McBride, and had one son, Lucius Earl McBride, Jr., who married Louise Barr; Laura Earl Curlin married, second, to Alfred M. Daniel, and had one child, Elizabeth Daniel). (2) Nina May Curlin, married William Ford Nolan, and has two children, Emma Catherine Nolan, and Wilford Allen Nolan, residence Dallas, Texas. (3) Irene Ethel Curlin married Marshall William Beedle, and has three children, Edward Marshall Beedle, Charles William Beedle, and Claude Allen Beedle. Their residence is in Dallas, Texas. (4) Pauline Belle Curlin had no children.

G. James Lemuel Curlin, residence Dallas, Texas, is unmarried.

b. Henry DeCab Sevier, son of John Garoutte Sevier and Mary Mayfield Sevier, married ――――――――――― and had a son, William Henry Sevier, who lives at Mayflower, Ark.

b. William J. Sevier, son of John Garoutte Sevier and Mary Mayfield Sevier married ――――――――――― and had two daughters, Laura Sevier and Drucilla Sevier, who live at Joplin, Mo.

d. John Michael Sevier, son of John Garoutte Sevier and Mary Mayfield Sevier, married ――――――――――― and had one son, Elbridge Sevier, who lives at Dexter, Mo.

e. James J. Sevier, son of John Garoutte Sevier and Mary Mayfield Sevier, was killed in the Battle of Vicksburg 1863 in the Confederate Army.

ELIZABETH CONWAY SEVIER

9. Elizabeth Conway Sevier, daughter of John Sevier, Jr., and her grandmother. She married ――――――――――― Byers.

SOPHIA SMITH GAROUTTE SEVIER

10. Sophia Smith Garoutte Sevier was the daughter of John Sevier, Jr., and his third wife, Sophia Smith Garoutte Sevier. She was named Sophia for her mother and grandmother, Sophia Smith, wife of Michael Garoutte. She was born 1815.

LOUISA REBECCA SEVIER

11. Louisa Rebecca Sevier, daughter of John Sevier Jr., and his third wife, Sophia Smith Garoutte Sevier, was born November 21, 1816. She married Major Byrd Brown (born October 20, 1801; died March 24, 1886). She died May 20, 1842, leaving two children,
 a. John Jacob Brown
 b. Sophia Louisa Sevier Brown

a. John Jacob Brown, son of Louisa Rebecca Sevier Brown and Major Byrd Brown was born February 23, 1840. He married January 1, 1866, Esther Eliza Wilson. They had ten children, namely:

 A. Thmoas Jefferson Wilson Brown
 B. Byrd Brown
 C. Embree Sevier Brown
 D. Nolachucky Brown, died in infancy
 E. Martha Rebecca Brown
 F. William Franklin Brown
 G. John Jacob Brown, Jr.
 H. Charles Vestal Brown
 I. Mariah Louisa Brown
 J. Ella Star Brown.

Of these:

A. Thomas Jefferson Wilson, born Oct. 2, 1867, married Genevieve Arnold, of Western West Virginia, August 14, 1907. No children.

B. Byrd Brown, born March 19, 1869, married Chloe Clark, of Nance County, Nebraska, February, 1904. One daughter, Mollie May, born 1905, married Dean Huddart, January, 1823. One son, Dean Duane.

C. Embree Sevier, born May 30, 1870, married April 2, 1919, Harriet Margaret Shields, daughter of David Shields, of Washington County, Tennessee. Their children, Nancy Esther, born December 1920, Jacob Embree, born Jan. 20, 1923; David Shelby, born January 28, 1924.

D. Nola Chuckey, born February 2, 1872. Died August 26, 1873.

E. Martha Rebecca, born October 6, 1873. Died March 27, 1901.

F. William Franklin Brown, born June 24, 1875.

G. John Jacob Brown, Jr., born March 26, 1877, married Oct. 1, 1901, to Nelia Fondren, of Washington County, East Tennessee. No children.

H. Charles Vestal, born July 25, 1881, married October 20, 1907, to Lillian Miller, of Washington County, Tennessee. Their children—Thomas Sherrill, born Oct. 18, 1909.

1. Mariah Louisa, born Jan. 19, 1883, married June 9, 1909 Herman Pierce of Sullivan County, Tennessee. Their children, Ella Rowena, born April 14, 1921 and Esther Louisa, born Feb. 10, 1924.

J. Ella Star, born July 10, 1887, married April 16.1919 Hugh Miller Cox of Sullivan County, East Tennessee.

(b.)   Sophia Louisa Sevier Brown, daughter of Louisa Rebecca Sevier Brown and Major Byrd Brown, was born January 14, 1842. She married Shelby McDowell Deaderick (see Deaderick Family Volume 1 Notable Southern Families) Her second husband was George Columbus Ward and her third husband was John A. Graham. Sophia Louisa Sevier Brown had children by each of her marriages. Her children were:

    A.   John Wallace Deaderick
    B.   Mary Louisa Ward
    C.   Nellie Ward died unmarried
    D.   Esther Ruth Ward, died in infancy
    E.   William Ward, died in infancy

The only surviving children of Sophia Louisa Sevier Brown were the son of her first husband and a daughter by the second husband.

Mary Louisa Ward, daughter of Sophia Louisa Sevier Brown Ward and George Columbus Ward (whom she married December 20, 1857) married a kinsman of her mother's third husband (John A. Graham) Mary Louisa Ward married Jonathan Summerfield Graham August 5, 1870, several years before her mother's marriage to John A. Graham took place.   Mary Louisa Ward Graham and Jonathan Summerfield Graham had eleven children, namely:

    1.   Roxie Inez Graham
    2.   Henry Jackson Graham
    3.   Sarah Lou Graham
    4.   Elizabeth Emmetta Graham
    5.   Esther Ruth Graham
    6.   John Wallace Graham
    7.   Shelby Franklin Graham
    8.   Jessie May Graham
    9.   Mary Lillian Graham
    10. Girtrude Graham
    11. Orlena Graham

these last children being twins.

Of the foregoing: Roxie Inez Graham married William Clyde Dishner, April 27, 1920. (their children are William Clyde Dishner, junior, Nola State Dishner and Harry Lee Dishner); Henry Jackson Graham married Jessie Eva Smith. September 10, 1922 (their children are John Smith Graham and Jackson Dale Graham); Sarah Lou Graham married Charles Andrew Dillow, July 1, 1923 (their child is Charles Graham Dillow.

MICHAEL ROBERT SEVIER

12. Michael Robert Sevier, son of John Sevier, junior and his third wife Sophia Smith Garoutte Sevier, was born June 18, 1822. He was named after his grandfather Michael Garoutte and for his paternal uncle Captain Robert Sevier who was killed at King's Mountain. Michael Robert Sevier accompanied his brother and sister, John Garoutte Sevier and Martha Ann Sevier to Obion County in 1845. In 1859 he moved with them to Conway County Arkansas.

He married, probably before he left East Tennessee, Sarah E. Bayless, of Jonesboro, Tennessee. They had several children some of whom died young. Their children were:

a. Elbridge Gerry Sevier, died about 1922
b. Sophia T. Sevier, born about 1850
c. Samuel Sevier, died about 1900
d. Robert E. Sevier, died about 1898
e. Abraham Sevier, died about 1884
f. John Sevier, died young
g. Archibald Sevier, died young
h. Anna M. Sevier, died young
i. Mary L. Sevier, died young
j. Martha E. Sevier, died young
k. Leonidas A. Sevier, died about 1878

Of the foregoing:

Elbridge G. Sevier, son of Michael Robert Sevier and Sarah E. Bayless Sevier married Elizabeth Compton. They had ten children, namely, Elbert E. Sevier, Oliver Sevier, Thomas R. Sevier, Mike Sevier, Archibald Sevier, Katherine Sevier, Caroline Sevier, John Sevier, Arthur Sevier and Joseph Sevier.

Sophia T. Sevier, daughter of Michael Sevier and Sarah T. Bayless Sevier, married twice. She first married William A. Lavendar and had four children, namely Joseph M. Lavendar, Sarah M. Lavendar, Benjamin L. Lavendar, and Ada L. Lavendar. She married for her second husband Albert A. Mosely and had six children, namely John Mosely, Robert Mosely, Lee Mosely, Lillian Mosely, Emma Mosely and Charles Mosely.

John S. Sevier, son of Michael Robert Sevier and Sarah E. Bayless Sevier, married Cynthia M. Hall. They had six children, namely, Laura Sevier, Frank Sevier, Beulah Sevier, Lilly Sevier Emory Sevier and Charles Sevier.

Robert E. Sevier, son of Michael Robert Sevier and Sarah E. Bayless Sevier, married Beulah Harrison and had two children namely: Ethel Sevier and Shelby Sevier.

The record of this branch of the family has been furnished by Mrs. Sophia T. Moseley, the only surviving child of Michael Robert Sevier and Sarah E. Bayless Sevier.

THE SEVIER FAMILY 195

GEORGE WASHINGTON SEVIER

13. George Washington Sevier, the son of John Sevier, junior, and his third wife Sophia Smith Garoutte Sevier, was born about 1823. He received the name of his paternal uncle, George Washington Sevier, first son of Governor Sevier by Catherine Sherrill Sevier.

ANNA MARIA SEVIER

14. Anna Maria Sevier, daughter of John Sevier, junior and his third wife, Sophia Smith Garoutte Sevier, was born about 1824. She married Henry Hoss, of Jonesboro, Tennessee. They had six children namely:

1. Amanda Fadora Hoss
2. Elijah Embree Hoss
3. Archibald Hoss
4. Sophia Hoss
5. John Isaac Hoss
6. Mattie Hoss

Of the foregoing:

(1.) Amanda Fadora Hoss married Samuel J. Kirkpatrick and had ten children, namely: Minnie Kirkpatrick, (who married Charles Kirkland, and had five children, Isabel Kirkland, Winifred Kirkland, Jesse Kirkland, Mollie Kirkland and William Kirkland); Hugh Henry Kirkpatrick, (who married Nina Bell Murphey and has two children, Mildred Kirkpatrick, married Max Maloney and has a daughter, Anna Bell Maloney, and a son, Hugh Henry Kirkpatrick, junior); Paul White Kirkpatrick, (who married Vesta Pennington and has one child. Mary Harris Kirkpatrick); Samuel Sevier Kirkpatrick (who married Anna Maria Panhurst and has no children); Jessie Eugenia Kirkpatrick (who married John Henry Bowman and has two children William Bowman and John Henry Bowman, junior); Archibald Hoss Kirkpatrick (who married Bessie Cruikshanks and has four children Anna Kirkpatrick, William Kirkpatrick, Dorothy Kirkpatrick and Bessie Kirkpatrick); William Reeves Kirkpatrick (who died unmarried. Anna Kirkpatrick (who died unmarried); Mary Kirkpatrick (who died young): and Charles Prescott Kirkpatrick (who married Essie Annie Schuessler).

(2.) Elijah Embree Hoss, son of Henry and Anna Maria Sevier Hoss was born in Washington County, Tennessee, April 14, 1849. He married Abbie Bell Clarke, daughter of Edwin R. Clarke and Mary Ann Sessler Clarke. He became a distinguished Bishop of the Methodist Episcolal Church South. Died at the home of his son, Dr. Sessler Hoss, at Muskogee Oklahoma, April 23, 1919. He had three children;

a. Mary Muriel Hoss was born at Santa Ross California in 1870. She married John Headman and has two children, Francis Headman and Embree Headman.

b.   Embree E. Hoss, junior, married Blanche Divine of Chattanooga and has one son, E. E. Hoss III.

c.   Sessler Hoss, a physician of Muskogee Oklahoma, married Irene Ewing Morrow of Nashville Tennessee (see Armstrong, Luttrell, McAdoo, Cockrill, Ewing, in Notable Southern Families Vol. I and III).   Dr. Hoss died at his home in Muskogee, Oklahoma Dec. 29, 1921.   He had two children, Sessler, junior, who died in infancy and Irene Ewing Hoss.

3.   Archibald Hoss, son of Henry Hoss and Maria Sevier Hoss, married Allie Susong and has three children, Henry Hoss, Anna Hoss and Dorothy Hoss.

4.   Sophia Hoss, daughter of Henry Hoss and Anna Maria Sevier Hoss, married George D. French, of Morristown, Tennessee and had four daughters, Virginia French, who married E. R. Taylor and has one son, E. R. Taylor, junior; Josephine French, who married W. C. Kreger, of Abingdon, Virginia and has three children, Jean Sevier Kreger, W. D. Kreger, junior, and George French Kreger; Mattie French who is unmarried; and Dora French, who married———— Barrow and has no children.   She lives in Morristown.

5.   John Isaac Hoss died unmarried.

6.   Mattie Hoss born March 24, 1855, married P. H. Prince June 11, 1878 and lived in Arkansas.   She had two children, Anna Prince and William Prince.

SARAH HUNDLEY SEVIER

15.   Sarah Hundley Sevier was the daughter of John Sevier, junior, by his third wife, Sophia Smith Garoutte Sevier.   She was born in 1826.   It will be observed that there was also a Sarah by the second wife.   Hundley was a name in the Conway family and is a favorite middle name to the present time among descendants. Sarah Hundley was the name of John Sevier,junior's first wife's mother.   He named one daughter for the first wife Elizabeth Conway and one for her mother.   Sarah Hundley Sevier married first, Robert E. Humphries, and second, Shelby Currey.   In documents in Washington concerning the Sevier estate, Emmetta Humphries, administratrix of the John Sevier Estate, says that she is the child of Sarah Hundley Sevier.

ARCHIBALD MCAFEE SEVIER

16.   Archibald McAfee Sevier, son of John Sevier, junior, and his third wife, Sophia Smith Garoutte Sevier, was born August 2, 1829.   He assumed the maintenance and education of his youngest sister Martha, while he was still quite young.   He moved to Missouri in 1856.   He lived in Neosha Mo. until his death.   He married Paulina Belle Sutton but had no children.

THE SEVIER FAMILY

MARTHA ANN SEVIER

17.   Martha Ann Sevier, daughter of John Sevier, junior, and his third wife, Sophia Smith Garoutte Sevier, was born November 3, 1831.   She married Thomas P. Price in 1850 in West Tennessee where she had accompanied her brother John Garoutte Sevier with whom she made her home after the death of their father, John Sevier, junior.   She removed with her husband to Neosho Mo.   They had eight children among them:

- a.   Frank J. Price
- b.   Albert H. Price
- c.   Henry T. Price
- d.   (a daughter) who married C. M. Harland of Memphis
- e.   (a daughter who married B. P. Armstrong of Neosho, Mo.

Mrs. Martha Ann Sevier Price lived until a few years ago. She resided in Memphis with her daughter, Mrs. C. M. Hart'and, after the death of Thomas P. Price in Neosho in 1905.

CHAPTER FOUR
Elizabeth Sevier

ELIZABETH SEVIER

Elizabeth Sevier, daughter of Governor John Sevier and his first wife Sarah Hawkins Sevier, was their eldest daughter. Her birth took place in Virginia about the year 1768. She came to the "Mountains" with her parents in 1773, arriving at the new home on Christmas day. Her marriage to William Clark said to be a veteran of King's Mountain and certainly a participant in other military expeditions of the time, took place about 1786. Her eldest child, Elizabeth Clark was born, according to family records, July 20, 1787.

William Clark was in Governor Sevier's Regiment at King's Mountain it is said and served at other times in Governor Sevier's Regiment. He was born in Shenandoah County Virginia, April 7, 1757. He lived in Pendleton District, South Carolina, but moved late in life to Hall County, Georgia, where he died June 4, 1843. It was while he was a resident of Washington County, North Carolina (now Tennessee) that he served with Governor Sevier and that his marriage to Elizabeth Sevier took place.

It is said that Elizabeth Sevier Clark died at For. Madison South Carolina and that all of her children were born in South Carolina. She died before 1792, for February 14, 1792 William Clark married Ruth Goodwin in Franklin County, Georgia.

Elizabeth Sevier Clark and William H. Clark had three children who are positively known and probably a fourth child. Documents in Washington concerning the Sevier estate mention her three children, Elizabeth, Sarah and John and omit the fourth child, Ruth. But family records give the name of this child and I therefore include her here. There may be an error in the list or Ruth may not have been living when the list was prepared. There are some errors and some omissions in the Washington documents.

I do not know the order in which these names should be p'aced but Elizabeth Clark it is said by descendants, was the eldest child.

Children of Elizabeth Sevier Clark and William H. Clark:

1. Elizabeth Clark
2. Sarah Hawkins Clark
3. John Clark
4. Ruth Clark

Elizabeth Sevier Clark probably died shortly after the birth of her last child as Major Clark married his second wife February 14, 1792.   It is said that at least one of Elizabeth's children, Sarah Hawkins Clark, was reared by Gov. Sevier and that she married from his house.   It is possible that all of Elizabeth's children lived with Gov. and Mrs. Sevier and that the little boy called "Sevier" by Gov. Sevier in his Journal was Elizabeth's son, John, who may have had Sevier as a middle name.   (Major Clark had a son however by his second wife named Sevier and also one named John.

January 25, 1795: Gov. Sevier in his Journal speaks of the "horses that ran away with Sevier and Ruthy"! Ruthy was his daughter. "Sevier" may be the son of Mary Ann Sevier who was a widow and seems to have made her home with her father, or he may be John (Sevier) Clark son of Elizabeth.

William Clark who married Elizabeth Sevier was born April 7, 1757, in Shanandoah County, Virginia.   While a resident of Washington County, North Carolina in 1777 he enlisted in Captain Thomas Price's Company. Col. John Sevier's Regiment.   In 1778 he served in Col. Valentine Sevier's Regiment.   June 1780 he served in Captain Asher's Company and in 1781 in Captain Williams' Company, Col. John Sevier's Regiment.

About 1785 he married Elizabeth Sevier who died) sometime before February 14, 1792.

February 14, 1792 he married in Franklin County, Georgia, Ruth Goodwin born May 14, 1771.   He died in Hall County, Georgia June 4, 1843.

The children of Major Clark and Ruth Goodwin Clark were:
John Clark born November 5, 1792·
Oliver Clark born October 5, 1794
Sevier Clark born September 11, 1797
Sabra Clark born March 3, 1799

"Major and Mrs. William H. Clark" were present at the wedding of Catherine Sevier to Richard Campbell, December 24, 1795, and at other times they were in the household of Gov. and Mrs. Sevier for visits, but this Mrs. Clark is evidently Major Clark's second wife.   Major Clark's widow, Ruth Goodwin Clark, was granted a pension in her application executed April 2, 1844.

ELIZABETH CLARK

Elizabeth Clark daughter of Elizabeth Sevier and William H. Clark was born in South Carolina, July 20, 1786.   She married John Elston in 1801.

The information which follows regarding the descendants of

Elizabeth Clark Elston and John Elston was furnished by Mr. Elston Luttrell ana is used in the form in which he prepared it.

John Elston and Elizabeth Clark Elston reared a family of eleven children, the first six born in Pendleton District, South Carolina, and the last five born in Habersham County, Georgia. They lived near the South Carolina and Georgia line, on the Tugaloo River, first on the South Carolina side in what was then the Pendleton, District, later Oconee County, until 1815-16, then on the Georgia side in Habersham County until 1834, at which date they moved to the Creek nation and settled in the upper Choccolocco. valley, in Benton (afterwards Calhoun) County, Alabama. Five of their children, namely, Sevier, William, John Clark, Ruth and Martha, came with them to Alabama.

The children of John and Elizabeth Clark Elston were eleven in number, as follows:

1. Allen Elston, born May 25, 1802.
2. Sally Elston, born August 8, 1805.
3. Neaty Elston, born June 29, 1807.
4. Nancy Elston, born September 16, 1809.
5. Sabra Elston, born April 8, 1812.
6. Sevier Elston, born December 27, 1814.
7. William Elston, born April 6, 1817.
8. Elizabeth Elston, born October 23, 1819.
9. John Clark Elston, born July 4, 1822.
10. Ruth Elston, born July 18, 1825.
11. Martha Elston, born April 17, 1831.

John Elston and his sons, were among the pioneer settlers of old Benton County, Alabama. They bought and entered large plantations of valuable land around the old Corn Grove postoffice in the upper Choccolocco Valley. John Elston died July 11, 1853; just seven days after signing his last will and testament. His wife Elizabeth died November 11 1845. They lie buried side by side in the family burying ground on the Allen Elston home place near the house. Several of their children and grandchildren are also buried there.

I—ALLEN ELSTON

Allen Elston, the eldest child of John Elston and Elizabeth Clark Elston, and grandson of David Elston, of New Jersey, was born in Pendleton District, South Carolina, May 25, 1802. He married Martha Humphreys of the same place in 1822 Martha Humphreys was born in South Carolina October. 23. 1806. They emigrated to the Choccolocco valley in Alabama about 1836, and settled in Benton (now Calhoun) County, near the Corn Grove postoffice, Here he died May 21, 1879, age 77 years.

Martha Humphreys Elston, wife of Allen Elston, died January 2, 1855. Mr. Elston afterwards married a second wife, Mrs. Minerva Gibson. The children of the first wife Martha Humphreys Elston, were ten in number, as follows:

1. Nancy Elston, born June 23, 1823.
2. Sabra Elston, born May 6, 1825.
3. Martha Elizabeth Elston, born June 8, 1827.
4. William Clark Elston, born March 6, 1829.
5. Sarah Elston, born June 17, 1831.
6. John Humphreys Elston, born June 18, 1835.
7. Kitty Hudson Elston, born October 31, 1837.
8. Susan Frances Elston, born February 14, 1840.
9. Eva Borders Elston, born Septeber 18, 1842.
10. Ann W. Elston, born October 24, 1844; died in infancy.

For further account of these see later.

II—SALLY (OR SARAH) ELSTON EDDINS

Sally Elston, second child of John Elston and Elizabeth Clark Elston, was born in Pendleton district, South Carolina, August 5, 1805. Her name is written "Sally" in the family Bible, but in her father's will she is mentioned as Sarah. She married James Eddins, of Franklin County, Georgia; died in Pickens District, South Carolina, in 1831 or 1832, leaving four daughters and one son. James Eddins afterwards married Salina Trimmer, of Toxaway Creek, South Carolina, and moved to Pickens County, Alabama, in 1835. He died December 22, 1877.

III—NEATY ELSTON DENMAN

Neaty Elston, the third child of John Elston and Elizabeth Clark Elston, was born in Pendleton District, South Carolina, June 29, 1807. She was married to Blake Denman near Cherokee Mountain, Habersham County, Ga. They lived there several years and then moved to Alabama and settled on a farm near Jacksonville. Here she died about 1852. Blake Denman died at the same place about 1886. They had seven or more children, whose names are not known.

IV—NANCY ELSTON

Nancy Elston, fourth child of John and Elizabeth Clark Elston, was born September 16, 1809. She is supposed to have died young.

V—SABRA ELSTON YOWELL

Sabra Elston, fifth child of John Elston and Elizabeth (Clark) Elston, was born in Pendeleton dist., S. C., April 8, 1812. She was married to James Allen Yowell, of Lincoln County, Tennessee. They had perhaps nine or ten children. She died there 1855-60.

VI—SEVIER ELSTON

Sevier Elston, sixth child of John Elston and Elizabeth (Clark) Elston, was born in Pendleton dist., S. C., December 27, 1814. He went to Alabama with his father in 1834. He married in S. C., Elizabeth B. Davis, of Pickens District, in 1847. They settled in Benton County, with others of the family, and acquired large agricultural interests. They had an only son, Harvey Davis Elston, born August 3, 1861, died July 11, 1869. Sevier Elston was postmaster at Corn Grove postoffice from 1842 to 1852. He died September 26, 1885.

VII—WILLIAM ELSTON

William Elston, seventh child of John Elston and Elizabeth (Clark) Elston, was born in Habersham County, Georgia, April 6, 1817; came to Alabama with his parents in 1834. He married there Miss Jane Worthington near White Plains, Calhoun County, Alabama, 18—. Had one daughter, Eleanor Elston, and an infant that died young. He died in 1854 of pneumonia. In 1857 his widow Jane and daughter Eleanor went out to Texas with some relatives. There Mrs. Elston married a second husband, name not known, and then a third named Broadus. They were yet living there in Burleson County, in 1881. The daughter Eleanor (later spoken of as Annie Elizabeth) married twice in Texas; 1st to A. Judson Jones, of Virginia. 2nd in 1879 to William Elston Taylor, her half-cousin from Talladega, Ala., he being a grandson of Allen Elston, Sr., of S. C. There were two sons by this union: (1) William Elston Taylor, Jr. (2) Andrew Law Taylor.

VIII—ELIZABETH (ELSTON) WEIR

Elizabeth Elston, eighth child of John Elston and Elizabeth (Clark) Elston, was born in Habersham County, Georgia, October 23, 1819. Was married to Dr. John R. Weir, of Blount County, Tenn., in about 1835. Had several children. About 1842 moved to Washington County, Texas Elizabeth died there April 20, 1851. Dr. Weir also died there in 1878-9. Two or three of their children were living in Texas in 1881. We find the following record of some of the children in the family Bible of John Elston, Mrs. Weir's father: (1) Mary Weir, born July 17, 1836, (2) Cullen Weir, born March 27, 1838. (3) Third child born February 26, 1840.

IX—JOHN CLARK ELSTON

John Clark Elston, ninth child of John Elston and Elizabeth (Clark) Elston, was born at Owl Swamp, in Habersham County, Ga., July 4, 1822. Moved with his parents to Alabama in 1834 He married January 21, 1846, Selina Jones, of Pendleton dist., S. C., a first cousin of James M. Jones, husband of his niece Nancy Elston. They lived in Benton (Calhoun) County, Alabama, till about 1869, then went to Johnson County, Texas, where he died March 19, 1896, Grandview postoffice. They had four children. For record of these and the grandchildren see later.

X—RUTH (ELSTON) MATTISON

Ruth Elston, tenth child of John Elston and Elizabeth (Clark) Elston, was born in Habersham County, Georgia, July 18, 1825. Migrated with parents to Alabama in 1834. Was married to Glover Mattison, in Alabama, about 1838. Reared four children. They moved to Denton County, Texas, in about 1866, and Ruth (Elston) Mattison died there July 8, 1870. Two of her children were living there in 1881. We have no further record of the children.

XI—MARTHA (ELSTON) HOLLINGSWORTH

Martha Elston, eleventh child of John Elston and Elizabeth (Clark) Elston was born in Habersham County, Georgia, April 17, 1831. Came to Alabama in 1834; was married at home about 1846 to Stephen P. Hollingsworth, of Rusk County, Texas, and they went at once to Texas to make their home, settling in Johnson County. Mr. Hollingsworth died there in the fall of 1879. Mrs. Hollingsworth was living there in 1881. They had three children.

CHILDREN OF ALLEN AND MARTHA (HUMPHREYS) ELSTON OF CALHOUN COUNTY, ALABAMA

I—NANCY (ELSTON) JONES

Nancy (Elston) Jones, daughter and first child of Allen and Martha (Humphreys) Elston, born in Pendleton District, S. C July 23, 1823; came with her parents to Alabama in 1836; was married to James Martin Jones, of Tennessee, July 3, 1838. They lived a few years in Petersburg, Tennessee; then came to Benton (now Calhoun) County, Alabama, and lived out their days in this county. James Martin Jones was born in Maury County, Tennessee, September 12, 1812; died in Jacksonville, Alabama, January 16, 1875, and was buried in Oxford, Alabama. Nancy (Elston) Jones died in Jacksonville, December 28, 1875, and was buried in Oxford cemetery. The children of this couple were seven in number. For further account of the children see later.

II—SABRA (ELSTON) HAYS

Sabra (Elston) Hays, daughter and second child of Allen and Martha (Humphreys) Elston, was born in Pendleton dist., S. C., May 6, 1825; came to Alabama with her parents in 1836; was married February 11, 1841, in Tennessee, to John B. Hays of that state while on a visit to her sister, Nancy Jones. John Hays was born Nov. 28, 1816. They settled at White Plains, Alabama. John Hays died April 9, 1863. Mrs. Hays died Sept., 26, 1886. They had nine children as follows, all born at White Plains:

1. Martha J. Hays, born January 14, 1842.
2. Allen A. Hays, born August 7, 1843.
3. Clifton C. Hays, born Dec. 6, 1845.
4. Infant daughter, born and died in 1847.
5. Alice V. Hays, born July 22, 1849.
6. Clara C. Hays, born December 24, 1852.
7. John Knox Hays, born March 4, 1855.
8. James W. Hays, born January 28, 1858.
9. Addie L. Hays, born Nov. 9, 1862.

III—MARTHA ELIZABETH (ELSTON) 1, DENDY; 2, DOYLE; 3, LUTTRELL

Martha Elizabeth (Elston) 1, Dendy; 2, Doyle; 3, Luttrell; third child of Allen and Martha (Humphreys) Elston, was born in Pendleton District, S. C., June 8, 1827. Moved to Alabama with her parents in 1836. Was married at home February 25, 1847, to James W. Dendy, of South Carolina. They had two children, one of whom died in infancy. The other child, James Allen Dendy, was born May 27, 1848; went out to Texas when a young man and reared a family there; was still living there in 1918 near Weatherford. James W. Dendy (the husband and father) was born March 21, 1823, and was a first cousin to his wife Martha E. Elston, their mothers being sisters.

Mrs. Martha E. (Elston) Dendy. married in 1863 a second husband, Dr. James A. Doyle, a widower with several grown children. They lived in Fort Madison, Oconee County, S. C., until Mr. Doyle's death about 1887. Mrs. Doyle then went to live with her son, James Allen Dendy, in Texas, where she remained until 1898. She then went to Oxford, Ala., where she was married to her widowed brother-in-law, Harvey W. Luttrell. They lived happily there until his death which occurred July 26, 1899. She again returned to Texas to make her home with her son, James A. Dendy, near Weatherford. Here she died October 8, 1916, aged 89 years. She had no children by her second and third marriage.

IV—WILLIAM CLARK ELSTON

William Clark Elston, son and fourth child of Allen and Martha (Humphreys) Elston, was born in Pendleton District, S. C., March 6, 1829; came to Benton County, Ala., with the family in 1836. He married Adline Findley, of Benton County, Alabama, in 1848. Adline was born Nov. 23, 1829. They moved to Arkansas in 1870 and settled in the Red River Valley near the Texas line. Here the mother Adline, died February 19, 1877. Mr. Elston, later moved over into Oklahoma, leaving most of his children (now grown up) in Arkansas and Louisiana. He died in Oklahoma in 1899.

The children of William Clark and Adline (Findley) Elston were nine in number, six sons and three daughters. The sons came to be very successful business men in and around Shreveport, La. For further account of these see later.

V—SARAH (ELSTON) BOWLING

Sarah (Elston) Bowling, daughter of Allen and Martha (Humphreys) Elston, was born in S. C. June 17, 1831; came to Alabama with her parents in 1836. She married February 25, 1847, Dr. William E. Bowling, of Georgia. They settled near the Corn Grove postoffice where they lived out their lives. Dr. Bowling was a farmer, school teacher and practicing physician. He died March 6. 1899. His wife died June 4, 1904. The children of this union were six in number. For further account of them and their offspring see later.

VI—JOHN HUMPHREYS ELSTON

John Humphreys Elston, son and sixth child of Allen and Martha (Humphreys) Elston, was born in S. C. June 18, 1835. He lived on the old home place with his father all his life. He was a leading and highly esteemed citizen and served in the Confederate States army in the War Between the States. He married Mollie Reagan, of Talladega County, Alabama, about 1876. They had two children: 1, Janie Elston, daughter, born March 16, 1878. 2, Louie Elston, son, born November 9, 1879. In the year 1880 Mr Elston went on a tour through Texas and died there May 10, 1880.

VII—KITTY HUDSON (ELSTON) HUDSON

Kitty Hudson (Elston) Hudson, daughter and seventh child of Allen and Martha (Humphreys) Elston, was born in Benton County, Alabama, October 31, 1837. She was married to J. Gip Hudson at home in 1868. She died November 5, 1874, leaving two or three small children.

VIII—SUSAN FRANCES (ELSTON) LUTTRELL

Susan Frances (Elston) Luttrell, daughter and eighth child of Allen and Martha (Humphreys) Elston, was born in Benton County, Alabama, February 14, 1840. She grew up intellectually active and was favored with good academic education. Her religious and moral ideals were high. She moved in cultured and refined circles of society. She was married December 14, 1856, to Harvey Wilkerson Luttrell, formerly of Knox County, Tennessee, but then of Oxford, Alabama. They lived in and near Oxford to the end of their lives. Mrs. Luttrell died at Oxford April 25, 1897. Mr Luttrell died same place July 26, 1899. The children of this union were eleven, as follows:

1. Corrie Luttrell, dau. born April 1, 1858.
2. Oscar F. Luttrell, son, born June 14 1859.
3. Elston Luttrell, son, born May 26, 1861.
4. Chester M. Luttrell, son, born October 8, 1862.
5. Bruce F. Luttrell, son, born July 13, 1868.
6. Rush Luttrell, son, born December 7, 1870.
7. A son, not named, born Jan. 14, 1872. Died 1872.
8. Katie Luttrell, dau., born July 4, 1875. Died 1875.
9. Marcy Luttrell, son, born January 16, 1877.
10 and 11. Frank and Fred Luttrell, twin sons, born March 28, 1879. Frank died Aug. 24, 1879. Fred died Aug. 14, 1879.
For further account of these children see later.

IX—EVA BORDERS (ELSTON) DeARMAN

Eva Borders (Elston) DeArman, daughter and ninth child of Allen and Martha (Humphreys) Elston, was born in Benton (later Calhoun) County, Alabama, September 12, 1842. She was married to James T. DeArman of the same county December 24, 1865. They lived out their lives in this county at different locations. Mrs. De-Arman died in Anniston, Ala., February 10, 1905. Mr. DeArman died same place a few years later. Of this union there were six children, as follows:

1. Alma Newell DeArman, daughter, born Nov. 14, 1866.
2. Cleff Elston DeArman, son, born June 21, 1869.
3. Kittie Turnipseed DeArman, dau., born July 20, 1873.
4. Louie DeArman, son, born October 31, 1876.
5. Retha DeArman, daughter, born July 9, 1878.
6. Pearl DeArman, daughter, born May 15, 1883.
For further account of these children see later.

X—ANN W. ELSTON

Ann W. Elston, daughter and last child of Allen and Martha (Humphreys) Elston, was born in Benton County, Alabama, October 24, 1844; died March 9, 1845.

CHILDREN OF JOHN CLARK ELSTON AND SELINA (JONES) ELSTON

1. Mary (Elston) Keith, daughter and first child, was born in 1847-8; was married to a Mr. Keith; died in Tennessee.

2. Roxie Carolina (Elston) Snow, daughter, and second child, was born August 14, 1849. She married in Oxford Alabama, Nov. 26, 1868, Clark Snow, youngest son of Dudley and Priscilla (Mounger) Snow, of Oxford. Here also they lived out their days. Roxie died in Oxford July 4th, 1909. Clark Snow died July 19th, 1919. They had seven children. See account of the children later.

3. Brazora (Elston) Heath, daughter, born————; was married to Chester Heath. Died in Cleburne, Texas; left children, one of them Arthur Heath of Artesia, New Mexico.

4. John Jabez Elston, son, born at Corn Grove December 24, 1853. Died January 24, 1856. Buried on the Allen Elston home place.

CHILDREN OF ROXIE CAROLINA (ELSTON) SNOW AND CLARK SNOW, OF OXFORD, ALABAMA

1. Kate Corinne Snow, daughter, born in Oxford, Alabama, Jan. 28, 1870; was married to Thomas Daniel Jackson June 17, 1896; died June 10, 1915. She left one daughter Joyce Elston Jackson born Dec. 5, 1904.

2. Ada Elston Snow, daughter, born December 8, 1871; was married to Charles Caleb Morgan November 17, 1897. To this union were born two sons: 1, Marechal Clark Morgan; 2, Norman Snow Morgan.

3. Ruth Snow, daughter, born in Oxford, Alabama, February 17, 1876; was married to Samuel Hallman December 15, 1910. Residence Oxford, Alabama. No children.

4. Julius Fane Snow, son, born March 22, 1878. Died January 13, 1879.

5. Maxie Snow, daughter, born July 19, 1879; was married to Joe L. Montgomery January 4, 1920.

6. Norman Lee Snow, son, born June 7, 1883. Not married.

7. Mary Winnifred Snow, daughter, born October 11, 1885; was married to James N. Griffin December 19, 1907. To this union one son, Jim Snow Griffin, born January 25, 1918.

CHILDREN OF NANCY (ELSTON) JONES AND JAMES MARTIN JONES

1. Mary Elizabeth (Jones) Hames,, daughter and first child, was born in Petersburg, Tennessee, April 18, 1843. Was married in Jacksonville, Ala., in 1866, to Captain William M. Hames and is yet living there. Had six children. Captain Hames died Feb. 8, 1908.

2. Joseph A. Jones, son, born in Alabama April 28, 1845. Married and had family of several children. Residence, Birmingham Ala.

3. Abner Gregory Jones, son, born in Alabama December, 1846. Died September 16, 1863.

4. Rowena (Jones) McClurkin, daughter, born 1848. Was married November 6, 1866, to James McClurkin. He lived near Oxford, Ala. for a number of years and raised a family of seven children. Husband died and she now lives in Jacksonville, Florida. The seven children are:

a. Curtis McClurkin, son, born 1867. Died in Anniston, Ala.

b. Joseph J. McClurkin, son, born December 10, 1868.

c. Burt McClurkin, son, born October 25, 1870.

d. Florence McClurkin, daughter, born August 30, 1875. Died———.

e. Walter McClurkin, son, born 1877.

f. Avery McClurkin, son, born October, 1881.

g. George P. McClurkin, son, born ———. Died———.

5. Mattie (Jones) Lester, daughter, born December 1, 1851. Was married February 4, 1885, to a Mr. Lester. Died in Jacksonville, Ala.

6. Alice (Jones) Camp, daughter, born December 2, 1862. Married.

7. Walter Jones, son, born June 1, 1864. Died in Anniston.

POSTERITY OF WILLIAM CLARK ELSTON AND ADLINE (FINDLEY) ELSTON OF ALABAMA

(1) FANNIE LEE (ELSTON) 1, HARRIS; 2, HARRIS

Fannie Lee (Elston) 1, Harris; 2, Harris, daughter and first child, was born in Alabama, in 1849; was married to Walter Harris, of Texas, and to this union were born two children, George and Walter O. Walter Harris died and then his widow Fannie Lee married a second husband, George Harris, brother of her first husband, and to this union was born one daughter, Golda. The mother died in Texas about 1878. For account of these children see later.

(2) (3) (4) (5) HENRY WORD ELSTON, WALTER ELSTON, HORACE ELSTON AND MARTHA ELSTON, four children of William Clark Elston are all mentioned as having died in childhood.

(6) JOSEPH WALKER ELSTON

Joseph Walker Elston, son, born in Alabama November 3, 1860. Went to Arkansas with his father's family about 1870. When reaching maturity began service as station agent with the V.S.&P. Railway in Louisiana. Was in this service a number of years and also engaged in mercantile business and was quite successful. He married at Haughton, La. December 8, 1886, Emily Ogilvie Moore, a school teacher from Georgia. To this union were born in Haughton, La., nine children. See later. The father moved to Shreveport, La and prospered with his brother-in-law until the family jointly were possessed of several large river bottom plantations, oil land, an interest in one several large river bottom plantations, oil land, an interest in one of the city banks, and the commercial business of Elston, Prince & McDade, (wholesale grocers and cotton factors) and seventeen producing oil wells, all located in the vicinity of Shreveport. Joseph W. Elston died September 16, 1922.

(7) PERCY PELHAM ELSTON

Percy Pelham Elston, son, born in Alabama, March 30, 1867. Lived most of his life in Haughton and Shreveport, La., where he was associated with his brothers in business. Died in 1898 at the age of 31. Was never married.

(8) ROSA PEARL (ELSTON), 1, ALLEN; 2, PRINCE

Rosa Pearl (Elston), 1, Allen; 2, Prince; daughter, born Jan., 5, 1870. She married first Pleasant D. Allen, of New Orleans, a railway trainman, and by him had two sons, Lawrence Elston and Joseph William. Mr. Allen was killed in a railway accident. Rosa Pearl later married a second time Joseph Wilson Prince. No children by this union. They lived on their two-thousand-acre plantation a few miles from Shreveport, La. For account of the Allen children see later.

(9) CHARLES H. ELSTON

Charles H. Elston, son, born April 5, 1873. Married Mamie Boone, and to this union was born one son, Charles Joseph Elston, April 21, 1898, at Doyline, La., and he married Peggy Eva Green February 18, 1921, and had one son.

CHILDREN OF FANNIE LEE (ELSTON) HARRIS

1. George Harris, son, by first husband Walter Harris, was born in Texas.

2. Walter Campbell Harris, born in Texas___———; married and had four children: (1) Fannie Lee Harris; (2) Juanita Harris; (3) Margaret Harris; (4) Walter Campbell Harris, Jr.

3. Golda Harris, daughter by second husband, George Harris, born in Texas————; m. George Frank Brooks and had two daughters: (1) Fannie Lee Brooks; (2) Margaret Brooks. The mother Golda (Harris) Brooks died in Temple, Texas.

CHILDREN OF JOSEPH WALKER ELSTON, OF LA

1. Julia Moore Elston, daughter, born in Haughton, La., Sept. 26, 1887. Married Buford Dean Battle in Shreveport, La., Aug. 27, 1919.

2. Dudley Clark Elston, son, born February 13, 1889. Married first Myrtle Lawrence April 29, 1907. To this union were born three children: (1) Ruth Elston, b. July 27, 1909. (2) Dudley Clark Elston, Jr., b. April 4, 1911. (3) Paul Lawrence Elston, b. June 7, 1912. Dudley Clark Elston married a second wife Una Lee Harrell, and to this union have been born three children: (1) Joseph Harrell Elston, b. September 28, 1918. (2) Robert Douglas Elston, b. March 2, 1921. (3) Evelyn Claire Elston, b. January 28, 1923.

3. Ethel Earl Elston, daughter, born at Haughton, La., September 12, 1890. Was married to Ross E. McDade May 24, 1911, and to this union have been born three daughters: (1) Ethel Elston McDade, (2) Emily Sarah McDade, (3) Juliet Adeline McDade.

4. Parks Moore Elston, son, born at Haughton, La., January 26, 1892. Married Lucy Nicholson, and to this union have been born three daughters: (1) Eleanor Earle Elston, b. May 7, 1917. (2) Ethel Lemerle Elston, b. January 5, 1920. (3) Dorothy Lilian Elston, b. March 28, 1922.

5. Joseph Walker Elston, Jr., son, born at Haughton, La., Nov., 9, 1894. Married Wilhelmina McDade. She was born January 22, 1898. To this union have been born four children: (1) Margaret Lindsey Elston, b. July 12, 1917. (2) Joseph Walker Elston (III), b. Nov., 22, 1919. (3) Mamie Elizabeth Elston, b. November 19, 1921. (4) Wilhelmina Elston, b. September 4, 1923.

6. William Word Elston, son, born December 27, 1894. Not married.

7. Robert Lee Elston, son, born February 15, 1897. Not married.

8. Harry Paul Elston, son, born July 15, 1899. He finished his education with A. B. degree at Washington University, St. Louis, Missouri, in 1923. Married Mildred Gibbons of St. Louis April 12, 1924. She was raised in London, England, and came to St. Louis with her parents in 1919. H. P. Elston is one of the managing heads of the large wholesale grocery and cotton business of Elston, Prince & McDade, of Shreveport, La.

9. Emily Elizabeth Elston, daughter and last child of Joseph Walker Elston, Sr, and Emily O. (Moore) Elston, was born in Haughton, La., September 5, 1901. She was married June 12, 1924, to Floyd Reynolds Hodges. Residence, Shreveport, La.

CHILDREN OF ROSA PEARL (ELSTON) 1, ALLEN

1. Lawrence Elston Allen, son, born in New Orleans, Nov., 12 1897. Not married. Lives in California.

2. Joseph William Allen, son, born in New Orleans Jan., 11, 1904. Married Mildred Love January 3, 1923. at Shreveport. Resides in California.

CHILDREN OF SARAH (ELSTON) BOWLING AND DR. WM. E. BOWLING OF CALHOUN COUNTY, ALABAMA

(1) MARTHA ELIZABETH BOWLING BARKER, the first child, was born December 29, 1847; was married to Abiah Morgan Barker September 26, 1865, in Alabama, but went at once to Texas, where the family afterward lived. She died in DeLeon, Texas, in 1922; husband yet living there in 1924, age 81. Their cihldren were five in number as follows:

a. George Ephraim Barker, b. July 20, 1866, married Cora Womble. Has several children and grandchildren. Residence, Waco, Texas.

b. Alban Eustace Barker, b. March 5, 1868. Married and has children. Residence, DeLeon, Texas (1924).

c. William Barker, b. September 26, 1869. Married and has children. Residence, DeLeon, Texas (1924).

d. Mollie Barker, b. —————. Married first a Ross; second a Hammett. Residence, DeLeon, Texas (1924).

e. Evan Barker, b. —————. Residence, DeLeon, Texas.

(2) GEORGE W. BOWLING, son, b. June 29, 1849. Died April 1861.

(3) VIRGINIA CUNNINGHAM (BOWLING) EVANS, third child born October 10, 1850; was married to Josephus M. Evans, October 19, 1871. They lived at Heflin, Alabama. The mother died there January 8, 1919. The children of this union were nine in number as follows:

a. Lena Georgia Evans, b. July 18, 1872; was married to W. Jack Vaughn November 24, 1892; Has two children. Residence, Heflin, Alabama.

b. Ewell Kirkham Evans, son, b. December 1873; d. 1875.

c. Jesse Evans, son, b. September 20, 1875; married Susie Belle Ingram, of Opelika, Alabama, December 23, 1902; has four children; residence Anniston, Alabama.

d. William Evans, son, b. 1877; died young.

e. Alex Olin Evans, son, b. July 23, 1880; married Minnie Lee Harris January 1, 1907; died March 30, 1914; had one child that died young.

f. Cynthia Elston Evans, daughter, b. February 11, 1883; died May 1, 1885.

g. Martin Josephus Evans, son, b. March 14, 1885; residence, Heflin, Alabama.

h. George Bismarck Evans, son, b. October 3, 1887; married Onnie Lou Black October 8, 1913; one child; wife died 1920. Residence, Heflin, Alabama.

i. Bruce Knox Evans, son, b. March 5, 1890; married Nellie Mae Grant November 3, 1914; one son; residence Anniston, Alabama.

(4) CYNTHIA BORDERS (BOWLING) WRIGHT, fourth child, was born Sept. 7, 1856; was married to Eli Martin Wright Dec. 17, 1874. Mr. Wright died within a few years. She died at Heflin, Ala., 1919. The children were two, as follows:

1. Lizzie Martin Wright, daughter, born July 9, 1880; married Ulysses Vaughn; has two children, Ruth and Martin. Lives at Heflin, Ala.

2. Elijah Allen Wright, son, born 1882; married ——————. Wife deceased. Two children, Flora and Allen. Residence, Heflin, Ala.

(5) SALLY JACKSON (BOWLING) FAULKNER, fifth child, was born December 10, 1861. Was married January 30, 1879, to John Thomas Faulkner. Residence, (1924) 1801 Copeland Avenue N, Birmingham, Ala. J. T. Faulkner was born in Cobb County, Ga., Feb. 7, 1856, and died in Birmingham March 23, 1912. The children of this union were eleven in number, as follows:

1. John Thomas Faulkner, Jr., born and died November, 1879.

2. Maud Virginia Faulkner, da., b. May 26, 1861; died May 28, 1882.

3. Thomas Byron Faulkner, son, b. April 9, 1883; married Katherine Gossett Dec. 2, 1906; one son, Thos. B., Jr., b. Oct. 12, 1909

4. Sarah Blanche Faulkner, da., b. Dec. 12, 1886, was married May 12, 1909, to Walter Douglas Miles; has one dau., Sallie Blanche, b. April 29, 1916.

5. William Ralph Faulkner, son, twin to Blanche, b. Dec. 12, 1886; married Nov. 20, 1910, Margaret Kathleen Saunders; has one da., May Christine, b. Aug. 12, 1912.

6. Jacob L. Faulkner, son, b. July 26, 1889. Not married.

7. Frank Elston Faulkner, son, b. Oct. 10, 1891; married April 2, 1910, Dora Williams; has one da., Hazel, b. Nov. 26, 1911.

8. May Faulkner, dau., b. May 6, 1894; died Nov. 30, 1898.

9. Ruth Elizabeth Fulkner, dau., b. May 20, 1896; was married June 10, 1916, to Melvin D. Jones; has one dau., Dorothy Elizabeth, b. Mar. 23, 1919.

10. Fred L. Faulkner, son, b. Mar. 4, 1900; married Nov. 10, 1920, Louise S. Collins, of Biringham, Ala.

11. George Randolph Faulkner, son and last child, b. Nov. 16, 1902.

(6)__WILLIAM BISMARCK BOWLING, son and last child of Sarah Elston and Dr. William E. Bowling, was born in Calhoun Co., Ala., Sept 24, 1870. Received high school education. Taught school, studied law, was elected to Congress several terms and is now (1924) serving. Married June 2, 1896, at LaFayette, Ala., Frances Steele Collins, whose parents were from London, Eng. Their children are four in number, as follows:

1. George Randolph Bowling, son, b. March 7, 1897; married Dec. 7, 1922, Sally Susan Dowdell; has one son, George Randolph Bowling, Jr., b. May 12, 1924. Residence, LaFayette, Ala.

2. Marian Elston Bowling, dau., b. Mar. 28, 1899; married to George Luckie Jenkins June 12, 1824. Residence, LaFayette, Ala.

3. Sarah Frances Bowling, dau., b. Jan. 18, 1901; not married.

4. Elizabeth Bowling, dau., died in infancy, 1904

CHILDREN OF SUSAN FRANCES (ELSTON) LUTTRELL AND HARVEY WILKERSON LUTTRELL, OF CALHOUN CO., ALA.

(1) CORRIE LUTTRELL SOWELL, daughter and first child, was born in Oxford, Ala., April 1, 1858. Was married to Charles L. Sowell, of Brewton, Ala., Oct. 22, 1885. Died May 8, 1903. Had no children.

(2) OSCAR FOWLER LUTTRELL, son, b. June 14, 1859. In 1889 he and others organized the Bank of Brewton, at Brewton, Ala., and he served as cashier of this institution for a period of twenty-four years. He married April 12 ,1893, Mollie Magill Oden, daughter of John P. Oden of Syllacauga, Ala. He died in Brewton, Ala., July 23, 1922. The children were four in number, all sons, as follows:

1. A son, not named, born May 20, 1895. Died in infancy.

2. John Oden Luttrell, born Sept. 10, 1896. Married. Residence, Denver, Colorado (1924).

3. Oscar Forney Luttrell, born June 13, 1899. Married in Atlanta, Ga., Aug. 23, 1922, Eliza M. Fariss. Residence, Atlanta.

4. Frank Alex Luttrell, born Dec. 16, 1901. Not married. Lives with his mother in Brewton, Ala.

(3) ELSTON LUTTRELL, third child, born near Oxford, Ala., May 26, 1861. Married in Florida July 15, 1886, Lucy Barber, daughter of James L. and Ellen M. Barber, of Kentucky. Lived some years in Oxford, Ala. Later located in Brewton, Ala., where he has since been engaged in mercantile business. The children of this union are five in number, as follows:

1. Randolph Luttrell, son, born in Oxford, Ala., May 29, 1888. Married Georgia Binion, daughter of J. T. Binion, of Dothan, Ala., July 4, 1907. Residence, Brewton, Ala., since 1897. The children of this union are: 1, Lucile Luttrell, born July 9, 1909. 2, Randolph Binion Luttrell, born March 26, 1912. 3, Joe Bell Luttrell, born March 1, 1918. 4, Clarence Reid Luttrell, born Feb. 1, 1923.

2. Corrie Luttrell, daughter, born in Oxford, Ala., June 7, 1889. Married Clarence M. Reid, of Fort Deposit, Ala., Dec. 16, 1908. Residence, 509 Finley Avenue, Montgomery, Ala. They have only one child, Lucy Olivia Reid, born Dec. 2, 1911.

3. Annie Laurie Luttrell, daughter, born in Oxford, Ala., December 15, 1891. Married in Brewton, Ala., Aug. 25, 1908, to William Marshall Strong. The children of this union are four: 1, Laurie Barber Strong, born June 23, 1916. 2, George Elston Strong, born Jan. 29, 1918. 3, Lutie May Strong, born Jan. 20, 1920. 4, Marshall Rush Strong, b. June 3, 1923.

4. Harvey Haynes Luttrell, born near Brewton, Ala., April 19. 1894. Served in the World War 1918-19. Married Mary Jane Adams, daughter of John A. Adams, in Montgomery, Ala., Sept. 24, 1919. Residence, Montgomery Ala. No children.

5. Alton Luttrell, born near Brewton, August 24, 1895. Died July 21, 1896.

(4) CHESTER McAULEY LUTTRELL, son, born Oct. 8, 1862. Followed mercantile pursuits all his life. Married October 5, 1886, Augusta Harwell, Oxford, Alabama. Present residence, Bradford, Pennsylvania. Their children are four in number, all daughters, as follows:

1. Juliet Luttrell, born July 31, 1887. Married to the Rev. Royal K. Tucker, of Mobile, Alabama, 1908. Residence (1924) Louisville, Kentucky. They have five children, all girls: (1) Lael Tucker, born March 28, 1909. (2) Ruth Tucker, born April 21, 1911. (3) Lucile Tucker, born October 29, 1912. (4) Juliet Tucker, born November 20, 1914. (5) Royal Leigh Tucker, born December 10, 1919.

2. Kattie May Luttrell, born January 18, 1900. Was married to Dr. Ernest E. Tucker, of Mobile, Alabama, ———. Residence (1924) New York City. They have two children: (1) Ernest Tucker, born March 20, 1921. (2) Katherine Tucker, born December 12, 1922.

3. Elizabeth Lynn Luttrell, born March 9, 1893. Was married to Lowell S. Langworthy, of Bradford, Pennsylvania, ———. There they yet live and have three children: (1) Mary Lynn Langworthy, born October 20, 1915. (2) Richard Langworthy, born May 21, 1919. (3) Lucile Langworthy, born October 20, 1921.

4. Ethel Lucile Luttrell, born April 28, 1898. Not married. Lives with her sister, Katie May Tucker, in New York City.

(5) BRUCE FRANCIS LUTTRELL, son, born near Oxford, Ala., July 13, 1868. Married at Evergreen, Alabama, August 4, 1896, Lena Crumpton, daughter of B. H. Crumpton. Has followed mercantile pursuits and is at present located in Tampa, Florida. The children are nine in number, as follows:

1. Suelston Luttrell, daughter, born July 26, 1897. Married October 10, 1920, to Charles A. Barker. Residence, Philadelphia, Pa.

2. Ralphine Luttrell, born January 28, 1899. Married July 22, 1915, to Ellis H. Till. No children. Residence, Tampa, Forida.

3. Rush Luttrell, son, born January 17, 1900. Died July 28, 1900.

4. Lucy Grace Luttrell, daughter, born September 12, 1901. Married December 16, 1918, to J. H. Fisher, of Virginia. Has one daughter, Bernadette, born April 1, 1921. Residence, Tampa, Florida.

5. Marcie Luttrell, daughter, born August 3, 1903. Married in Tampa, Florida, June 29, 1921, to Willis W. Henderson. Has two children: (1) Dorothy, born 1922. (2) Geraldine, born 1923.

6. Bruce Luttrell, Jr., son, born August 6, 1905. Not married.

7. Boardman Luttrell, son, born November 28, 1906.

8. Ernestine Luttrell, daughter, born August 17, 1908. Married in Tampa, Florida, May 10, 1924, to Barney Tapp, of Tampa.

9. Lena Luttrell, daughter, born December 25, 1912.

(6) RUSH LUTTRELL, son, born near Oxford, Ala., December 7, 1870. Spent his life in railroad train service. Married in Calera, Alabama, Lutie Blevins. Died May 13, 1924. No children.

(7) A son, not named, born January 4, 1872. Died July, 1872.

(8) KATIE LUTTRELL, daughter, born July 4, 1875. Died August 18, 1875.

(9) MARCY LUTTRELL, son, born January 16, 1877. Was an electrical and mechanical engineer. Electrocuted by accident in Selma, Alabama, December 14, 1903. Not married.

(10 & 11) FRANK and FRED LUTTRELL, twin sons, born March 28, 1879. Fred died August 14, 1879. Frank died August 24, 1879.

CHILDREN AND GRANDCHILDREN OF EVA BORDERS (ELSTON) DeARMAN AND JAMES T. DeARMAN OF CALHOUN COUNTY, ALABAMA

(1) ALMA NEWELL (DeARMAN) BORDERS, daughter, born Nov. 14, 1866. Was married to William C. Borders, Jan. 23, 1884. Died June 14, 1891, in Anniston, Alabama. She had two children, as follows:

1. Sam J. Borders, son, born June 14, 1885. He is an R. F. D. mail carrier and resides at DeArmanville, Alabama.

2. Salie Borders, daughter, born May 2, 1887; was married —— —— to W. O. Chitwood. Residence, DeArmanville, Ala.

(2) CLEFF ELSTON DeARMAN, son, born June 21, 1869. Married Lucy Methvin, of Senoia, Ga., December 28, 1898. Cleff Elston died April 28, 1901, and his wife Lucy died April, 1911. They had no children.

(3) KITTIE TURNIPSEED (DeARMAN) METHVIN, daughter, born July 20, 1873. Was married to D. R. Methvin, of Senoia, Ga., December 27, 1894. Present residence, Anniston, Alabama. There were six children to this union, as follows:

1. Eva Lucile Methvin, born October 4, 1895. Married a Mr. Dye. Residence Anniston, Alabama.

2. D. T. Methvin, born August 12, 1897.

3. Cleff Leon Methvin, born September 26, 1899. Married and resides in Anniston, Alabama.

4. Roy Methvin, born April 22, 1901.

5. Paul Methvin, born September 3, 1903.

6. Kittie Ruth Methvin, born October 14, 1909.

(4) LOUIE JONES DeARMAN, son, born October 31, 1876. Married Ida Rosila Brightmon, of Anniston, Ala., June 27, 1899. Residence Fairfield, Alabama. Their children are seven in number as follows:

1. Hubert Pryor DeArman, born October 29, 1900.

2. Evelyn Louise DeArman, born September 18, 1902; was marred to James Newton Smith, February 15, 1922; has one son, James Newton Smith, (Jr.) born October 3, 1924.

3. Cleff Elston DeArman, (Jr.) born December 15, 1904.

4. Retha Gertrude DeArman, born November 3, 1906.

5. Ida Margaret DeArman, born April 6, 1911.

6. Louie Jones DeArman, (Jr.) born April 6, 1911. (Twin).

7. Virginia Loraine DeArman, born June 29, 1913.

(5) RETHA EVELYN (DeARMAN) McCLURKIN, daughter, born July 9, 1878. Was married to James Walter McClurkin, Anniston, Alabama, April 4, 1906. They resided in Anniston and have four children as follows:

1. James Avery McClurkin, born June 7, 1907.

2. Evelyn Pearl McClurkin, born May 31, 1910.

3. Louie Walter McClurkin, born January 14, 1918.

4. Sarah Retha McClurkin, born May 10, 1918.

(6) PEARL (DeARMAN) OWENS, daughter, born May 15, 1883; married December 20, 1910, to Foster Pierce Owens, of Heflin, Alabama. They now reside at Heflin and have three children as follows:

1. Foster Pierce Owens (Jr.), born August 25, 1913.

2. Retha Eva Owens, born November 18, 1916.

3. Annie Pearl Owens, born January 14, 1920.

FAMILY OF ALLEN ELSTON, SR., OF SOUTH CAROLINA AND ALABAMA

Allen Elston, one of the younger sons of David Elston, of New Jersey, was born in Eizabeth, New Jersey, January 13, 1782. He naturally followed the fortunes of his father's family in their migrations, first to Wilkes County, North Carolina, then to Tennessee and Kentucky. The father David Elston seems to have finally located in Kentucky near Lexington, possibly then embraced in "The State of Franklin", and ta have lived out his life there. But the two sons, John and Allen, in about 1798, being then 24 and 16 years of age respectively, went on further southward and settled in upper South Carolina, in Pendleton District, on the Georgia line. We find these two brothers and their families lived quite close together for several succeeding generations. About 1815 John Elston crossed over the line into Habersham county, Georgia. Allen Elston may have done likewise. They both developed large and valuable agricultural and mercantile interests. Later they decided to try their fortunes further west and in a yet newer country. Accordingly in 1833, "the year the stars fell," Allen Elston moved to the Creek nation and located in the Choccolocco valley in Tal'adega county. His brother, John Elston, followed him in 1834 and located in the same valley in Benton county. Here their good fortunes followed them. Allen and his sons amassed valuable agricultural and mercantile properties and all lived out their lives in this county. The father, Allen Elston, Sr., died December 9th, 1868, aged nearly 87 years.

Allen Elston (Sr.) of South Carolina, son of David Elston of New Jersey, as best we can determine from the evidence before us, which however is not absolutely conclusive, married in South Carolina, a first wife who was Ruth Clark, a daughter of Major William H. Clark and a grand-daughter of Governor John Sevier, of Tennessee. We have no record of any children by this marriage, and the probabilities are that Ruth did not live long after the marriage. Allen married a second wife, Mrs. Annie Blair Terrell, a widow with one daughter, Elizabeth Terrell. This daughter afterwards married William Johnson and had children, one of them Harriet Johnson, who married Charles J. Cooper, of Oxford, Ala., and had a large family.

This completes the record of the children of Elizabeth Clark who married John Elston and Ruth Clark who married Allen Elston which was furnished by Elston Luttrell a descendant of Elizabeth Clark Elston and John Elston. This splendid record has been of material assistance in the compilation of the Sevier Family History.

SARAH HAWKINS CLARK

2. Sarah Hawkins Clark, daughter of Elizabeth Sevier Clark and Major William H. Clark was born about 1788.   She seems to have spent much time in her grandfather, Gov. John Sevier's, home and is certainly very frequently mentioned by him as "Sally Clark".

She married possibly about 1804 in Knoxville in the Governor's mansion.   She married   General   James   Rutherford   Wyly,   a grandson of Colonel Benjamin Cleveland of King's Mountain fame. Descendants of this couple have therefore three lines to King's Mountain. (John Sevier, Major Clark and Col. Cleveland) General Wyly was also a distinguished officer of the war of 1812.   He was the son of James and Jamima Cleveland Wyly, Jamima Cleveland Wyly being the daughter of Col. Benjamin Cleveland and Mary Graves Cleveland.

Sarah Hawkins Clark Wyly   and   General   James   Rutherford Wyly had twelve children. eight sons and four daughters, namely:

1. William Clark Wyly

2. Oliver Cromwell Wyly

3. Benjamin Cleveland Wyly

4. John Henry Wyly

5. James Rutherford Wyly, junior

6. Robert Wyly

7. Walton Wyly

8. Augustine Clayton Wyly

9. Elizabeth Wyly

10. Louisiana Wyly

11. Mary Ann Wyly

12 Sarah Catherine Wyly

13. Florence Wyly

Of the foregoing:

1. William Clark Wyly, son of Sarah Hawkins Clark Wyly and General James Rutherford Wyly was born———.   He married——— Amelia Starr and had two children.

A. Robert Wyly

B. Eliza Hanna Wyly lived and married in the West.   She died some years ago.   She married William Tipman Trammell, son of Jehu and Elizabeth (Fain) Trammell. Jehu Trammell was the son of William Trammell. Elizabeth Fain the daughter of Ebenezer and Mary (Black) Fain. Ebenezer Fain was a soldier in the Revolution. According to D. A. R. Books Eliza Hannah Wyly had at least four daughters, all of whom belong to D. A. R., as follows

1. Augusta Josephine Trammell, born Georgia, married John William McWilliams.

2. Anna Eliza Trammell, born in Georgia, married Charles Parmelee Beeks

3. Rosalind Clark Trammell, born in Georgia, married Benjamin Rush Blakely.

4. Amelia Elizabeth Trammell, born in Georgia, married Charlie Reed Johnson.

2. Oliver Cromwell Wyly, son of Sarah Hawkins Clark Wyly and General James Rutherford Wyly was born about 1808. He married for his first wife Lucy Edins in 1828 and had three daughters and five sons, namely: Newton Cromwell Wyly, born 1829; Benjamin F. Wyly, born 1830; James A. Wyly; Carolyn M. Wyly; Sarah Amelia Wyly; Louise Wyly; Robert A. Wyly and William Sevier Wyly.

Newton Cromwell Wyly, born 1829, married in 1849, Malinda Townsend and had one son, Homer Virgil Miller Wyly.

Benjamin F. Wyly, born in 1830, married in 1858, Sallie Williams and had three sons, Eugene Wyly, Newton Wyly and ———Wyly.

James A. Wyly married for his first wife a Miss Williams and had no children and married for his second wife Miss Verner and and had a son and a daughter.

Carolyn M. Wyly married Henry Alexander Fuller and had three sons, Oliver Clyde Fuller (who married Kate Fitzhugh Caswell and has Edythe Fuller, Elizabeth Fuller, Inez Fuller, Lytie Fuller, and Robert Fuller); Henry Walter Fuller; Clarence Paul Fuller; and Annie Raily Fuller (deceased).

Sarah Amelia Wyly married Henry Lamar Smith and had two sons; Victor Lamar Smith (who married Carolyn Johnson); and Alexander Wyly Smith (who married Ida Kendrick and has Alexander Wyly Smith. junior, married Hellen Hill Payne and has three children and was a Captain in the United States Army; Kendrick Smith was in the United States Aviation Corps; and Ester Smith).

Lula or Louise Wyly married Colet Carter and had a daughter, Florence Carter, who married Judge Frank Carter of Asheville North Carolina.

Robert A. Wyly married———Hatchett and has six sons.

William Sevier Wyly married ———Hatchett, a sister of his brother Robert Wyly's wife, and had two sons of whom only one is now living.

2. Oliver Cromwell Wyly married for his second wife, Ade'ine Byrd, a daughter of Colonel Thomas Byrd and had four children, two sons and two daughters.

Oliver Cromwell Wyly married for his third wife———————— and had ten children, all but one of whom were living in Texas in 1918.

3. Benjamin Cleveland Wyly, son of James Rutherford Wyly and Sarah Hawkins Clark Wyly, married first Ann McGee and had one son, John McGee Wyly, who married Amelia Forney and had four children; Annie McGee Wyly (who married David Lowe and has a daughter Annie Wyly Lowe, married Walker Willis); Benjamin F. Wyly (who married Ellie Peck and has three children, Lottie Wyly, Catherine Wyly, married————————, and Forney Wyly); Sadie Swope Wyly (who married F. M. Billings and has Wyly Billings and F. M. Billings, junior; and Henry Forney Wyly (who married Sallie Dunlap and has two children, Henry Forney Wyly, junior, and Sallie Dunlap Wyly.)

Benjamin Cleveland Wyly married for his second wife Eliza Snow and had Samuel Snow Wyly; Frank Wyly (a daughter) who married Tom Garlington; Ella Wyly married ————————Brothers; Ida Wyly married Joe Clay King, and Jennie M. Wyly married William Murrary Davidson.

4. John Henry Wyly, son of Sarah Hawkins Clark Wyly, and General James Rutherford Wyly was born 18————————.

5. James Rutherford Wyly, junior, son of Sarah Hawkins Clark Wyly and General James Rutherford Wyly was born 18————————.

6. Robert Wyly, son of Sarah Hawkins Clark Wyly and General James Rutherford Wyly was born 18————————. He married unmarried.

7. Walton Wyly, son of Sarah Hawkins Clark Wyly and General James Rutherford Wyly was born 18————————. He married Mary Johnson and had no children.

8. Augustine Clayton Wyly, son of Sarah Hawkins Clark Wyly and General James Rutherford Wyly, was born 18————————. He married Josephine Taylor Hamilton and had three children, Madeline Wyly, Nell I. Wyly, who married Montagu Gammon and Thomas Hamilton Wyly.

9. Elizabeth Wyly, daughter of Sarah Hawkins Clark Wyly and General James Rutherford Wyly, was born 18————————. She married Thomas Sparks.

10. Louisiana Wyly, daughter of Sarah Hawkins Clark Wyly and General James Rutherford Wyly, was born 18————————. She married————————Byrd.

11 Mary Ann Wyly, daughter of Sarah Hawkins Clark Wyly and General James Rutherford Wyly was born 18————. She married 18————. Judge William Henderson Underwood and had Helen Underwood (who married M.A. Nevin and had William Henry Nevin, beceased; James Banks Nevin (who married first Alace Wells and is deceased); Thomas O'Connor Nevin, deceased; Sarah Hawkins Nevin, deceased; James Banks Nevin (who married first Alace Wells and married second Mary Bryan); Mary Michell Nevin (who married Randolph Wright); Wyatt Holmes Nevin, deceased); Annie Lou Underwood (who married Captain C. Rowell and had William Sinclair Rowell; Neal Rowel', deceased; Mary Wyly Rowell; Martha Cheatham Rowell, deceased; Elizabeth Clifton Rowell, deceased; and Annie Lou Rowell, deceased); Florence Wyly Underwood (who married E. M. Eastman and has Zoe Eastman, married Charles Robin Pitner, John Eastman married Laura Hume, Helen Eastman, unmarried, and Guy Eastman married Emma Hume); Mary Corde'ia Underwood (who married D. D. Plumb and had Rosa Milledge Plumb, married J. H. O'Neill); Ida Underwood (who married George H. Snyder and had Wyly Snyder, George Snyder and Clifford Snyder ; Wilhemina Underwood (who married John H. Pitt and has no children); Rose Underwcod who marr!ed C. R. Clark and has one son, Charles Richard Clark, junior); John James Underwood (who died young); Charles Walton Underwood (who married Martha Moore and has John Underwood, Charles Walton Underwood, junior, William H. Underwood, Robert Wyly Underwood, Valentine Xavier Underwood; Mary Underwood, married William Anderson and Evelyn Underwood, married Ralph Tanner.)

12. Sarah Catherine Wyly, daughter of Sarah Hawkins Clark Wyly and General James Rutherford Wyly was born 18————. She married William Addison Rogers and had two daughters, Zoe Rogers, who married William Clifton Mansfield and A!ah Rogers, who married———————— Daniel.

The chi'dren of William Clifton Mansfield formerly of Cleveland and Sweetwater, Tennessee, but now of Atlanta, Georgia, and his wife, Zoe Sevier (Rogers) Mansfield are as follows:-

1. William Mansfield, died in infancy
2. Zoe Sevier Mansfield, died 1914, unmarried
3. Katherine Louise Mansfield,who married Samuel Tipton Jones of Sweetwater, Tennessee and had four children:-

    a. Clifton Martin Jones
    b. Florine Mansfield Jones
    c. Sevier-Tipton Jones, who died in infancy

4. Felice Mansfield who died unmarried in 1918 of influenza.
5. Eston Sevier Mansfield who married Ellie Patterson of Atlanta. They were the parents of three children:-

    a. Sevier Mansfield who died in infancy
    b. Marian Mansfield
    c. William Denton Mansfield

In the marriage of these two are united the families of the two bitter political opponents, John Sevier and Colonel Tipton and the

THE SEVIER FAMILY

erroneously called "Tipton-Sevier feud" comes to a happy end, Samuel Tipton Jones being a lineal descendant in the sixth generation from Col. John Tipton while Katherine Louise Mansfield, his wife, is, likewise in the sixth generation, a lineal descendant of Governor John Sevier. In recognition of this union one of their children bore the name Sevier-Tipton Jones.

13. Florence Wyly. It appears that another child of Sarah Hawkins Clark Wyly and General James Rutherford Clark was Florence Wyly, born 18————. She married Dennis Joseph O'Callagham and had a daughter, Mary Lilly O'Callagham, born in Clarksville, Ga., who is a member of the D. A. R. through this record.

JOHN CLARK

3. John Clark, son of Elizabeth Sevier Clark and Major William H. Clark, was born ————. By accounts that some members of the family have sent me he married———— and had at least one daughter who was called by descendants of this family "Cousin Kittie Clark". However this may be a mistake. If he died young, it would account for his father naming another son John Clark.

RUTH CLARK

4. Ruth Clark, daughter of Major William H. Clark, was born————. In the records in Washington concerning the Sevier estate, Elizabeth Sevier Clark is mentioned as having three children and the names are given: Elizabeth, Sarah and John. But an error may have been made. Ruth may have been accidentally omitted or Ruth may have been deceased when the list was prepared. Some errors in regard to other heirs do occur in these records, some names being repeated and some omitted.

Ruth Clark married, Allen Elston, brother of her sister's husband, John Elston, by family tradition and by the record prepared by Elston Luttrell, see page 220. By Mr. Elston's account she was the first wife of Allen Elston and probably died young without issue.

Allen Elston and Ruth Clark Elston settled about 1834 in the Choccolocco valley in Talladega County, Alabama, where he lived until his death, surviving his first wife by many years.

225

CHAPTER FIVE
Sarah Hawkins Sevier

SARAH HAWKINS SEVIER

Sarah Hawkins Sevier, daughter of Governor John Sevier and his first wife, Sarah Hawkins Sevier, was born in Rockinkham, Virginia, July, 1770. She received her mother's full name. She was about ten years of age when her mother died in January or February 1780, and she was raised after her father's second marriage by Catherine Sherrill Sevier, her step-mother. She married early as all the Sevier girls did, probably about 1787, when she was seventeen years of age. The Sevier girls married from fourteen and fifteen up. Their mother, Sarah Hawkins, married John Sevier when she was about fifteen and John Sevier was sixteen.

Sarah Hawkins Sevier married Benjamin Brown, known as and usually called, Judge Benjamin Brown. She died before 1839. In letters from some members of the family she is called Dolly Sevier and she evidently had that diminutive.

In 1818 she must have been a widow as in the Sheriff's Bill of Sale for her father's property she is mentioned alone, while the other daughters are all mentioned with the names of their husbands.

A Benjamin Brown aged 87 was a pensioner in the 1840 list. This puts his birth in 1753, and would make him seventeen years older than Sarah Hawkins Sevier Brown, so I presume this Benjamin (who is not called Judge) was her husband's kinsman.

Mr. and Mrs. Benjamin Brown are frequently mentioned by Governor Sevier in his Journal. They are recorded as dining and lodging in the Sevier household and they evidently lived not too far away for frequent visits.

Sarah Hawkins Sevier Brown and Judge Benjamin Brown had ten children but I have not the names of any of them.

CHAPTER SIX
Mary Ann Sevier

MARY ANN SEVIER

Mary Ann Sevier, daughter of Governor John Sevier and his first wife, Sarah Hawkins Sevier, was born in Virginia. By the authority of Mrs. Sophia Hoss French she was born in 1771 or 1772. I have no other record of her birth date and therefore place her as the sixth child. Governor Sevier in his Journal refers to her as Mary Ann, while the other older daughters, (his Journal, so far as it has been preserved, begins in 1790), are called by their married names. Mrs. Benjamin Brown, Mrs. Walter King, etc. He does not mention Mary Ann's wedding and therefore if she were born in 1771 or 1772, I conclude that she was married before the first recorded date in the Journal, but became a widow early and was an inmate of his household. This would account for his reference to her as "Mary Ann"; and for less frequent references than he bestows upon the comings and goings of Mr. and Mrs. Benjamin Brown, who frequently dine or "lodge" with him. Only once, later in his Journal, (September 1812) does he call the name of "Mrs. May". So her marriage to her second husband, John Corland, took place after that date.

According to the record of Mrs. French, Mary Ann Sevier married for her first husband, Samuel May. There are few references to this marriage and I conclude that Samuel May died very young. Samuel May appears on the tax list of Greene County, Tennessee, in 1783. This may have been her first husband or his father. She is better known by the name of her second husband, who was Joshua Corland.

The name of her second husband is sometimes given as Joshua Corlin and sometimes Joshua Corland. As will be noted in other instances, the spelling of many names varied. Her brother, George Washington Sevier, speaks of her as living July 23, 1739, when he writes to Dr. Draper.

I do not know the names of her children. There is, however, a reference in Governor Sevier's Journal———— to a child named "Sevier", that could only be a grandchild and, of course, only the child of a daughter. As the other married daughters certainly did not make their home in his home, it is possible that this child "Sevier", who was evidently about the age of his daughter Ruth, was the daughter of Mary Ann who was then, or later, the widow of Samuel May.   This is only supposition.   Some of the descendants may have data that will link "Sevier" to the family tree.   He may have been the son of Elizabeth, who named her son John Clark for Governor Sevier.   He may have been named John Sevier Clark and called by his middle name.

In the bill for the Sheriff's Sale, February 10, 1818, are mentioned "Joshua Corland and Mary Ann his wife".

CHAPTER SEVEN
Valentine Sevier

VALENTINE SEVIER

Valentine Sevier, son of Governor John Sevier and his first wife, Sarah Hawkins Sevier, was born in Virginia in 1773. He was a child when he accompanied his family to the "Mountains", now Tennessee, arriving Christmas day, 1773. Valentine Sevier was born in 1773 which was the year his father's entire family moved from Virginia to "the Mountains". He received the name Valentine which is identified with his family for centuries, but the result is almost hopeless confusion to students of the family history as at least four of his first cousins, his grandfather, and his uncle had exactly the same name. The two older men can be identified as they appear in the records, because of their age or other circumstances, but the five young men all about the same age and all named Valentine Sevier offer a puzzle that is frequently not to be solved. Even in his marriage this Valentine is confused with Valentine, the son of Abraham Sevier, for it is said that Valentine the son of Governor John married————Arnott (Arnett?), while it is established that Valentine, the son of Abraham, married Elizabeth Arnett. Whether these two Valentines married sisters or cousins of the same surname, or whether descendants have merely confused one Valentine with the other is more than I can say.

In the absence of information to the contrary however I will say that Valentine Sevier, son of Governor John Sevier, married, according to statements made to me,———— Arnott. His marriage took place about 1795, when he was about twenty-two years of age.

Valentine Sevier went to Overton County, Tennessee, where Governor Sevier had immense holdings, fifty-four thousand acres at least. Joanna Sevier Wendell and John Wendell were I think the pioneers of the family in opening up this new territory and possibly Valentine Sevier accompanied his sister and brother-in-law. This was several years before his father's death. After that event, "Bonny Kate" and other members of the family joined the Overton

237

County colony . In the meanwhile many Seviers had moved to Overton and among them were Abraham Sevier and his family, including his son Valentine. Therefore the location of Valentine Sevier records in Overton County is not conclusive. Valentine Sevier, son of Ayraham, was however younger than Valentine, son of Governor John Sevier.

Valentine Sevier was living in 1818 when the Sheriff's Bill of Sale was published, and George Washington Sevier in a letter to Dr. Draper in 1839 says that he was living then.

I think it probable that Valentine Sevier (subject of this chapter) married in East Tennessee about 1795. A descendant of Martha Sevier, who was I think his daughter, says that Martha was born in 1799. This would put her father's marriage about the date 1795.

Joseph Sevier in a letter to Bishop Hoss in 1916, said that he was a descendant of Henry Sevier, son of Valentine Sevier, son of Governor John Sevier. I have not been able to hear from this man.

Mrs. Martha Sevier Price, of Memphis, a grand daughter of Governor Sevier (daughter of John Sevier, junior) wrote in 1907 that her brother Michael Sevier raised a great-grand-daughter of Valentine Sevier. She was the daughter of a Federal soldier———— Sevier, who died in Little Rock, Arkansas, during the War Between the States. In his last hours he begged Michael Sevier to get his little motherless girl and raise her. Michael Sevier agreed to do this and as soon as peace was declared went for the child. (Mrs. Price does not say in her letter where he went, so we have not that clew). This child was named Mary Sevier and she was raised in the family of Michael Sevier.

Mrs. Price's letter also says that at one time a grandson of Valentine Sevier, Samuel Sevier, was living in Camden Arkansas. He was possibly the father or grandfather of Joseph Sevier who wrote to Bishop Hoss in 1916, but who has answered no recent letters.

From the foregoing information, the children of Valentine Sevier were:

1. Henry Sevier
2. Martha Sevier, born about 1799
   and others.

THE SEVIER FAMILY
HENRY SEVIER

Henry Sevier, son of Valentine Sevier, was born about 1797. He must have grown up in Overton County with his sister Martha Sevier and other young kinspeople. He married about 1715 and had a son Joseph J. Sevier, who had a son Joseph J. Sevier, who wrote to Bishop Hsos from Rockford Mo., in 1916, giving this information. He has answered no recent letters however.

MARTHA SEVIER

Martha Sevier, born about 1799, was probably the daughter of Valentine Sevier.

She must have grown to maturity in Overton County with dozens of her young kinspeople. Her step grand-mother "Bonny Kate was domiciled in Overton County in what must have been a handsome home for the period and this home probably provided a meeting place for the young people of the entire neighborhood.

Martha Sevier married———— Poindexter about 1815. Mrs. F. A. Birdsall of Yazoo City, Miss. is her descendant.

CHAPTER EIGHT

Richard Sevier

RICHARD SEVIER

Richard Sevier, son of Governor John Sevier and his first wife, Sarah Hawkins Sevier, was born in 1775.

A list of Governor Sevier's children prepared by Mrs. Sophia Hoss French, of Morristown, a descendant of Governor Sevier through his third son, John Sevier junior, gives Richard as dying in December, 1792. He would then have been less than twenty years of age.

In another reference it is said that he died of a fever contracted in an Indian Campaign when he was eighteen years of age, this would place his death in the fall or winter of 1793.

His death while still a youth accounts, of course, for only brief mention of him.

Governor John Sevier makes but one reference to his son Richard in the Journal. Under date of January 14, 1794, he gives details of a dream of being in an unknown country, evidently Heaven, and his son "Dicky" meeting him there. The dream shows that his father's mind was still deeply concerned with his recent sorrow.

CHAPTER NINE
Rebecca Sevier

REBECCA SEVIER

Rebecca Sevier, daughter of Governor John Sevier by his first wife, Sarah Hawkins Sevier, was born in Virginia probably about the year 1777. She died November 17, 1799, just four and one half years after her marriage, while still a young woman.

Young women at that period married as a rule at an early age and I judge therefore that at her marriage in 1795, she was not more than seventeen or eighteen years old. It is for that reason that I place her birth about 1777. Several of Governor Sevier's daughters were married even before they were seventeen, two of them at fifteen, which was at that time a frequent custom. Rebecca Sevier was a small child if not a baby when her mother died in 1780 and she was raised by her step-mother, Bonny Kate Sevier. She married John Waddell, or Waddle, as it was sometimes spelled, Thursday, February 26, 1795, just one week after her sister, Nancy Sevier, married Walter King.

Governor Sevier mentions the marriage in his Journal as follows:

(1795, February)

"Thursday, 26, Rebecca's wedding to John Waddle. Friday cold. Saturday very cold. Came home from Rebecca's wedding."

Rebecca, it seems from that record, was married away from home, presumably in Jonesboro, as that is the point most frequently mentioned when the family journeyed forth. No reason is given or suggested by any information that I have for the marriage to take place away from the family residence. It would seem that John Waddle was an accepted visitor to the house as he was among the guests at Nancy Sevier's wedding to Walter King, just one week earlier.

John Waddell was born in Philladelphia about 1765. He was the eldest of ten children of John Waddell I and his wife, Rachel Quee Waddell. John Waddell I was born of Scotch parents in County Donegal, Ireland, in 1736. He emigrated to America and settled near Philadelphia where he married Rachel Quee, the daughter of a Scotchman and his wife who was Hester Rittenhouse. They soon emigrated to what we now know as Tennessee and settled in Washington District. They were Presbyterians and educated their son John Waddell II to be a Presbyterian minister. He did not however follow this profession. He was too young to be in the earlier part of the Revolution, but he served, it is said in the later campaigns with the young Seviers, whose neighbor he was, under Col. John Sevier who was later his father-in-law. He survived his wife Rebecca Sevier, more than half a century, dying in 1855 in Hot Springs, Ark. He married a second time and had children, who have descendants but these do not come in the Sevier line and so they are not included in this history.

Rebecca Sevier Waddell died November 17, 1799, just four and a half years after her marriage to John Waddell II, leaving two children namely:

1 Sarah Rebecca Sevier Waddell
2 John Sevier Waddell.

SARAH REBECCA SEVIER WADDELL

Sarah Rebecca Sevier Waddell, daughter of John Waddell II and Sarah Rebecca Sevier Waddell, was born April 25, 1796. She was given her mother's name and Rebecca's mother's name, Sarah (Hawkins). She died May 1883. She married about 1815, or a little earlier, Abram Hair and has numerous descendants. It is said that the children of Abram Hair and Sarah Rebecca Sevier Waddell Hair were:

Martha Hair

Mary Hair

Minerva Hair

Elizabeth Hair

I do not know if there were other children of if these came in this order.

Elizabeth Hair, daughter of Sarah Rebecca Sevier Waddel Hair and Abram Hair, was born 18——.   She married about 18——, —— —————— Chandley and had a daughter, Nancy Chandley, born 18——, who married————— Weed.   They had a daughter, Opal Weed, born 18——, who married George A. Sprinkle and lives now in Weaversville, North Carolina.

JOHN SEVIER WADDELL

John Sevier Waddell, only son of Rebecca Sevier Waddell and John Waddell II, was born February 14, 1799.   His mother died when he was nine months old.   He and his sister, Rebecca, went to live with their paternal grandparents, John Waddell II and Rachell Quee Waddell, who lived near Jonesboro, Tennessee.   John Sevier Waddell married January 6, 1831 Sophia Doak, daughter of John Doak and Jane Montgomery Doak and grand-daughter of Dr. Samuel Doak, founder of Washington Cllege.   In 1838 John Sevier Waddell with his wife and two children, Samuel Waddell and Rebecca Jane Waddell emigrated to Henry County, Missouri.   He purchased land near Calhoun, Missouri and there he spent the remainder of his life. He died February 11, 1864.   He married twice.   His first wife, Sophia Doak Waddell, died June 27, 1843.

They had three sons and one daughter, namely:

a. Samuel Whitefield Waddell, born December 5, 1831 in Tennessee, died out west November 1877.

b. Rebecca Jane Waddell

c. Alexander Nelson Waddell

d. James Newton Waddell

Of these:

a. Samuel Whitfield Waddell, son of John Sevier Waddell and Sophia Doak Waddell, born December 5, 1831 in Tennessee, died out west November 18, 1877 unmarried.

b. Rebecca Jane Waddell, daughter of John Sevier Waddell and Sophia Doak Waddell, was born March 13, 1835 in Tennessee, died in Coronodo, California, October 1, 1918.   She married, October 6, 1853, James Monroe Duncan.   They had nine children but of these only three daughters lived to maturity, namely:

Ella May Duncan, born September 12, 1864, died December 26, 1919 in California, married Dr. Joseph P. Gray and had a daughter, Rebecca Gray, born in Nashville, Tennessee, who married Arthur

Lowell Endicott July 7, 1914, and they have a daughter, Margaret Elinor, born April 5, 1925. They make their home in Pasadena, California.

Jennie Doak Duncan born September 4, 1867 in Henry County, Mo., married Rev. Sterling Price Brite, August 30, 1893, in Windsor, Mo. Their children are: Mary Louisa Brite, born November 17, 1898; John Duncan Brite, born march 4, 1901; Joseph Landes Brite, born July 9, 1903, married Cordelia Metcalf; Katherine Duncan, born October 7,1879 near Windsor, Mo.

c. Alexander Nelson Waddell, son of John Sevier Waddell and Sophia Doak Waddell, born December 21, 1838 near Calhoun Mo., died February 15, 1913 near Windsor, Mo. He married January 5, 1868, Eliza Frances Carter in Missouri. She was born in Virginia and went with her parents, Thomas Carter and Eliza Carter, to Missouri in 1861. Alexander Nelson Waddell and Eliza Carter Waddell had six children, three sons and three daughters, namely:

Robert Doak Waddell, born near Windsor Mo., July 22, 1869, married October 12, 1904. They had no children. He lives at Bartlesville, Okla.

John Carter Waddell, born August 27, 1871, died August 27, 1915.

Eliza Jane Waddell, born April 16, 1873, near Windsor, Mo., married Avery Finks, of Calhoun, Mo., in 1902. They have Frances Avery Finks, born 1912.

Alice Nelson Waddell, born January 8, 1875 near Windsor, Mo., died in St. Louis, Mo., December 14, 1918. She married December 19, 1919, Arthur J. England. They had one child, Frances Hall England, born February 1915.

Annie May Waddell, born October 21, 1876, near Windsor, Mo., died at Liberty, Mo., August 26, 1918. She married March 3, 1915, Dr. Robert E. Sevier, son of Henry Sevier of Liberty, Mo. She left two children, Helen May Sevier, born January 4, 1917 and Robert Ann Sevier, born August 8, 1918.

Alexander Thomas Waddell, born October 26, 1882 near Windsor, Mo., married Doris Mathews, of Sedalia, Mo. They have one child, Alice Lee Waddell, born January 20, 1908.

d. James Newton Waddell, son of John Sevier Waddell and Sophia Doak Waddell, was born, May 1, 1843 near Calhoun, Mo. He died January 28, 1915, in Henry County, Mo. He married

Martha Box.   They had one daughter Bettie Waddell, born 1884.

John Sevier Waddell, after the death of Sophia Doak Waddell, married Mary Ann Pinkston, November 1,1844.   She was born in Estell, Ky., November 19, 1823, and moved with her parents, Bassel Lee Pinkston and Elizabeth Norland Pinkston, to a farm near Calhoun, Mo.   Mary Elizabeth Pinkston Waddell died October 1, 1866 leaving seven children, namely:

- e. Thomas Jefferson Waddell
- f. Sarah Elizabeth Waddell
- g. John Franklin Waddell
- h. William Wilson Waddell
- i. Isora Waddell
- j. Medora Waddell
- k. Mary E. Waddell

Of these:

e. Thomas Jefferson Waddell, son of John Sevier Waddell by his second wife, Mary Ann Pinkston Waddell, was born August 20, 1845, died April 4, 1862, near Calhoun, Mo.

f. Sarah Elizabeth Waddell, daughter of John Sevier Waddell by his second wife, Mary Ann Pinkston Waddell, was born August 13, 1850, near Calhoun, Mo.   She died July 2, 1909.   She married August 31, 1871, Thomas Preston Kairns, of Canada.   They had no children.

g. John Franklin Waddell, son of John Sevier Waddell by his second wife, Mary Ann Pinkston Waddell, was born January 13, 1852, near Calhoun, Mo., he married in Brownsville, Texas about 1883.

h. William Wilson Waddell, son of John Sevier Waddell by his second wife Mary Ann Pinkston Waddell, was born March 10, 1854, near Calhoun, Mo.   He married Augusta Florence Duncan March 20, 1878.   She was the daughter of John Duncan and Mary Frances Crews Duncan.   William Wilson Waddell and his wife had six children though only four lived to maturity, namely:

Leslie Waddell

Clay Duncan Waddell

Marie Elizabeth Waddell

Augusta Florence Waddell

Of these:

Leslie Waddell, born August 30, 1879 near Windsor, Mo.   He married Virginia Bohn, of Brighton, Ill., December 24, 1907.   They had two children: Eleanor Louisa Waddell, born November 8, 1909 and William Clay Waddell, born March 23, 1911.   Their mother, Virginia Bohn Waddell, died November 29, 1921.   She was born February 14,1880.   Dr. Leslie Waddell married, December 25, 1922, for his second wife, Alice Corinne Power of Kansas, born September 16, 1892.   Dr. Leslie Waddell is located in Pittsburg, Pa., and is a member of the faculty of the University of Pittsburg.

Clay Duncan Waddell, born near Windsor, Mo., April 28, 1885. He married Lydia Peak, of Nevada, Mo., September 21, 1911. Lydia Peak was born, January 4, 1893, in Boon County, Missouri. She was the daughter of Judson Davis Peak and Emily Jane Ford Peak.   They had three children, Mary Frances Waddell,born October 20, 1913; Virginia Nadene Waddell, born May 14, 1916, died December 14, 1922 and Clay Peak Waddell, born November 20, 1918.

Marie Elizabeth Waddell was born near Windsor, Mo., September 24, 1894 .

Augusta Florence Waddell was born near Windsor, Mo., October 19, 1897.   She married Cleveland S. Cotter, March 11, 1917, in Jefferson City, Mo.   They had one child, William Waddell Cotton, born May 10, 1918.

i. Mary Isora Waddell, daughter of John Sevier Waddell and his second wife Mary Ann Pinkston Waddell, was a twin to Medora Waddell.   They were born May 20, 1856, near Calhoun Mo., Isora Waddell married November 6, 1872, Alexander Brame of Kentucky. They had five children, three of whom grew to maturity, namely:

Gertrude Brame, born April 21, 1875, died in Visalia, Cal., married March 25, 1902 in Clinton, Mo., Henry Taylor.   They had one son, Richard Taylor.

Bessie Brame, born near Windsor, Mo., March 12, 1880, married Claude B. Hall, September 27, 1906, died March 24, 1910 in Portland, Oregon.

Ruth Brame born December 29, 1891, married Noel Sheats, October 26, 1918 in Seattle, Washington.

j. Medora Waddell, daughter of John Sevier Waddell and his second wife Mary Ann Pinkston Waddell, was a twin to Isora

Waddell.   They were born, May 20, 1856 near Calhoun, Mo.   She married September 29, 1875, Earhart, son of Dr. Earhart, of Texas. They had six children, only five of whom lived to maturity: namely:

William Earhart, born near Nevada, Mo., August 1876.

Ethel Earhart, born near Nevada, Mo., August 1882, died in Nevada, Mo., November 1, 1915

Murry Earhart, born near Nevada in 1882

Frank Earhart, born in Nevada, Mo., 1890

k. Mary E. Waddell, youngest child of John Sevier Waddell, and Mary Ann Pinkston Waddell, was born, August 15, 1858 near Calhoun, Mo., and died, April 10, 1872.

CHAPTER TEN
Nancy Sevier

NANCY SEVIER

Nancy Sevier, the daughter of Governor John Sevier and his first wife, Sarah Hawkins Sevier, was born about 1779. She lived in the household of her step-mother, Bonny Kate, until her marriage. She is frequent'y mentioned in her father's Journal and her marriage to Walter King is noted as taking place, February 19, 1795. After that date she and her husband are very often mentioned in the Journal. Walter King owned and operated the Iron Works near the Sevier plantation and frequent trips are made to the Works by various members of the family.

Nancy's marriage was quite a social event many relatives and neighbors assembling for the ceremony. The Journal gives this entry concerning it:

"February 19, 1795.
Thursday, 19, Mr. King and Nancy married. Jimmy Weir's family here. Mr. Harril', Mr. Waddell, Mr. Claiborne, Mr. Weir's family here, Cousin Jack and Mr. Doak."

"Mr. Weir" refers to Colonel Samuel Weir. Jimmy Weir was another neighbor. Mr. Waddell is John Waddell or Waddel, who married Rebecca Sevier a week later. Mr. Doak was doubtless the officiating minister. "Cousin Jack" may be the nephew of the Governor, known in this record and familiarly at that period as Devil Jack. "Cousin" was used interchangeably with "nephew" for many years, or the Governor may have called the young man by the name by which he was called by the young Seviers. I do not know of any real Cousin Jack that Governor Sevier possessed.

I understand that descendants of Nancy Sevier King and Walter King lived in Knoxville and that a Walter King, who must be IV or V, in Knoxville has their family Bible. Nancy Sevier King was living in 1818, as she is listed in the Sheriff's Bill of Sale. A son of Nancy Sevier King, Austin King was Governor of Missouri and was living in Missouri in 1853. A letter from him is on file in the New York City Library.

"The Encyclopedia of the State of Missouri" says: "Austin A. King, lawyer, legislator, Governor of Missouri and member of

Congress, was born in Tennessee, September 21, 1801. He died in Richmond, Missouri, April 22, 1870. His father was a soldier in the Revolutionary War, and from him he inherited a strong national spirit. While a young man he came to Missouri and settled in Columbia, where he practiced law with success. In 1837 he removed to Richmond, Ray County, and was appointed circuit judge and served on the bench for eight years. In 1848 he was chosen Governor'.

If Walter King, father of Austin served in the Revolution, as stated in the foregoing paragraph from "Encyclopedia of the State of Missouri," he must have been considerably older than his wife. I have no confirmation of his Revolutionary service and am inclined to think this biographical note is in error as he was probably too young. It was probably his father who served.

Mrs. Emma King Turner, wife of Emmitt Turner, joined the D. A. R. on the record of Gov. Sevier and her lineage is given in the D. A. R. Lineage Books as follows: She is a daughter of Thomas Benton King and Clara Bingham, grand daughter of Austin Augustus King and Nancy Roberts, great grand daughter of Walter King and Nancy Sevier and great great grand daughter of Governor Sevier.

From the foregoing information Nancy Sevier and Walter King had at least two sons.

Walter King, junior.

Austin Augustus King.

WALTER KING, JUNIOR

Walter King, junior, son of Nancy King and Walter King married and had descendants who lived in East Tennessee.

AUSTIN AUGUSTUS KING

Augustus King, son of Nancy Sevier King and Walter King, was born September 21, 1801. He died in Richmond, Mo., September 22, 1870. He was Governor of Missouri and was a member of Congress from Missouri. He married Nancy Roberts.

CHAPTER ELEVEN
Catherine Sherrill Sevier

CATHERINE SHERRILL SEVIER

Catherine Sherrill Sevier, was the daughter of Governor John Sevier and his second wife, Catherine Sherrill Sevier. In the list of Gov. Sevier's children, prepared by George Washington Sevier (son of the Governor) for Dr. Lyman C. Draper, Catherine is given as the second child of her mother and she appears in practically all lists in this order. However Mrs. Ellett, author of Pioneer Women of the West , says in her sketch of Ruth Sevier that Ruth was the second child of her mother, leaving the first place for Catherine. Also, Ruth's marriage took place two years after Catherine's, indicating that Ruth was the junior, for marriage took place early in life at that period and from the time a girl was fifteen she was considered ready for marriage. I therefore place Catherine Sherrill Sevier before her sister, Ruth, in this record placing her as the first child of her mother and the eleventh child of her father Gov. John Sevier.

She grew to womanhood on her father's plantation, "Plum Grove", near Jonesboro, Tennessee. She is frequently mentioned in her father's Journal. He has various endearing names for her, calling her Catty, Cattery, Kitty and the like.

She married twice. Her first marriage is recorded in Governor Sevier's Journal, with considerable detail. He gives the officiating minister's name and the list of guests present. He sets down the groom as "R. Campbell", but we know from other records that he was Richard Campbell, son of Richard Campbell, senior, and that he was a first cousin to the elder Sevier children, as their mother, Sarah Hawkins, was a sister to the elder Richard Campbell's wife, Mary Hawkins. Also a letter from George Washington Sevier to Dr. Lyman Draper confirms this knowledge for he states that his sister, Catherine married Richard Campbell.

The marriage of Catherine Sherrill Sevier to Richard Campbell took place, Thursday 24, 1795, which was quite a marrying year for the Seviers, Nancy and Rebecca having married in February, 1795. Dr. Samuel Doak officiated and evidently the ceremony was an event of general interest in the neighborhood. Governor Sevier records many guests present, among them: Major John Sevier and his wife (this was the third son of the Governor), Mrs. Waddell

261

(this was the daughter, Rebecca), Mr. Harrill, (he was also a guest at Nancy's wedding), Mr. J. A. Anderson, Mr. McKee and his lady, Miss Peggy, Mr. Sherrill, (this was the father or brother of Bonny Kate), Mr. and Mrs. Wear (Col. Samuel Wear and his first wife Mary Thompson Wear), Major James Sevier and his lady (this was the Governor's second son, his wife was Nancy Conway), Mrs. William Clarke (this was Major Clarke's second wife. He married first, the Governor's eldest daughter, Elizabeth), Benjamin Brown and his wife, (this was the daughter, Sarah Hawkins Sevier), Josiah Allen and John Ficks. (The inclosures are mine. Ed.)

This makes quite a social item. If the Governor had only been thoughtful enough to describe the bride's costume and to name the members-of the household who were present there would be nothing left to sigh for. I should so like to know what children were living in his home, as well as these names of the sons and daughters who evidently came from their own homes to be present.

Catherine Sherrill Sevier Campbell and Richard Campbell had one son, of record. Whether there were other children by this marriage I do not know. If so none lived to maturity probably. The one son was named George Washington Campbell in compliment to Catherine's brother, George Washington Sevier.

George Washington Campbell married ——————— and has descendants, one of whom, George Washington Campbell, was Lieutenant Governor of Missouri in 1903.

Governor Sevier in his Journal makes frequent mention of Mr. and Mrs. R. Campbell. He goes to a ball at their home in Knoxville, Christmas evening, 1799. In June 1800, he makes the last reference to R. Campbell, when he goes to "a little hop at R. Campbell's". Evidently the Campbell's were socially inclined and evidently the Governor saw them frequently. Shortly after this last date there is a break in the Journal and afterwards frequent breaks. After several years, in 1808, the name of A. Rhea begins to appear. Richard Campbell had died and Catherine's second marriage had taken place in the interim.

Thursday, December 12, 1799 Mrs. R. Campbell is mentioned in the Journal and Pater Campbell. Pater may be her son although I have record of only one son, George Washington Campbell. "Pater" may be a nickname for him.

Catherine Sherrill Sevier Campbell married Archibald Rhea, junior, about 1803. His sister, Jane Rhea, married Catherine's brother, Dr. Samuel Sevier. Archibald Rhea, junior, is mentioned many times in Chalkley's Abstract of Augusta Records. He received land October 21, 1771. (Page 516, Volume III.) This Archibald Rhea, junior, however, I consider a generation older than the Archibald, junior, who married Catherine Sevier. He was possibly father to Archibald who married Catherine   There were evidently many successive members of the family named Archibald Rhea.

I have not the exact date of the second marriage, but as the third child by Archiabald Rhea was born January 1, 1809, I conclude that the marriage took place about 1803.   Catherine Sevier Campbell Rhea died May 1, 1827.   Archibald Rhea died January 25, 1833.

The children of Catherine Sevier Campbell Rhea were:

1. George Washington Campbell
2. James White Rhea
3. John Sevier Rhea
4. Ann Eliza Rhea.

Further records of Catherine Sevier's children have been sent to me by Mrs. Ida Barclay Tucker as this chapter is going to press. They will be found in full in the appendix, though received too late for inclusion here.   By Mrs. Tucker's record Catherine Sevier had two other Rhea children, one of whom, Mary Rhea was her grandmother.   The names supplied by Mrs. Tucker are:

5. Mary Rhea
6. Jane Rhea

GEORGE WASHINGTON CAMPBELL

George Washington Campbell, son of Catherine Sevier Campbell and Richard Campbell was born in East Tennessee, about 1797, the marriage of his parents taking place Christmas eve, 1795.   He received his name in compliment to his mother's favorite brother who was himself quite young (fourteen) in 1796.   This was George Washington Sevier, eldest son of "Bonny Kate".

George Washington Campbell married and had children, though I do not know their names.   A grandson of one of them was George Washington Campbell, who was Lieutenant Governor of Missouri in 1903.   Mr. C. Schiller Campbell of Lincoln, Nebraska writes that he is the son of James C. Campbell, born August 19, 1834, who was a grand son of Catherine Sevier Campbell and Richard Campbell.

JAMES WHITE RHEA

James White Rhea, son of Catherine Sevier (Campbell) and Archibald Rhea, junior, is said to be the first son by Catherine's second marriage.   He was born in East Tennessee.   He died in Galveston, Texas.

JOHN SEVIER RHEA

John Sevier Rhea, son of Catherine Sevier (Campbell) Rhea and Archibald Rhea, junior, was born in East Tennessee.   He was named in compliment to Gov. John Sevier.

ANN ELIZA RHEA

Ann Eliza Rhea, daughter of Catherine Sevier (Campbell) Rhea, was born January 1, 1809.   She married Thomas Hooper Merrill, ——————— 18——.   They had eight children.   Ann Eliza Rhea Merill, died September 7, 1887, and is buried in Courtland, Alabama.

The children of Ann Eliza Rhea Merrill and Thomas Hooper Merrill:

a.   Angelina Merrill

b.   Orlando Merrill

c.   Edwin Merrill

d.   Ellen Merrill

e.   Emma Merrill

f.   William Merrill

g.   Thomas Merrill, junior

h.   Laura Merrill.

MARY RHEA AND JANE RHEA

The history of Mary Rhea and Jane Rhea will be found in the Apendix.

CHAPTER TWELVE
Ruth Sevier

RUTH SEVIER

Ruth Sevier, daughter of Governor John Sevier and his second wife, Catherine Sherrill Sevier, was their second child. She is usually given as the first child of the second marriage, but Mrs. Ellet, in Pioneer Women of the West, says she was the second.

She was raised at the beautiful Plum Grove residence of her parents and enjoyed a very novel life for a young girl even in that interesting period. She learned in her childhood to speak the Indian tongue and could, in fact, converse in several dialects with the chiefs of the various nations. At one time her father had taken prisoner thirty Indians and having no place to take them, he brought them home! They so thorough'y enjoyed the Plum Grove plantation that they refused to leave, and little Ruth became their adoration. They taught her all they knew of woodcraft and legend and they christened her "Chuckey's Rutha", Chuckey being their name for John Sevier, while Rutha was his pet name for his small daughter whom he seems to have especially adored. The Indians called her a princess and prophesied that she would marry a Chief and be one of them, a prophesy which was singularly fulfilled, for she did marry a young man who, though of the white people, had been raised by Indians, adopted into their tribe and made a Chief.

Ruth Sevier was so adept in the Indian tongues that on several occasions she acted as interpreter and was consulted very frequent y in important matters even when she was not absolutely the offi:ial interpreter.

She married twice. Her first marriage was to the young man who had grown up with the Indians. He was Richard Sparks. He had been captured at four years of age and was given the name of Shawtunte. He was a childhood playmate of Tecumseh and The Prophet, two of the great chiefs and two of the most dangerous. He was reared in the family of Tecumseh until he was sixteen. He was then released and he went to the Kentucky settlements and later into East Tennessee and to the settlement on the Holston and Nollachucky Rivers. His mother, seeing him, recognized him instantly by a mark. He took the name Richard Sparks after his release from Indian captivity, and under that name Governor

Sevier took him into his family and made use of his knowledge of Indian character and his familiarity with the country. Governor Sevier obtained for him an appointment in the United States Army. In the meanwhile Rutha had taken great interest in the newcomer with his romantic history, being at first the only one who could communicate with him. She taught him to read and write and gave him in fact the benefit of all her own schooling.

They were married about the time that Governor Sevier obtained an appointment for him in the Army. Governor Sevier very frequently mentions "Rutha" in his Journal, and "my daughter, Mrs. Sparks". Richard Sparks was a Colonel and was stationed at Fort Pickering on the Mississippi River in 1801 and 1802. He was afterwards sent with his regiment to New Orleans, Baton Rouge and Fort Adams. Ruth Sevier Sparks accompanied him and made loyal friends. She seems to have inherited her father's faculty of acquiring friendship. Colonel Richard Sparks died at Staunton, Virginia, in 1815.

Ruth Sevier Sparks married for her second husband, Daniel Vertner, of Mississippi, near Fort Gibson. He is said to have been a wealthy planter. In 1834, Ruth Sevier Sparks Vertner was visiting friends or relatives in Maysville, Kentucky, when she died.

She had no children. She has many namesakes, however, among the descendants of her brothers and sisters, the name Ruth occuring frequently in the family annals. Her second husband was also extremely popular with the Seviers and his name is perpetuated as "Daniel Vertner Sevier," the name having been used for several generations.

CHAPTER THIRTEEN

George Washington Sevier

GEORGE WASHINGTON SEVIER

George Washington Sevier, son of John Sevier and Catherine Sherrill Sevier, was born February 1, 1782. He was John Sevier's thirteenth child. After his father's death he removed to Overton County, Tennessee with his mother and he was Clerk of the Circuit Court in that county for several years. His military record is as follows: Ensign of the Second Infantry, March 26, 1804; Second Lieutenant, August 22, 1805; First Lieutenant, May 31, 1807; Captain of Rif'e Company, May 3,1808; Lieutenant Colonel, July 6, 1812; Colonel, January 24, 1814. His descendants are eligible to the Societies of 1812.

Much of the early history of the Sevier family is based upon his letters to Dr. Lyman G. Draper. These are now in the Draper Collection in Madison, Wisconsin. He was employed by Governor Claiborne, of Mississippi, and died in Mississippi while in his service.

He married Catherine Weatherly Chambers, by whom he had eleven children, namely:

(1) George Washington Sevier, junior
(2) Catherine Anna Sevier
(3) William C. Sevier, never married
(4) Thomas K. Sevier, never married
(5) Cornelia V. Sevier
(6) John Vertrees Sevier, never married
(7) E iza M. Sevier
(8) Marion F. Sevier, never married
(9) Laura J. Sevier
(10) Putman M. Sevier, never married
(11) Henry Clay Sevier, never married.

Of the foregoing:

DR. GEORGE WASHINGTON SEVIER, JUNIOR

Dr. George Washington Sevier, junior, married Sarah Knox, of Nashville, niece of Mrs. Andrew Jackson, who was raised at the Hermitage by President and Mrs. Jackson. They had six children, namely: George Washington Sevier, III, William Sevier, Andrew

Jackson Sevier, Mary Catherine Sevier, Eliza Donelson Sevier and
Jennie Vertner Sevier.   Andrew Jackson Sevier married Columbia
Dobys, and they had seven children: Columbia Sevier (who
married Willard H. Utz, of Louisiana); Andrew Jackson Sevier,
Second, (who married J. S. Agee, of Alabama); Jennie Vertner
Sevier (who married T. F. Young, of Vicksburg); Mary Catherine
Sevier (who married W. J. Ward, of Arkansas); and Ada Elizabeth
Sevier (who married A. C. Williamson, of Arkansas); one daughter,
Sarah Knox, died unmarried many years ago.   Mary Catherine
Sevier married Robert Dunbar, leaving two children, Robert Dunbar,
Second, and Nannie Bells Dunbar, both living in Missouri.   Jennie
Vertner Sevier married George Clarke for her first husband and for
her second husband married Adolphus Harris, of Virginia.   They
had one daughter, Sarah Knox Harris, who married Captain George
Sager, of Port Gibson, Mississippi.   Eliza Donelson Sevier married
W. T. Jefferies, of Port Gibson, Mississippi, and left two children,
Mary Sevier Jefferies and Evan Shelby Jefferies.   Mrs. Jefferies
and Mrs. Utz are the only living children of Dr. George W. Sevier
and his wife, who was Sarah Knox, and are among the oldest
descendants of Governor John Sevier, and the nearest to him in point
of relation, being great-grand daughters.   They also represent other
early Tennessee families in their relation to the Jackson, Shelby,
Knox, and Donelson families.

CATHERINE ANN SEVIER

Catherine Ann Sevier, married Albigence Waldo Putman,
a grandson of General Israel Putman.   They had two children:
Julia (who married William O'Niel Perkins, lived in Nashville for
many years and had no children) and Waldo Washington Putman
(who married Eliza Jane Smith and had three daughters: Emma,
Agnes and Caroline.   Misses Emma and Agnes Putman are not
married.   Miss Caroline Putman married Robert Morrison, of
Chattanooga, and had four children, Kenneth Morrison, who died
young.   Harold   Morrison,   who   married   Sterling   Milne,
Louise Morrison, who married Roy L. Baker and has one child, Roy
L. Baker, junior, and Putman Morrison, who married Elizabeth
Venneble and has five daughters: Elizabeth, Agnes, Mary, Esther
and Ruth.

3.   William C. Sevier, never married

4.   Thomas K. Sevier, never married

5.   Cornelia V. Sevier

6.   John Vertrees Sevier, never married

7.   Eliza M. Sevier, married John F. Donald

8.   Marion F. Sevier, never married

THE SEVIER FAMILY
LAURA J. SEVIER

9. Laura J. Sevier married Henry L. Norvell and had Joseph A. Norvell (who married Mary Slinkard and had Louise Norvell and Nita Norvell, of Colorado, neither of whom is married; Cornelia Sevier Norvell, (who married Albert B. Payne and had Albert B. Payne, Second, never married; Ida Payne, married Minor Scovel, Amy Payne married Charles Rosse and Douglas Payne married Annie Alexander); Aduella B. Norvell (who never married); Sarah Woods Norvell (who married N. W. Leonard); Moselle Norvell (who married Frank Porterfield Elliott, and is now living in Nashvil'e. Her children are Laura Norvell Elliot and Elizabeth Porterfield El iott.

10. Putman M. Sevier, never married

11. Henry Clay Sevier married twice, first Mary Clark and second Mary Nash.

CHAPTER FOURTEEN
Samuel Sevier

SAMUEL SEVIER

Samuel Sevier, son of Governor Sevier and his second wife Catherine Sherrill Sevier, was born in East Tennessee, June 26, 1785. He died October 25, 1844. Governor Sevier in his Journal makes frequent mention of Samuel. On 28th of September,1795, which by the Journal, fell on Monday, an oratorical contest was held at Martin Academy. The prizes were $3.00, $2.00 and $1.00 and they were captured by James Anderson, James Trimble and Samuel Sevier. Governor Sevier fails to record the amount of the prize, which I find mentioned elsewhere, however, and though he says there were three winners in the contest, he apparently gives the names of but two, "James Anderson Trimble, and Samuel Sevier". This is only a seeming error, he merely forgot the first name of the Trimble boy, who was James Trimble, and punctuation was not the Governor's strong point.

Odd that after a hundred and thirty years we find recorded in history and the Governor's Journal the prowess of three little boys in oratory!

Samuel Sevier became a physician and moved to Alabama to reside. His mother, late in life, went to his home to live with his family near Russellville, Alabama, and there she died and was buried. It is said that Samuel was her favorite son. He had settled on a large grant of land made to Gov. Sevier and several members of the Sherrill family also went to that section.

Dr. Samuel Sevier married in 18——, Jane Rhea, whose brother, Archibald Rhea married Samuel's sister, Catherine Sevier as her second husband. About the time of his marriage Samuel Sevier moved to Alabama to a plantation near Russellville and there he lived until his death, in 1844. He was buried in the old cemetery near that place and his mother was buried beside him. In 1922, through the efforts of Colonel S. G. Heiskall, of Knoxville, the body of Catherine Sherrill Sevier, widow of Governor Sevier and mother of Dr. Samuel Sevier, was moved from the Russellville cemetery to Knoxville and reinterred beside her husband.

Catherine Sherrill Sevier had moved from Tennessee in June

277

1836, to spend the "rest of her life" with this favorite son, but she lived only a few months, passing away in October of the same year.

Dr. J. G. M. Ransey, of Annals of Tennessee fame, is authority for the statement that Samuel Sevier married a sister of Archibald Rhea, who married Catherine Sevier.   He makes reference to this in his history of Lebanon Church.

Dr. Samuel Sevier and Jane Rhea Sevier had ten children, namely:

1. John Sevier, who married Mildred Merrill

2. Catherine Ann Sevier, who married Branham Merrill

3. Margaret Sevier, who married Charles B. Tenant

4. Joanna Sevier, who married Hugh Dickson

5. Archibald Rhea Sevier, who married Malinda Chisholm

6. Benjamin Brown Sevier, who married Drucilla Ewing

7. Daniel Vertner Sevier, who married Sophronia Chisholm

8. Branham Merrill Sevier, who married a Spanish girl in Mexico

9. Jane Sevier, who married Lewis C. Chisholm

10. Samuel Sevier, who married Jane Desprey.

Once again the family habit of naming children for various in-laws is illustrated.   Benjamin Brown Sevier, for instance, is evidently named for Sarah Hawkins Sevier's husband and Daniel Vertner Sevier is named for Ruth Sevier's second husband and Archibald Rhea Sevier is named for Catherine Sevier's husband, though in this instance, Archibald Rhea was also maternal uncle to the namesake and Mrs. Samuel Sevier (Jane Rhea) was a daughter of Archibald Rhea, senior.

JOHN SEVIER

John Sevier, son of Dr. Samuel Sevier and Jane Rhea Sevier, married Mildred Merrill.   Their children were:

a. Ruth Sevier, who married ———— Wilder, and for her second husband ———————— Colins and lived in Louisville, Kentucky.

b. Mary Sevier, who married ———— Knight.   She died in Memphis.

c. "Tib" Sevier, who married ———— Wiggins. She died in Memphis.

d. John Sevier, who lives in Wasihngton.

e. Sallie Sevier, who lives in Louisville.

f. Edgar Sevier, who died.

CATHERINE ANN SEVIER

2. Catherine Ann Sevier, daughter of Dr. Samuel Sevier and Jane Rhea Sevier, married Branham Merrill. Their children were:

a. John Merrill, who married Miss Fannie Hopgood

b. Branham Merrill, Junior.

c. Mildred Jane Merrill, who married ———— Didlake.

DR. DANIEL VERTNER SEVIER

7. Dr. Daniel Vertner Sevier, son of Samuel Sevier and Jane Rhea, was born 18————. He married twice, first, Mary Sophronia Chisholm and second, Catherine Keelen. By his first marriage he had four children:

a. Adelia Sevier, who married Joseph Baumer.

b. Cullen Sevier, who died in infancy.

c. Daniel Vertner Sevier, junior, who married Media Watkins.

d. Dr. Samuel Gillington Sevier, born December 19, 1854, who married M. J. Benson, January 19, 1885. Their children were Bessie Cordelia, died in infancy; Annie Esther, died in infancy; Mary Sophronia, married W. T. Kirk; Samuel Prentice, who married Cathleen Morris; James Henry, Edgar and Tommie Camille, a daughter.

Dr. Daniel Vertner Sevier married for his second wife, Catherine Keelen and had three daughters:

e. Katie Sevier, who married Dr. Caterbury.

f. Nancy Sevier, who married Thomas Hyde.

g. Jennie Sevier, who died in young womanhood.

Daniel Vertner Sevier, junior, has in his possession a beautiful miniature painting by Peale, of Governor John Sevier. It was given by the widow, Catherine Sherrill Sevier to her son Dr. Samuel Sevier and by him to his son, Dr. Daniel Vertner Sevier and by him to his son, Daniel Vertner Sevier, junior. He loaned this miniature to the Tennessee Historical Society in 1924.

JANE SEVIER

9. Jane Sevier, daughter of Dr. Samuel Sevier and Jane Rhea Sevier, married Lewis C. Chisholm and had Joanna Chisholm, who married G. Lueddemann.

SAMUEL SEVIER, JUNIOR

10. Samuel Sevier, junior, son of Dr. Samuel Sevier and Jane Rhea Sevier, was born 18————. He moved to Aberdeen, Mississippi,

to reside and became a dentist. For many years he was the most prominent dentist in that whole section of the country. He married Josephine Desprez, daughter of William Desprez, a prominent physician and surgeon of his time. Dr. Samuel Sevier, junior, and Josephine Desprez Sevier had four children, namely:

a. Samuel Sevier III, born February 16, 1874, who married Mary Louise Fogarty and has three daughters, Josephine Desprez Sevier, Susan Rhea Sevier and Mary Louise Sevier.

b. William Rhea Sevier, who is a druggist and lives in Birmingham, Alabama. He married ———— ———— and has three children, Nell Davidson Sevier, Anne Rhea Sevier and William Kearney Sevier.

c. Susan Gaffney Sevier, of Birmingham, Alabama, who is unmarried.

d. Jane Desprez Sevier, who married W. H. Clarke, of Aberdeen, Mississippi, and has four daughters and one son, namely: Evelyn Willoughby Clarke, Josephine Etheridge Clarke, who married W. L. Watkins; Louise Desprez Clark and Susan Elizabeth Clarke, all of Aberdeen, Mississippi, and the one son, Rufus Gordon Clarke, who makes his home in Columbus, Mississippi.

CHAPTER FIFTEEN

Polly Preston Sevier

POLLY PRESTON SEVIER

P olly Preston Sevier was the fifteenth child of Governor John Sevier and the fifth child of his second wife, Bonny Kate Sevier. Polly is not a nickname for Mary in this case, as it frequently is, as she had an older sister named Mary Ann Sevier. Governor Sevier had a sister Polly and he probably named his little daughter for this sister. The name Preston compliments some favorite "in-law", doubtless, as the Sevier family habit is to name children for in-laws into the third and fourth generation.

Polly Preston Sevier was born about 1789 in East Tennessee. She married William Overstreet, junior, September 18, 1806, and it was the custom of the period for girls to marry about sixteen, not much later, at least, and frequently earlier. She was living in 1818, as she is mentioned as an heir, in the Sheriff's Bill of Sale. According to information furnished by a descendant, Mrs. J. R. White, of Glasgow, Kentucky, she had several children, at least four, three daughters and a son.

These children were:

1. Rebecca Burden Overstreet

2. Ruth Sparks Overstreet

3. Catherine Overstreet

4. George Overstreet

Nancy Overstreet, possibly a sister of William Overstreet, married Robert Neilly, December 29, 1797.

These names all show the usual tendency toward naming children for the in-laws. Rebecca Burden shows the connection with John Borden, (for Burden is Borden differently spelled), whose two wives were of the Sevier blood, the first, Catherine Matlock and the second, Catherine Sevier. Rebecca Sparks Overstreet was named for her aunt, Ruth Sevier, whose first husband was Richard Sparks.

REBECCA BURDEN OVERSTREET

Rebecca Burden Overstreet, daughter of Polly Preston Sevier Overstreet, and William Overstreet, junior, was born 18———. She married Micajah Armstrong, sometimes spelled Misija. They had at least one daughter, Mary Ann Armstrong, who married D.. Lemuel Hughes and had a son, W. B. Hughes.

W. B. Hughes married————— ————— and had six children, namely:

a. Grace Hughes, who married J. Robert White, of Glasgow, Kentucky, and has five daughters, Elizabeth White, who married Guy C. Miller, Julia White, Mary Hope White, Ruth Sevier White and Grace Roberts White.

b. Mary F. Hughes, who married E. B. Trigg and has two children, Catherine Sevier Trigg and Anne Ballard Trigg.

c. Robert Bonner Hughes, who married——————————— and lives in Portersville, California.   He has three children, Frank Hughes, Dorothea Hughes and ————— Hughes.

d. Dr. James Lemuel Hughes, who married— ——————. ———— and lives in Madera, California.   He has four children.

e. Dr. W. C. Hughes, who married—————. - and lives in Madera, California.   He has two children.

f. Cora Hughes, who is unmarried and lives in Dinuas, California.

RUTH SPARKS OVERSTREET

Ruth Sparks Overstreet, daughter of Polly Preston Sevier Overstreet and William Overstreet, junior, was born 18———.   She married William Dill Jourdain as his first wife.   She had five sons and one daughter.   She died in 1849.   Dr. Jourdain married for his second wife her niece, the daughter of her sister Catherine Overstreet who had married Absolom Holman.   I do not know the names of the children of Ruth Sparks Overstreet Jourdain.

CATHERINE OVERSTREET

Catherine Overstreet, daughter of Polly Preston Sevier Overstreet and William Overstreet, junior, was born 18———.   She married Absolom Holman of Salina, Tennessee.   They had two daughters, Catherine Holman and ————— Holman.   Catherine Holman married Dr. William Dill Jourdain as his second wife, his first having been Ruth Sparks Overstreet, her mother's sister.   Catherine Holman Jourdain had by her marriage to Dr. Jourdain, two children, namely: Ruth Catherine Jourdain and Robert Lee Jourdain.   Ruth Catherine Jourdain married ————— Hoyt and lives in California.   Robert Lee Jourdain lives in St. Louis, Missouri.

William Dill Jourdain, who married twice into the Sevier-Overstreet connection was born in the Greeneville District, South Carolina, January 31, 1799.   He moved with his parents to Smith County, Tennessee, in 1808.   He began to study medicine at twenty years of age at Murfreesboro, Tennessee. After graduating from the Nashville School of Medicine, he practiced medicine in Nashville for two years and then removed to Glasgow, Kentucky. He married twice, first Ruth Sparks Overstreet, by whom he had five sons and one daughter. After her death in 1849, he married her niece, her sister Catherine's daughter, Catherine Holman, daughter of Absolom Holman, of near Salina, Tennessee.

Dr. Jourdain subsequently removed to Missouri and entered the ministry of the Christian Church. He died in Norbonne, Missouri, January 21, 1889.

GEORGE OVERSTREET

George Overstreet, son of Polly Preston Sevier Overstreet and William Overstreet, junior, was born 18———. He married——————————— and lived in Overton County, Tennessee, He left a large family. He was given Power of Attorney by several heirs, May 5, 1857, and his post office address was then Locust Shades, Tennessee.

CHAPTER SIXTEEN
Eliza Conway Sevier

ELIZA CONWAY SEVIER
(also called Betsey)

Eliza Conway Sevier, daughter of John Sevier and his second wife, Catherine Sherrill Sevier, was born in East Tennessee, November 11, 1790.   She married, August 9, 1810, Major William McClellan of the United States Army.   They lived for a while in Knoxville and later at various Army posts.   Mrs. Ellet, in "Pioneer Women of the West", speaks of her as living in the year in which the book was published in Van Buren, Arkansas. George Washington Sevier says in his letter to Dr. Draper that Eliza Conway Sevier McClellan was living in 1839.   When John Sevier was inaugurated Governor of Tennessee, in 1803, his son-in-law, Major McClellan "was living in his brick house in Knoxville".   Eliza Conway Sevier McClellan, died June 26, 1860.

Governor Sevier, in his Journal, frequently mentiones "Betsey" and "my daughter Betsey" when he evidently means a child.   At this time (the dates of the Journal), his eldest daughter Elizabeth, who is frequently called Betsey, was married and had children of her own.   I conclude that the Governor used Betsey as a dimunitive for Eliza Conway Sevier.

Eliza Conway Sevier McClellan and Major William McClellan had five children, namely:

1. John McClellan

2. Ann McClellan

3. Catherine McClellan

4. Mary Jane McClellan

5. Lida McClellan

Of the foregoing:

JOHN MCCLELLAN

John McClellan married a Miss Gregg and lived in Texas.   He had no children.

ANN MCCLELLAN

Ann McClellan married Judge Brown and had children.   She lived in Marshall, Texas.

NOTABLE SOUTHERN FAMILIES

MARY JANE MCCLELLAN

Mary Jane McClellan married Captain Gabrial Rains, United States Army, afterwards General Gabriel Rains, Confederate States Army. He was a son of General Gabriel Rains. Captain Rains was a distinguished officer of the Army and a graduate of West Point. Immediately upon the breaking out of the War Between the States he resigned from the United States Army and offered his services to the Confederacy and became a Brigadier General. General Gabriel Rains and Mary Jane McClellan Rains had six children, namely: Stella Rains. (who died unmarried); Leila Rains (who married first,——— Randall and had a son, Charles Rains Randall, died unmarried, and married second, Judge William Watkins Smythe, of Augusta, and has four children, James Haris Smythe, died young, Bonita Smythe, married Lee Hankinson and has four children, and Josephine Smyth, who married James Weiborn Camak, and died, leaving one child, a son); Sevier McClellan Rains (who was killed in the West in an engagement with Indians. He was an officer in the United States Army and was unmarried); Catherine McClellan Rains (who married Kirby Tupper, a Captain in the United States Army); and Fanny May Rains (who married Colonel Walter Chatfield, of the United States Army)

LIDA MCCLELLAN

Lida McClellan married John Gregg, a planter in Texas and had three children, Willie Gregg (who was killed in Battle in the War Between the States); Alla Gregg (who died unmarried) and Nola Gregg (who married ——— Nelson).

CHAPTER SEVENTEEN
Joanna Goode Sevier

JOANNA GOODE SEVIER

●anna Goode Sevier, daughter of Governor John Sevier and his second wife, Catherine Sherrill Sevier, was born November 11, 1792. She had at least two cousins of exactly the same name and possibly other young kinswomen of the same name and she is therefore continually confused with namesakes. Her uncle, Abraham Sevier, named a daughter Joanna Goode Sevier and another uncle, Colonel Valentine Sevier III, seems to have had a daughter of the same name. Histories of these Joannas will be found in other chapters of this book.

Queerly enough in one list of Governor Sevier's children two Joannas appear. This is thought by some members of the family to be merely an accidental error. Others claim that a grand-daughter lived in the home of Governor Sevier, while still others think that the second Joanna is a niece, possibly the daughter of Colonel Valentine Sevier III. The additional Joanna in the list mentioned, gives John Sevier nineteen children, but it is well known that there were only eighteen. The same list makes two other errors, though these can be explained. Elizabeth is given twice and Mary is given twice. The explanation of these apparent errors is simple, Elizabeth was the oldest daughter. A younger daughter Eliza, was nicknamed Betsey. Someone, in preparing the list has translated "Betsey" into Elizabeth and, omitting Eliza entirely, has given two children as named Elizabeth There was also a daughter named Mary Ann in the first group of children, while Polly is one of the younger daughters. Polly is frequently a nickname for Mary and the person who prepared this record, probably so construed it, giving two Marys and omitting Polly. Polly however, was evidently a name given in compliment to Governor Sevier's sister Polly.

Governor Sevier mentions his daughter Joanna many times in his Journal. Mrs. French, of Morristown, who has collected much information, gives Joanna's birth as occuring November 11, 1794. She died July 31, 1823. Her obituary now in possession of her grand-son, Joseph Windle Sevier, gives the date of her death "July 31, 1823, in the thirtieth year of her age", thus placing her birth in 1792. The date, November 11, 1794, as given by Mrs. French, seems to me to be wrong for this reason Governor Sevier's Journal gives full, if crisp information concerning the happenings of November 11, 1794 and the days before and after. He would not have failed to mention the birth of a daughter, and particularly one to whom he gave his mother's full name. He says: "Tuesday 11, November, Rain. Finished halg. corn. Frank ran away." Frank was one of the slaves. He is mentioned at other times. Early in the next year, 1795, Joanna is mentioned as going to meeting with the Governor "and wife", so she must have been larger than a babe in arms. I conclude therefore, that she was born in 1792 but probably on November 11, as Mrs. French indicates.

She married about 1810, when she was possibly sixteen or seventeen. She married Joseph Hawkins Windle, who was the first cousin of the elder Sevier children, whose mother was Sarah Hawkins, before her marriage. Joseph was the son of Caroline Hawkins, who married Joseph Windle.

Joseph Hawkins Windle prepared a statement of his children's names which is dated February 2, 1826. In it he says that his wife is deceased.

The eight children of Joanna Goode Sevier Windle and Joseph Hawkins Windle by the father's statement were:

1. Daniel S. Windle
2. Juliet Windle
3. Robert A. Windle
4. Samuel W. Windle
5. Catherine Windle
6. Mary Windle
7. Ruth V. Windle
8. Joanna Goode Sevier Windle

With one exception, Mary Windle, I have not the descent of these children, but I will list them here in order that dates and names can be added by descendants who have the information.

DANIEL S. WINDLE

Daniel S. Windle, son of Joseph Hawkins and Joanna Goode Sevier Wind'e, was born 18——. His middle initial doubtless stands for Sevier.

JULIET WINDLE

Juliet Windle, daughter of Joanna Sevier Windle and Joseph Hawkins Windle, was born 18——.

ROBERT A. WINDLE

Robert A. Windle, son of Joanna Goode Sevier Windle and Joseph Hawkins, was born 18——.   A power of attorney was given to a Robert A. Windle by several Sevier heirs, May 5, 1857.

SAMUEL W. WINDLE

Samuel W. Windle, son of Joanna Goode Sevier Windle and Joseph Hawkins Windle, was born 18——.

CATHERINE WINDLE

Catherine Windle, daughter of Joanna Goode Sevier Windle and Joseph Hawkins Windle, was born 18——.

MARY WINDLE

Mary Windle, daughter of Joanna Goode Sevier Windle and Joseph Hawkins Windle, was born 18——.   She received the name Hawkins, according to records in the family of her descendants, her full name being Mary Hawkins Windle.   Mary was of course, for Joanna's sister.   She married in 18——, her second cousin, Alfred C. Sevier, son of Joseph Sevier, Sr., son of Valentine Sevier II.

Alfred C. Sevier and Mary Hawkins Windle Sevier had at least two children:

1.   Joseph Windle Sevier

2.   Amanda Sevier

Of these:

Joseph Windle Sevier, son of Alfred C. Sevier and Mary Hawkins Windle Sevier, was born 18——.   He is now living, (1923), at Livingston, Tennessee, and has furnished this part of this record.   He had five daughters, namely: Mrs. Lillian Sevier Stewart, of Livingston; Mrs. A. E. Speck, of Sheriden, Arkansas; Mrs. J. S. Arms, of Celina, Tennessee; Mrs. John Lee Bowman, of Crawford, Tennessee; Miss Leuce E. Sevier, of Livingston, Tennessee.

Amanda Sevier, daughter of Alfred C. Sevier and Mary Hawkins Windle Sevier, was born 18——.   She married ——————— Abeton, and lives at Willow Grove, Tennessee.

RUTH V. WINDLE

Ruth V. Windle, daughter of Joanna Good Sevier Windle and Joseph Hawkins Windle, was born 18——.   She was given the name Ruth in compliment to her mother's sister, Ruth, whose second husband was Daniel Vertner.   I conclude that Ruth V. means Ruth Vertner.

JOANNA GOODE SEVIER WINDLE

Joanna Goode Sevier Windle was the daughter of Joanna Goode Sevier Windle and Joseph Hawkins Windle, and was born 18——. She was given her mother's full name.

CHAPTER EIGHTEEN
Robert Sevier

ROBERT SEVIER

Robert Sevier, son of Governor John Sevier and his second wife, Catherine Sherrill Sevier, was born in East Tennessee, about 1789. He was living in 1818 when the Sheriff's sale of his father's property took place. Also his brother, George Washington Sevier, mentions him as living July 23, 1839, when G. W. Sevier writes to Dr. Draper. I have no other information concerning him.

Appendix

APPENDIX

EXPLANATION OF TITLES USED

Valentine Sevier I, refers to the first Valentine Sevier of direct record. He emigrated from France to England and there married Mary Smith.

Valentine Sevier II, refers to the son of Valentine I. He was the Valentine who emigrated to America and married Joanna Goode.

Colonel Valentine Sevier, brother of Governor John Sevier, is usually called Colonel Valentine Sevier in histories and always in this book. In this book he is always given the suffix III, also, as he was the third Valentine Sevier in direct line.

Governor John Sevier is usually called Governor John Sevier. However, he appears in various histories, sometimes as General, sometimes in his earlier years as Captain and Colonel.

Nollichucky Jack, refers to Governor John Sevier. It was a name bestowed upon him by Indians and taken up by his friends and admirers.

James Sevier, son of Governor John Sevier, is usually called Major Sevier.

John Sevier, junior, means the son of Governor John Sevier. Though there are many Johns, all historians unite in giving Governor Sevier's son the suffix "Junior".

"Devil Jack" Sevier, refers to Governor John Sevier's nephew, John Sevier, son of Valentine Sevier III.

Bonny Kate Sevier, refers to Governor John Sevier's second wife, who was Catherine Sherrill.

ADVERTISEMENT OF THE SHERIFF'S SALE

An advertisement in the Knoxville Register, February 10, 1818, by the Sheriff of Knox County, John Callaway, is interesting as it gives the names of fifteen of the eighteen children of Governor John Sevier, as living at that date. This advertisement is often referred to in the foregoing pages.

"I expose for public sale on Saturday the 14th of March next, at the Court House in Knoxville, all the right and title that Joseph Sevier, James Sevier, John Sevier, Joshua Corland and Maryann, his wife, Sarah Brown, Valentine Sevier, Walter King and Nancy his wife, Daniel Vertner and Ruth his wife, Archibald Rhea and Catherine his wife, George W. Sevier, Joseph H. Wendell and Joanna his wife,

LAST RECORD OF JOANNAH SEVIER

Samuel Sevier, Wm. Overstreet, junior, and Polly his wife, and
Robert Sevier, the heirs of John Sevier deceased, have in a tract of
land containing 290 acres on the South side of the Holston River on
the waters of Stock Creek known by name as the Marble Spring Place".

This advertisement proves that only three of the children of
Gov. Sevier, namely: Elizabeth, Richard and Rebecca, had passed
away before February 10, 1818.

Joannah Sevier was a witness in court August 20, 1773, Vol. I,
Page 174 Abstracts of Augusta County, Virginia.   This is the last
record concerning her in Virginia.   The family moved to the
"Mountains" in a short time arriving Christmas day 1773.   I have
never seen any reference to her in accounts of the moving or thereafter.   Her name is spelled Joana, Joannah and Joanah, while her
family name is spelled Good, Goade and Goode.

THE BORDEN GENEALOGY

Hattie Borden Wells in the Borden Genealogy, gives John
Borden, son of John and Mary Borden and great grandson of
Benjamin Borden, to whom Gov. Gooch, of Virginia granted
Borden's Manor, as marrying for his second wife "Catherine Sevier,
daughter of Gov. John Sevier". about 1824.   This is manifestly
impossible, as Governor Sevier's daughter Catherine was a generation
elder and had been married twice long before this date.   She first
married Richard Campbell and later married Archibald Rhea.

John Borden married twice and probably his two wives were
cousins.   The first wife was "Catherine Matlock, daughter of
William Matlock".   I think she was a grand daughter of Catherine
Sevier (sister of Governor Sevier, who married William Matlock),
and that his second wife, Catherine Sevier, was a grand daughter
instead of a daughter of Governor John Sevier.

In case this supposition is correct she was probably the daughter
of Robert Sevier (son of Gov. Sevier).   I have no data of his
family, though it is said that he married and left children.   He lived
near the family of Matlock, so that the widowed John Borden would
very likely have known Robert Sevier's family.   However the same
statement applies to Valentine Sevier (son of Governor Sevier) for
he also married and lived near the Matlocks and I have very little
record of his family.

NICHOLAS SEVIER

Volume II, Page 383, of Chalkley's Abstract of Augusta,
Virginia Records, shows that Nicholas Sevier entered land, February
22, 1750.

MICHAEL SEVIER

Michael Sevier is refered to in Governor Sevier's Journal as M.
Sevier.   Michael Sevier is mentioned in Chalkley's Abstract of
Augusta Records, Volume II, Page 381. One Michael Sevier was killed
by Indians June 26, 1792, near Ziegler's station, two miles from
Bledsoe's Lick, Sumner County, Tennessee.   In Governor Sevier's
Journal under date, December 14, 1794, he says, "M. Sevier's wife
delivered of a son".

"TOBY"

A history of John Sevier would not be complete without mention of Toby, who was evidently his body servant. Toby is very frequently spoken of in the Journal and he accompanies his master on every occasion. No doubt he participated in many of the dramatic events of the period and he too should be remembered as a pioneer, for "they also serve who only stand and wait."

One quotation from the Journal is an example of many.

(July 1798)

Wed. 11, Myself, Washington and Toby set out for Tellico Block House to the treaty—staid that night at Maryville—Pd expenses 12.

Toby was a trusted servant and was sent to and fro on many missions in addition to accompanying his master as will be seen by the reference to Willam Sevier.

LUCINDIA SEVIER

Mrs. Effa Pegram Carter Breed, of Ithaca, New York, writes:

"My mother, Ann Eliza Carter, was born November 17, 1825, at Scotland Neck, Surry County, Virginia, opposite the place of. Jamestown Settlement. Scotland Neck, being the name of the homestead, named in honor of Scotland Neck, North Carolina. She was the daughter of William Carter and Lucy, or Lucindia Sevier. Lucy, or Lucindia Sevier, died when her daughter, Ann Eliza was a small girl and William Carter married a second wife. Therefore she knew very little of her ancestry, but was told she was a grand-daughter of Governor John Sevier. She remembers that in her childhood, an old lady lived at her home who was called Aunt Winnie Sevier. She does not know whether this was her deceased mother's sister or aunt.

Records both at the homestead and in Surry County, Virginia, were burned during the War Between the States.

"Ann Eliza Carter married Ebenezer Thompson, of Portsmouth, Virginia, about 1849. He was born August 6, 1817, and died March 7, 1912. She died December 24, 1895. They had five children, namely:

1. Emma Thompson, born 1850, died 1852.

1. Carter Sevier Thompson, born December 6, 1855 died September 7, 1912. He married Miriam McWilliams, of Philadelphia. They had no children.

3. Effa Pegram Thompson, born July 6, 1861, married Arthur M. Breed, April 8, 1896. He died October 3, 1919. They had four children, Paul Thompson Breed (born January 14, 1897); Monroe Thompson Breed, (born July 18, 1898); Ebenezer Thompson Breed, (born March 1, 1903.)

4. Lozier Thompson, born July 28, 1863, died March, 1908. He married Eva Alexander about 1895. They had one child, Lozier Thompson, junior, born July, 1897, who married Helen——— about 1919. They have one child, Lozier Thompson III, born February 1921.

5. Ellie Wilson Thompson, born May 30, 1868,
(Editor's Note: Lucindia or Lucy Sevier was not the daughter of Governor John Sevier as he had no daughter by that name. She was possibly a grand-daughter or niece. Zella Armstrong)

DESCENDANTS OF REBECCA SEVIER WHO MARRIED
JOHN RECTOR
(See Page 45)

Robert D. Hull of Moshiem, Tennessee, furnishes me with the following information of Rebecca Sevier (daughter of Valentine Sevier II) who married John Rector.

Rebecca Sevier Rector and John Rector had several children, among them:

1. George Rector

2. Frank Rector

3. Susan Rector

Of these:

1. George Rector, son of Rebecca Sevier Rector and John Rector

2. Frank Rector, son of Rebecca Sevier Rector and John Rector

3. Susan Rector, daughter of Rebecca Sevier Rector and John Rector, married Isaac Dearstone and had nine children namely:

a. John Dearstone

b. Crist Dearstone

c. Robert Dearstone

d. Isaac Dearstone, Jr.

e. Mattie Dearstone

f. Martha Dearstone

g. Rachel Dearstone

h. Margaret Dearstone

i. Elizabeth Dearstone

Of the foregoing:

a. John Dearstone married Nannie Hull. They had five children, George, Robert, Nannie, Bertha, and Lona.

d. Isaac Dearstone, junior, married Linda Sevier. They had o sons, John Dearstone and Charles Dearstone.

e. Mattie Dearstone married Alfred Roberts.

f. Mattie Dearstone married —————————Susong and had one aughter, Hattie Susong.

g. Rachel Dearstone married Gabriel Susong. They had six children, John, Melvin, Carl, Ella and Nannie.

h. Margaret Dearstone married————————— Bullen. They had three children, Charles, Guy and Etta.

i. Elizabeth Dearstone, married David M. Hull. They had six children, Robert D. Hull, George Hull, John Hull, Kittie Hull, Maggie Hull and Cora Hull. Of these: Robert D. Hull married Mary Ellen Kelton, and has two daughters, Samantha Hull and Arnold Guy Hull. George Hull died when a young man. John Hull married Bess Wright. They have four children: Daniel Hull, Robert Hull, Luella Hull and Loreine Hull. Kittie Hull died young. Maggie Hull married John Wampler. They have three children: Earl Wampler, Pearl Hull Wampler and Viola Hull Wampler. Cora Hull married John Gray. They have no chidren.

ABRAHAM SEVIER FAMILY
(See Page 73)

Mrs. G. L. Wing of Browning, California, has sent a list of children of Abraham Sevier which is not exactly like the list furnished me earlier. She is a great grand daughter of Abraham Sevier. She writes: "The following is recorded in my father's Bible." She then gives the names as they appear on Page 73 with the following changes:

Elizabeth Sevier, born November 12, 1790, married Mr. Scriggins November 21, 1805.

Mary Ann Sevier married ————— Holterman, November 21, 1813.

Joanna Goode Sevier born April 3, and died December 29, 1836. She married Alfred Robison January 5, 1823.

Valentine Smith Sevier, born November 20, 1801, married Elizabeth Arnett August 25, 1819.

Abraham Rutherford Sevier, born January 12, 1807, married Mary Coulston January 31, 1833

Catherine Sherrill Sevier, born March 17, 1809, married Jasper Rowland 1842.

Mrs. Wing adds one child not given in the other record, namely:

Robert B. Sevier, born July 7, 1812, died 1821.

CHILDREN OF VALENTINE SEVIER AND ELIZABETH
ARNETT SEVIER
See Page 74

Valentine Sevier, junior, son of Valentine Sevier and Elizabeth Arnett Sevier, was born August 3, 1841, Morgan County, Illinois and died April 2, 1891. He was a minister of the Southern Methodist Church. He married three times. It is said that he had three children by one marriage, and that he had a son Charles. Mrs. George L. Wing gives this record: Valentine Sevier, junior, married Rebecca Jenkins, August 3, 1876 in Shelby County, Illinois and had:

a. Elbert V. Sevier, born September 5, 1878, died August 31, 1879.

b. Daisy Sevier, born October 13, 1880. Lives in Banning California, and married George L. Wing in 1904, in Nevada, Missouri. They have one son Fredrick Sevier Wing, born 1906.

c. Mina Sevier, born November 1884, married Charles L. Bell, 1908 in Nevada, Missouri, and had no children.

d. Buford V. Sevier, born June 2, 1887, married Virgie Middleton, 1919 and had Robert Jean Sevier and Betty Jane Sevier.

e. Earl J. Sevier, born August 23, 1889, married Alberta Flory, 1918.

LAURA EVELYN HALE
(See Page 178)

After the chapter concerning James Sevier and his children was printed Mrs. Clara D. Silverthorne sent me the names of the nine children of Laura Evelyn Hale and her husband Thomas T. Gosnell, namely:

Frances Elizabeth, died at eighteen

William, died young

Douglass, died young

Emma Josephine, died young

Mathew, died at twenty-six

Lemuel

Frank

Clara Douglas

Clara Douglass Gosnell married first Samuel McLaughlin and had no children and married second, William Custis and had Harry Douglass Silverthorne (who married Caroline M. Raffo and has no children), Carl Douglass Silverthorn, (who is a Lieutenant in the Army and is not married).

JAMES SEVIER

The following record is furnished by M. R. Woodland, of Rahway, New Jersey, who is descended from James Sevier, one of four brothers born in Virginia early in 1800.   I do not know the names of their parents.   The four brothers as given by Mr. Woodland:

    I.   James Sevier, born 1811 (?)

    II.   Bethel Sevier, born 1813 (?)

    III. George Sevier, born

    IV.   John Sevier, born

    I.   James Sevier, born 1811 (?), died 1881, married in Virginia about 1840, Mary Ann Boiles, or Biles.   Her brothers and sisters were Gilbert Boiles, Peggy Boiles, (who married William Waggoner) Eddie Boiles and Sally Boiles.   Mary Ann Boiles Sevier (born 1812 (?) died 1875.

The children of James Sevier and Mary Ann Boiles were:

    1.   Mary Sevier

    2.   Sarah Sevier

    3.   Elizabeth Sevier

    4.   Nancy Sevier

    5   Joseph Best Sevier

    6.   John Wesley Sevier

    7.   Perry Sevier

    8.   Isaac Sevier

    1.   Mary Sevier, daughter of James Sevier and Mary Ann Boiles Sevier, was born in Virginia, 1841 (?).   She died July 1, 1903.   She married Edward Paterson, born 1838, died 1894.   Their children were:

    a.   Ann Paterson, born 1868, died 1921, married William Bayer.

    b.   James Paterson, born 1870, died

    c.   Lucy Paterson, born 1872, died 1888

    d.   George Paterson, born 1876

    e.   Joseph Paterson, born 1880, died 1898.

    2.   Sarah Sevier, second daughter and second child of James

Sevier and Mary Ann Boiles Sevier, was born in Virginia in 1848 (?), She died 1861.

3. Elizabeth Sevier, daughter of James Sevier and Mary Ann Boiles Sevier, was born in Virginia in 1844. She married, January 25, 1866, William Thomas Woodland (born 1846, died 1911) a Veteran of the War Between the States.

Their children:

a. John William Woodland, born December 12, 1866, married twice, first Hulla Shank, by whom he had no children, and second Maggie Gunning, by whom he had one child, Catherine Woodland, born June 19, 1903, who married Harold Fox and has two children, William Thomas Fox, born 1920 and Roy Franklin Fox, born 1922.

b. Manford R. Woodland, born May 3, 1868, married Luna May McCormack, August 30, 1891.

c. Jasper Newton Woodland, born December 5, 1870, married Grace ——————. Their children are Manford Woodland and —————— Woodland.

d. Lillie Ann Woodland, born February 28, 1872, married Elmer E. Orice, December 30, 1899.

4. Nancy Sevier, daughter of James Sevier and Mary Ann Boiles Sevier, was born in Virginia, in 1846. ?. She married —————— Cupp.

5. Joseph Best Sevier, son of James Sevier and Mary Ann Boiles Sevier, was born in Virginia in 1847 (?). He was a Veteran of the War Between the States. He married Emma Linn. Their child, Bessie Sevier, married George Perry. They had four children, namely: Tollis Perry, born October 1, 1901, who married Glen Ruby, and had Margaret Ruby, Paul Ruby, Pauline Ruby and —————— Ruby. Ruth Perry, born April 3, 1903; John Perry, born June 18, 1905 and Russell Perry, born February 2, 1907.

6. John Wesley Sevier, son of James Sevier and Mary Ann Boiles Sevier, was born in Virginia, in 1849. He died in prison at Andersonville during the War Between the States.

7. Perry Sevier, son of James Sevier and Mary Ann Boiles Sevier, was born in Virginia, in 1850. He died November 29, 1908, He married twice, first Jennie Miller and second Matilda Bull. By his first wife, Jennie Miller (born 1855, died 1884) he had two children:

a. Mamie Sevier, born August 26, 1879, who married Frank Nugent and had a daughter, Bessie Nugent, born 1900, who married John Schwartz in 1921. They have one child, Genevieve Rose Schwartz, born 1921, died young.

b. Orie Sevier, born February 5, 1882, married Pearl Roney, and has two children, Manford Sevier, born 1907 and Orrie Sevier, junior, born 1904.

Perry Sevier by his second wife, Matilda Bull has three children:

c. Easter Sevier, born May 21,1899, married Frank Culliflower, and had children.

d. Joseph Ray Sevier

e. Dale Sevier, born, ————————. Married Pearl Howard.

8. Isaac Sevier, son of James Sevier and Mary Ann Boiles Sevier, was born in Virginia in 1852. He died in 1882 (?).

LOULA SEVIER

Mrs. F. M. Gibson, Harlem, Ky. P. O. Box 548 writes:

"My grandmother was Loula Sevier, who married a Methodist minister by the name of ———————— Bijreo, (my mother's father). They had a daughter, Cornelia Sevier Bijreo and a son,Robert Bijreo. Cornelia Sevier Bijero married ———————— and has a daughter ———————— who married F. M. Gibson of Harlan, Ky.

ISAAC SEVIER

Mrs. Mary C. Green of Danville, Ky., has written me that her grandfather:

Isaac Sevier, born November 3, 1789 was a first cousin of Governor John Sevier. Isaac Sevier was the son of ———————— Sevier and Elizabeth Taylor Sevier. Isaac Sevier married———————— and had a daughter, Agnes Sevier, who married ———————— and had a daughter, Mary————————. who married ———————— Green and lives in Danville, Ky.

(Editor's Note. Isaac Sevier born November 3, 1789, is too young to be the first cousin of Gov. John Sevier. He was possibly a son of a first cousin and in that case he is a grand son of the Emigrant William Sevier.) See Part Two.)

SOME "SEVIERS"

Mrs. John M. Combs, of Cambridge, Ohio is deeply interested in a branch of the Sevier family, spelling the name Seviers with a final s. She has sent the following interesting information:

"————————Seviers married Jane Hultz. She was born 1743, died 1824. At her death she had one hundred and six descendants. ————————Seviers and Jane Hultz had only one son, John Seviers, born 1764, died 1884. He married Elizabeth or Betsy Vlery. She died 1853. They settled in Beaver Dam, Pensylvania and had twelve children:

1. Charles Seviers
2. Polly Seviers
3. Jesse Seviers
4. John Seviers, born July 30, 1800
5. Jane Seviers, who married James Sankey
6. Cyrus Seviers
7. Henry Seviers
8. Betsy Seviers

9. George Seviers

10. Rebecca Seviers

11. Milton Seviers

12. Hiram Seviers

Of the foregoing:

John Seviers married Nancy Huffman and settled in Ohio. They had six children: Jacob Seviers, Elizabeth Seviers, Mary Seviers, John Seviers and Sarah Seviers.

It is said that George Seviers the ninth child of ———— Seviers and Jane Hultz Seviers visited his kin in Virginia, (Note by editor. There were not any of the Sevier family living in Virginia when George would have been of age to visit. He may have visited his mother's kin).

Mrs. Combs thinks that residence among Pensylvania Dutch people caused the spelling Seviers with the final s.

(Note by editor. If this ————Seviers who married Jane Hultz was born about the same year as his wife, 1743, he was a little older than Gov. John Sevier who was born 1745. ———— Seviers could be a possible first cousin to Gov. Sevier (in that case the son of William Sevier) or he could be a half brother to Gov. John Sevier, if Valentine Sevier the Emigrant married before he married Joanna Goode. Valentine Sevier in some of the records is said to have married a Baltimore lady shortly after his arrival in America, but his marriage to Joanna Goode took place in Virginia, about 1744,, when he was forty-two years of age. At that period marriage took place early in life and I think it very probable that he did marry "a Baltimore lady" before his marriage in Virginia to Joanna Goode.

FROM LIFE OF GOODPASTURE

In the Life of Jefferson D. Goodpasture, written by his two sons will be found this in reference to the children of Governor John Sevier who lived on the Governor's 57000-acre tract of land in Overton County where "Bonny Kate" also lived, to-wit:

"Among his sons and daughters there were Catherine Campbell, whose second husband was Archibald Rhea; Joanna Windle, and Valentine Sevier who lived on Iron's Creek; Mary Overstreet who lived on Obed's River; George W. Sevier who lived on Sulphur Creek and afterwards removed to Nashville; Sarah Brown, who lived at the James McMillan place, and Ann Corlin who lived on Ashburn's Creek."

The same authority says that Abraham Sevier lived ten miles north of Livingston, and that Joseph Sevier (brother of Gov. Sevier not the son) lived near the mouth of Ashburton's Creek.

VERA FAY TURNER

(See Page 119)

Vera Fay Turner married, 1925, Dr. I. G. McCutcheon of St. Louis.

ANOTHER JOHN SEVIER

This interesting record has been sent to me but I have no means of knowing where this branch of the Seviers should be placed.

John Sevier, born in Tennessee, lived at one time in Kentucky, then in Brown County, Illinois and later in Missouri. Date and place of birth not known, though he may have been born as late as 1800. The name of his first wife, by whom he had seven children, is unknown. His children by first marriage, (names may not be in order of birth):

a. Archibald Sevier, b. Sept. 18, 1820, in Kentucky

b. Helen Sevier

c. Lucinda Sevier

d. Jane Sevier

e. John Sevier

f. Will Sevier

g. Valentine Sevier.

Children by second marriage; (names may not be in order of birth):

h. Moses Davis Sevier born, Mt. Sterling, Illinois

i. Frank Sevier

j. Newton Sevier

k. Jasper Sevier

l. Sarah Sevier.

Of the foregoing:

a. Archibald Sevier, oldest child of John Sevier and his first wife, was born Sept. 18, 1820, in Kentucky. He moved to Brown County, Illinois and in April 1887 was living at Indian Grove, Chariton County, Missouri. He died 1901. He married Emily Medlin about 1839. She was born about 1822 and died Aug. 1900, in Missouri. Names of their children and dates of births from the Bible of Archibald Sevier:

A. Catherine Sevier, b. Oct. 30, 1840

B. Sally Sevier b. July 4, 1843

C. Emily Josephine Sevier, b. Sept. 7, 1844

D. John Wesley Sevier, b.Feb. 18, 1847

E. Elizabeth Jane Sevier b. Feb. 12, 1849

F. Nancy Minerva Sevier b. Feb: 14, 1851

G. Lou A. Sevier b. Jan. 9, 1853

H. William Thomas Sevier b. Jan. 28, 1855

I. —————— Sevier, twin, b. Dec. 28, 1856

J. —————— Sevier, twin, b. Dec. 28, 1856

K. James Madison Sevier, b. Oct. 7, 1858.

Of these:

A. Catherine Sevier, daughter of Archibald Sevier and Emily Medlin Sevier, was born Oct. 30, 1840.

B. Sally Sevier, daughter of Archibald Sevier and Emily Medlin Sevier, was born July 4, 1843 and died about 1922, at Clayton, Illinois.   She married —————— Stiffey and had three children, namely; Alva Stiffey, of La Grange, Missouri; Oliver Stiffey, of Clayton, Illinois; Mary Stiffey, of Timewell, Illinois, who married John Woodworth.

C. Emily Josephine Sevier, daughter of Archibald Sevier and Emily Medlin Sevier, was born Sept. 7, 1844 and died about 1922 at Clayton, Illinois.   She married John Graham and had two children; Frank Graham, who married a cousin, Ida Sevier, the daughter of William T. and Delilah Fannie Johnson Sevier, on April 19, 1895 in Morgan County, Illinois (they had a daughter, Letha Graham, who is unmarried, and another child .   The second child of Emily Josephine Sevier Graham is Fred Graham.

D. John Wesley Sevier, son of Archibald Sevier and Emily Medlin Sevier, was born Feb. 18, 1847 and died at Precept, Nebraska. He married Mary Elizabeth Beckman, Nov. 10, 1868, Mt. Sterling, Illinois.   She now lives at Beaver City, Nebraska.   Their children; 1. Hettie Sevier, born April 25, 1871, Timewell, Illinois, lives at Forest Grove, Oregon; married Leo Umscheid, who is deceased, and had children; Clarence Umscheid, who is married and has three children; Margaret Umscheid, who is married and has two children; Myrtle Umscheid, who is married and has two children; Guy Umscheid, Ralph Umscheid, Alice Umscheid and Robert Umscheid.

2, William Henry Sevier born Oct. 1, 1873, Alexander, Illinois, lives Beaver City, Nebraska, married Sarah Malone; 3, Guy Lee Sevier, born April. 27, 1875, Exeter, Illinois, lives Beaver City, Nebraska, married Edith Garrett and had four children; Ruby Sevier, Marie Sevier; Irene Sevier and Lucille Sevier; 4, John Sevier born June 6, 1877, Exeter, Illinois, who lives at Hudson, Colorado and is not married; 5. Robert Sevier, born April 28, 1879, Alexander, Illinois, who lives Chicago, Illinois and is unmarried; 6. Rose May Sevier, born Oct. 5, 1881, Elk Creek, Nebraska, lives Beaver City, Nebraska, married Ben W. Hardin and had nine children: Harold Hardin, Gerald Hardin, Nellie Hardin, Warren Hardin, Wayne Hardin, Maxine Hardin, Dorothy Hardin, Donna Hardin and Doris Hardin; 7. Emma Sevier, born Sept. 27, 1883, Elk Creek, Nebraska, lives Beaver City, Nebraska, married Fred W. Shafer and has Fred W. Shafer, junior; 8. Katherine Sevier born July 29, 1885, Beaver City, Nebraska, lives at Cook, Nebraska, married Guy Hall and has a daughter, Hazel Hall; 9. Mable Sevier born Nov. 4, 1889, Burlington, Colorado, lives on Grand Island, Nebraska, married Grove O'Neil and has two children, Althea June O'Neil and Cecil James O'Neil.

E. Elizabeth Jane Sevier, daughter of Archibald Sevier and Emily Medlin Sevier, was born Feb. 12, 1849, Brown County, Illinois and died on her birthday, Feb. 12, 1925, Alexander, Illinois. She married Charles Hagen, Aug. 17 1870 at Alexander, Illinois. He was born April 21, 1843, Strasburg, Germany. Their children: 1. Rose Hagen, born Nov. 24, 1871 in Sangamon County, Illinois, lives at Arcadia, California, married Ellis Martin Mawhinney, the son of Joseph and Amy C. (Wiley) Mawhinney, Brunswick, Missouri. He was born Jan. 12, 1864, Parkersburg, West Virginia. Their children, a son and a daughter, born at Brunswick, Missouri, died in infancy; 2. Minnie Hagen, born May 1873, Sangamon County, Illinois, lives at Sims, Illinois, married, I. N. Sumner, who died June, 1924 at Sims, Illinois and had seven children: Charles Sumner, unmarried, of Lone Pine, California; Florence Sumner, of Little Rock, Arkansas, married Billy Milam and had two children, Billy Milam, junior. and Jaunett Milam; Ellis Sumner, of Little Rock, Arkansas, married Lillian ———— and has no children; Rose Sumner, of Little Rock, Arkansas, married Henry Mines and has an only child, Ruby Mines; Earl Sumner, married ———— ———— and has two sons, one of whom is William Sumner; Robert Sumner, unmarried; Clarence Sumner; 3, Catherine Hagen, born April 30, married Fred R. Wallbum, a prominent farmer of Morgan County, Illinois, April 26, 1905, Morgan County Illinois. He was born Feb. 8, 1870, Morgan County, Illinois and is the son of Fred and Barbara (Reiser) Wallbum. Their five children were born near Alexander, Illinois; Charles Fredrick Wallbum, b. Feb. 9, 1906,

Barbara Elizabeth Wallbum, b. March 2, 1908; Catherine Marguerite Wallbum, b. April 3, 1911, d. April 10, 1911; George Elder Wallbum b. Feb. 28, 1913; Nellie Rose Wallbum b. Aug. 1, 1916; 4. Elizabeth Hagen born and died the same day, in 1880, near Alexander, Illinois; 5. Charles Hagen, junior, born 1881, Sangamon County, Illinois, lives at Quincy, Illinois, married Hattie Whorl and had three children: Carl Hagen, who married Mary ———— and had a daughter Mary; Helen Hagen and Catherine Hagen; 6. Nell Hagen, born April 7, 1885, Morgan County, Illinois, lives at Lynnville, Illinois, married Earl Landis and has an only child, Maxine Landis; 7. Will Hagen, born 1887, Chariton County, Missouri, lives at Canton, Illinois, married Amy Cooper and has four sons: Basil Hagen, Lewis Hagen, Robert Hagen, George Hagen.

F. Nancy Minerva Sevier, daughter of Archibald Sevier and Emily Medlin Sevier, was born Feb. 14, 1851 and died Nov. 20, 1920 in Springfield, Illinois. She married James Brown Sept. 4, 1872 in Morgan County, Illinois and had no issue. Mr. Brown lives near Alexander, Illinois.

G. Lou A. Sevier, daughter of Archibald Sevier and Emily Medlin Sevier, was born Jan. 9, 1853 and lives near De Kalb, Illinois. She married Henry Ferguson Nov. 15, 1868, Mt. Sterling, Illinois and had six children: 1. Artie Ferguson born Dec. 28, 1869, lives Kingston, Illinois, married Guy Gossett, 1917, Rockford, Illinois and had no children. Their adopted son is Lowell A. Dearinger; 3. Mary Ferguson, born March 29, 1876, lives, Wichita, Kansas, married Ezra Henry, 1894, Wichita, Kansas and has an only child; 4. Marguerite Ferguson, born March 16, 1878, lives, De Kalb, Illinois, married John H. Cooper Oct. 1, 1893, Quincy, Illinois and has an only child, Hazel Cooper born Oct. 2, 1896, St. Louis, Missouri, of De Kalb, Illinois, who married Leslie Cutlip July 5, 1918; 5. Joe Feruson born Oct. 31, 1880, lives at Sparland, Illinois, married Laura Beaumont 1903, Sparland, Illinois and has four children: Edward Ferguson, who married ———— ———— and has one child, George Ferguson; Denny Ferguson; Anna Ferguson; 6. Della Ferguson born Aug. 4, 1885, lives, De Kalb, Illinois, married first, Jesse Kindhart 1910 in Oklahoma and had an only child, Keith Edward Kindhart, born May 25, 1912, Molin, Illinois. She married second, James Thornton, June 20, 1919, Sycamore, Illinois.

H. William Thomas Sevier, son of Archibald Sevier and Emily Medlin Sevier, was born Jan. 28, 1855 and died in Missouri. He married Delilah Fannie Johnson, June 4, 1872, Morgan County, Illinois and had seven children: 1. John Sevier, of Triplett, Missouri; 2. Will Sevier; 3. Lou Sevier, lives, Springfield, Illinois, married Patsy Ryan and had five children, including Carl Ryan, Ethel Ryan and Mamie Ryan; 4. Mary Sevier married Mike Rustenmeyer;

5. Ethel Sevier married ——— ———; 6. Ida Sevier died near Triplett, Missouri, married her cousin, Frank Graham, April 19, 1895; 7. Cora Sevier, of Ashland, Illinois, married ——— ———.

I. ——— Sevier, twin child of Archibald Sevier and Emily Medlin Sevier, born Dec. 28, 1856, died 1856.

J. ———Sevier, twin child of Archibald Sevier and Emily Medlin Sevier, born Dec. 28, 1856, died 1856.

K. James Madison Sevier, Son of Archibald Sevier and Emily Medlin Sevier, born Oct. 7, 1858, married Lula Kidd, daughter of John and Mary (Joiner) Kidd, April 8, 1880, Morgan County, Illinois.

b. Helen Sevier, the daughter of John Sevier and his first wife.

c. Lucinda Sevier, the daughter of John Sevier and his first wife.

d. Jane Sevier. The daughter of John Sevier and his first wife.

e. John Sevier, the son of John Sevier and his first wife, lived, at one time, near Champaign, Illinois. He married ——— ——— and had at least one child, a daughter, Minnie Sevier.

f. Will Sevier, son of John Sevier and his first wife, moved out West and was never heard from.

g. Valentine Sevier, son of John Sevier and his first wife, lived near, Champaign, Illinois. He married ——— ——— and had several sons and at least one daughter, Kate Sevier.

h. Moses Davis Sevier, son of John Sevier and his second wife, Mary Bass Sevier, was born at Mt. Sterling, Illinois. He married ——— ——— and had a son, Daniel or David Sevier, who lived in Kansas.

i. Frank Sevier, son of John Sevier and his second wife, Mary Bass Sevier.

j. Newton Sevier, son of John Sevier and his second wife, Mary Bass Sevier.

k. Jasper Sevier, son of John Sevier and his second wife, Mary Bass Sevier.

l. Sarah Sevier, daughter of John Sevier and his second wife, Mary Bass Sevier, lived at Hiawatha, Kansas. She married ——— Quigley. She is credited by some of the Seviers, as being the daughter of Moses Davis Sevier. Others say she was the daughter of his father.

ARCHIBALD SEVIER

Descendants have furnished me with the following information concerning Archibald Sevier, thought to be a son of John Sevier, junior, but his approximate birth antedates John Sevier, junior's son, Archibald's, birth by forty years.   Also Archibald Sevier, son of John Sevier, junior, though married, died without children.   This information is valuable and it is printed in full as some descendant may be able to place this Archibald Sevier.

Archibald Sevier was born about 1789 and died near Burksville, Kentucky, when his children were small.   He married Hannah Webb, who married for her second husband, Elmond Brezee, of Barzee, and there were four children of her second marriage.   She is said to have died in Washington or Oregon.   Archibald Sevier and Hannah Webb Sevier had two children:

a.   Moses Webb Sevier born 1809

b.   George Washington Sevier, born Jan. 5, 1816.

Of the forgoing:

a.   Moses Webb Sevier, son of Archibald Sevier and Hannah Webb Sevier, was born 1809, near Burksville, Kentucky and died Sept. 11, 1877 in Texas.   For a number of years he lived near Clinton, Henry County, Missouri, where others of the Seviers lived.   He married Susan Glum Hibbler in 1846, born 1819 in St. Louis, Missouri, died Oct. 15, 1886, Seagoville, Texas.   Their children:

A.   Hannah Melissa Sevier, born Sept. 24, 1848

B.   Margaret Ann Sevier, born Jan. 19, 1851

C.   Nancy Jane Sevier, twin of Margaret Ann Sevier

D.   Charlotte E. Sevier born Feb. 19, 1854

E.   Susan Laura Sevier born March 18, 1856

F.   Martha Pauline Sevier born March 9, 1858

G.   Fieldon Moses Sevier born March 11, 1861

H.   George Washington Sevier born Jan. 20, 1866

I.   Rosa Lee Sevier born Feb. 14, 1870.

Of these:

A.   Hannah Melissa Sevier, daughter of Moses Sevier and Susan G. Hibbler Sevier, was born Sept. 24, 1848 in Osage County, Missouri.   She lives at Urich, Missouri.   She married first, Archibald Bethel Colson June 24, 1863, in Henry County, Missouri, who died in that county Nov. 15, 1908, and had children born in Henry County, Missouri: 1.   Dr. J. R. Colson born Dec. 11, 1865, of Schell City, Missouri, married Ara Morrison, 1894 and has four children, none of whom is married; Eugene Colson, who served in World War with overseas service; Archie Colson; Wilbur Colson; Cassell Colson; 2. Martha Jane Coleson born Jan. 16, 1867, lives, Clinton, Missouri, married first, Meredith Anderson and had four children; Arthur Anderson married Gertrude ———; Earl Anderson married Alpha Coontz; Archie Anderson married Mary Middleton; Rhote Anderson married Mollie Warner; and married second, ——— Angle; 3. Laura Susan Colson born March 2, 1869 married Dr. T. L. Crissman and had two sons; Archie Chrissman, of Fayetteville, Arkansas, served as musician in the Navy during the World War, married first, Alice ———, who died; and second, Nina Strong; Harry Crissman, of Dallas, Texas, married Mary ———; 4. Mary Charlotte Colson born July 7, 1871, married first, Tom Clyer, and second ——— Biggs. Her children; Eugene, of Pueblo, Colorado, served in the 35th Division in the World War overseas, married Georgia Salmon; Melissa, of Clinton, Missouri, married Glenn Knouse; 5. Gertrude Colson born March 27, 1873, lives, Montrose, Missouri, married Joseph Harness Oct. 18, 1893 and has; Glum Harness, who served in World War, and Richard Preston Harness, namesake of his uncle; 6. Boss Colson born April 19, 1875, lives Nevada, Missouri, married Maud Frost and had; Byrle Colson, of Calhoun, Mo., served in 35th Division Overseas in World War, married Ida Brockway; Archie Colson, who died when about eight; Sevier Ellen Colson, of Kansas City, Missouri; 7. Richard Preston Colson born Sept. 21, 1880, unmarried. Hannah Melissa Sevier married second, Archibald Byrum Redford Aug. 28, 1913.

B. Margaret Ann Sevier, daughter of Moses Sevier and Susan G. Hibbler Sevier was born Jan. 19, 1851, Osage County, Missouri and died a number of years ago. She was a twin.

C. Nancy Jane Sevier twin with Margaret Ann Sevier, daughter of Moses Sevier and Susan G. Hibbler Sevier, was born Jan. 19, 1851, Osage County, Missouri and died in Kaufman, Texas. She married Thomas Wess at Kaufman, Texas and had no children.

D. Charlotte E. Sevier, daughter of Moses Sevier and Susan G. Hibbler Sevier, was born Feb. 19, 1854, in Henry County, Missouri and died in Bonham, Texas. She married Lum Thomas at Kaufman, Texas and had three children who lived, at one time, at St. Charles, Missouri.

E. Susan Laura Sevier, daughter of Moses Sevier and Susan G. Hibbler Sevier, was born March 18, 1856 in Henry County, Missouri and died at Kaufman, Texas. She married William Anderson and had an only child, Fannie Lee Anderson, who is dead.

F. Martha Pauline Sevier, daughter of Moses Sevier and Susan G. Hibbler Sevier, was born March 9, 1858 near Clinton, Missouri and lives at Seagoville, Texas. She married Curtis Hanes son of William and Mary Jane (Hawthorn) **Hanes**, at Kaufman, Texas, was born June 2, 1858, and has children, born, Seagoville, Texas; 1. Claude Hanes born March 6, 1882, lives Fredrick, Oklahoma, married Susie Ayres May 17, 1803, Kaufman, Texas and had eight children born, Manitou, Oklahoma; Vaughn Hanes, Dean Hanes, Carroll Hanes, Maupane Hanes, Reba Hanes, Therman Hanes, Evelyn Hanes and C. C. Hanes; 2. Flora Hanes born June 28, 1885, lives Dallas, Texas, married John J. Fletcher April 17, 1902 Dallas, Texas and had children born Vinyard, Texas; Curtis C. Fletcher born 1905; John J. Fletcher, junior, born 1910; Patrick Fletcher born 1912; Paul Burnett Fletcher born 1915; 3. Sula Hanes born May 19, 1888, lives Tulsa, Oklahoma, married C. B. Fallis Feb. 29, 1906, Seagoville, Texas and has; Frances Fallis born 1907, Jacksonville, Texas and Sevier Fallis born 1911 Dallas, Texas; 4. Bsyan Hanes born Oct. 29 1897, lives Seagoville, Texas, married Ethel Farr July 29, 1920, Clinton Missouri and has Betty Jo Hanes born 1923 Seagoville, Texas.

G. Fieldon Moses Sevier, son of Moses Sevier and Susan G. Hibbler Sevier, was born March 11, 1861, Henry County, Missouri and died near Mesquite, Texas. He married Annie Bodine, of Savoy, Texas and had: 1. Glynn Sevier; 2. Connie Sevier, living near Bonham, Texas.

H. George Washington Sevier, son of Moses Sevier and Susan G. Hibbler Sevier, was born Jan. 20, 1866, Dallas County, Texas and died in Texas. He was not married.

I. Rosa Lee Sevier, daughter of Moses Sevier and Susan G. Hibbler Sevier, was born Feb. 14, 1870 in Texas and died, unmarried in Kaufman County, Texas.

b. George Washington Sevier, son of Archibald Sevier and Hannah Webb Sevier, was born Jan. 5, 1816 near Burksville, Kentucky and died Sept. 4, 1893. He moved to Missouri when a small boy. He married Jane Catherine Tolle Sept. 24, 1840. She was born Sept. 21, 1822 and died Feb. 27, 1902. Their children were born in Missouri.

A.   George Archibald Sevier born Aug. 20, 1841

B.   Moses N. Sevier born Feb. 8, 1844

C.   Chloe H. Sevier born Oct. 29, 1845

D.   Parmenas Sevier born May 24, 1847

E.   Sagisman M. Sevier born Jan. 27, 1851

F.   Milton L. Sevier born Nov. 27, 1853

G.   Robert E. L. Sevier born Jan. 27, 1864

Of these:

A. George Archibald Sevier, son of George Washington Sevier and Jane Catherine Tolle Sevier, was born Aug. 20, 1841 in Missouri.

B. Moses N. Sevier, son of George Washington Sevier and Jane Catherine Tolle Sevier, was born Feb. 8, 1844 and died May 19, 1902.

C. Chloe H. Sevier, daughter of George Washington Sevier and Jane Catherine Tolle Sevier, was born Oct. 29, 1845, and lives at Monrovia, California. She married F. M. Monroe.

D. Parmenas Sevier, son of George Washington Sevier and Jane Catherine Tolle Sevier, was born May 24, 1847 and died Nov. 14, 1847.

E. Sagisman M. Sevier, son of George Washington Sevier and Jane Catherine Tolle Sevier, was born Jan. 27, 1851 and lives at Monrovia, California. He married Ellen ————.

F. Milton L. Sevier, son of George Washington Sevier and Jane Catherine Tolle Sevier, was born Nov. 27, 1853 and lives at Los Angeles, California. He married Helen C. Mefford.

G. Robert E. L. Sevier, son of George Washington Sevier and Jane Catherine Tolle Sevier, was born Jan. 27, 1864 in Marion County, Missouri and lives at Rosamond, California. At the age of four he moved to Southeast Iowa for four years, then returned to Marion County, Missouri and later to Monroe County, Missouri where he lived for a number of years. He married first, Annie M. Christian Oct. 1, 1891 and had; 1. Roger Walter Sevier born July 27, 1893 in Missouri; and married second, Lucile D. Colson, a niece of Archibald Bethel Colson, May 3, 1905 in Missouri and had children born in California: 2. Robert M. Sevier born Feb. 20, 1906; 3. Lucile M. Sevier, twin with Earl M. Sevier, born Sept. 26, 1911; 4. Earl M. Sevier, twin with Lucile M. Sevier, born Sept. 26, 1911; 5. Donald C. Sevier born Oct. 31, 1914; 6. Betty Lee Sevier born June 1, 1917; 7. John H. Sevier, twin with George Bryan Sevier, born Jan. 30, 1920; 8. George Bryan Sevier, twin with John H. Sevier, born Jan. 30, 1920.

MARY RHEA
(See Page 263)

Mrs. Ida Barclay Tucker writes that Catherine Sevier and Archibald Rhea had a daughter, Mary Rhea and a daughter Jane Rhea.

Mary Rhea born ———— died 1858, married William Barclay and had two sons, Archibald Rhea Barclay and Hugh G. Barclay. Archibald Rhea Barclay married but had no children. Hugh G. Barclay married Margaret Chilton. Their children were:

1 Frances Barclay

2. Alice Barclay

3. Septima Barclay

4. Hugh G. Barclay, junior.

Of these:

Frances Barclay married Joseph Davidson.

Alice Barclay married Henry Hammond of Mobile, Ala. Their children: Hugh G. Barclay, III, Lucile, Alice, Louise, Helen and Hugh.

Septima Barclay married Philip Huston, of Louisville, Ky. Their children: Chilton, Ellen, Philip, Edith, Rowland, Margaret and Cecil.

Hugh G. Barclay, junior, married Carrie Brannon. Their Children: Hugh G. Barclay, III, Lucile, Alice, Louise, Helen and Lee.

Ida Barclay married Thomas Tudor Malcolm Tucker. Their Children:

a. Margaret Chilton Tucker, who married William Fitzgerald, Mayor of Toledo, Ohio.

b. Lucy Glover Tucker, who married Richard Crays, Effingham, Ill.

c. Allene Piatt Tucker.

d. Mary Chilton Tucker.

e. Hugh Barclay Tucker, who married Lucy Cory and lives in Little Rock, Ark.

f. Douglass M. Tucker.

g. Philip Tucker.

MARTHA SEVIER
(See Page 237)

Martha Sevier, said to be a granddaughter of Governor Sevier and thought by descendants to be a daughter of his son Valentine

Sevier, married ————— Poindexter. She had a daughter Sarah Poindexter who married Hugh Cowan and they had a daughter Josephine Cowan who married G. W. Dorsey.

SARAH CATHERINE WYLEY

See Page 224

Sarah Catherine Wyly and William Addison Wily Rogers had four children, Zoe, Minnie, Ada and Walter. Walter died unmarried about 1890. Minnie married Stanley Owen of Yadkin College, and had one child, William Mansfield Owen. Minnie died about 1895. Ada married Mathew Daniels. They have four children, Katie Wyly, Vera, William and Zoe.

Elston Sevier Mansfield married Frances Langston, in 1920, his first wife dying soon after the birth of William.

Florine Mansfield Jones, married Harry Avis Hall of Charlston, West Va., October 19, 1924.

Samuel Tipton Jones and Katherine Louise Mansfield Jones had a fourth child, Samuel Tipton Jones, junior.

WILLIAM SEVIER

William Sevier is mentioned by Gov. Sevier many times in his Journal, though at no time in a way that he can be identified. For instance:

(March 1797 (He was then in Knoxville and was Governor of Tennessee) "Tues. 28, cool, sent Toby home to assist Wm. Sevier down; also sent with him 6 crowns and four dollars to Mrs. Sevier, a muslin pattern to Joanna and a dimity one to Polly."

That seems a very human touch for the great warrior and statesman, thinking of his little daughters (they were about twelve and fourteen) and sending them a "pattern" of goods for new frocks from the great metropolis and trading center of Knoxville. I can imagine they were wild with delight over the muslin and dimity!

WILLIAM VALENTINE BAXTER

William Valentine Baxter said to be a descendant of the Seviers was born in Greene County. His grand daughter says he was a grandson of Governor John Sevier. He was killed in the War Between the States.

NANCY SEVIER
(See Page 257)

(See Page 257)

Nancy Sevier who married Walter King had a son not listed on Page 257 who was called for her father John Sevier. John Sevier King was born May 30, 1815 in Roane County, Tenn. and died April 15, 1884 in Louden, Tenn. The date of his birth in Roane County shows that Nancy Sevier King and Walter King had moved to Roane County by that date. John Sevier King married Martha Earnest (born April 1, 1814, died May 30, 1880). The marriage took place December 2, 1834. They had eight children, among them W. H. King who was the third child. I do not know the names of the other seven children. W. H. King was born in Kingston, Roane County, Tenn. August 31, 1843. He married November 27, 1864, Cynthia P. Fryar. They had six children, namely:

W. H. King, Jr.

Charles W. King

Martha Earnest King

Ann M. King

Nancy Sevier King

———— King died young

W. H. King married October 7, 1874 for his second wife, Sarah E. Foster.

Kingston the County seat of Roane County, Tenn. was established in 1799 on land belonging to Robert King.

Mrs. Clara King Bowdry of Fort Worth, Texas sends me further information of the descendants of Walter King and Nancy Sevier King. She writes:

Walter King and Nancy Sevier King had several sons and daughters who removed to Missouri:

Dr. Thomas A. King

Amanda King, who married ———— Brazeale

Martha King, whose second husband was Major Robert Sevier.

Austin Augustus King.

Other sons remained in Tennessee.

Austin Augustus King was Governor of Missouri from 1848 to 1853. He was born in Sullivan County, Tenn (1801). He married in Jackson, Tenn., later removing to Richmond, Mo. He was twice married. He first married Nancy Harris Roberts. His second marriage was to Mattie Woodson.

His children by his first marriage were:

1. Walter King who married Annie Miles

2. Elizabeth King who married three times, ———— Moore, ———— Lackey, and ———— Richberg.

3. William A. King who married twice, Theodora Pence, and Kate Denley Clark

4. Edward King who married Jennie Lule

5. Thomas Benton King who married Clara Bingham

6. Henry King who died in infancy

7. Austin Augustus King, Jr. who married Dorothy Lyle.

His child by his second marriage was:

8. Mary Bell King who married Harry Toole.

Of the foregoing:

William A. King removed to Texas in 1873 settling in Stephenville, Erath County.

Mrs. Elizabeth King Richberg went to Chicago to reside.

Mrs. Mary Belle King Tootle resides in New York City

Thomas Benton King removed to Texas to reside in 1873, settling in Stephenville, Erath County. He married Clara Bingham, daughter of George Caleb Bingham, a noted artist of Missouri and his first wife Elizabeth Hutchinson of Booneville, Mo.

Thomas Benton King had ten children namely:

a. Horace B. King married Stella Pitts

b. Alice King married E. S. Newton

c. Emma C. King married Emmett Turner

d. George Bingham King married Florence Morris

e. Austin A. King, deceased

f. Thomas Benton King, Jr. died in infancy

g. Clara Louise King married W. P. Bowdry

h. Donald King married twice, Berta Davis and Elizabeth Jones

i. Laura Rollins King

j. Frances R. King married J. P. Burt, Jr.